American Behavioral History

American Behavioral History

An Introduction

EDITED BY

Peter N. Stearns

New York University

NEW YORK AND LONDON

NEW YORK UNIVERSITY PRESS
New York and London
www.nyupress.org

Library of Congress Cataloging-in-Publication Data
American behavioral history : an introduction /
edited by Peter N. Stearns.
p. cm.
Includes bibliographical references and index.
ISBN–13: 978–0–8147–9843–0 (cloth : alk. paper)
ISBN–10: 0–8147–9843–8 (cloth : alk. paper)
ISBN–13: 978–0–8147–9844–7 (pbk. : alk. paper)
ISBN–10: 0–8147–9844–6 (pbk. : alk. paper)
1. Psychology—United States—History.   2. United States—
Social conditions.   3. United States—Social life and customs.
I. Stearns, Peter N.
HN57.A5847   2005
306'.0973—dc22   2005012783

New York University Press books are printed on acid-free paper,
and their binding materials are chosen for strength and durability.

Manufactured in the United States of America
c 10 9 8 7 6 5 4 3 2 1
p 10 9 8 7 6 5 4 3 2 1

To the memory of Linda W. Rosenzweig, 1942–2005,
colleague and friend,
an imaginative historian and educator

Contents

Preface

This is a book about a new way of using history, to understand basic aspects of human and social behavior—in this case, in the United States, but potentially more widely. Of course, like most novel endeavors, it is not fully new. We all use history to explain phenomena such as current voting patterns (which often seem surprisingly, even troublingly, rooted in the past). We readily see certain current institutions emerging from a combination of change and continuity from the past. But we have typically subjected only a fraction of relevant behaviors to historical scrutiny, and for their part some of the most imaginative historians, when opening new topics in the past, have been a bit timid about bringing them forward to explicate the present.

The book thus springs from recognition of the utility of the explosion of historical knowledge over the past forty years, though it focuses on deliberately grasping the present as emerging from the past. The book does not invite all historians to do behavioral history and does not claim that history alone explains key behaviors. But there is a missed opportunity in the current gap between historical innovations and the range of vantage points available on distinctive features of contemporary values and actions. Behavioral history requires quite explicit analysis from historians, beyond some of the conventional presentations in the discipline, and this can be truly exciting. It requires new openness from scholars in other disciplines—and happily, there are many signs of this trend already, in fields such as alcohol or obesity studies. It deserves new attention from interested users of history, alongside the more familiar entertainment fare of battles and biographies. There is nothing wrong with the latter, but there are opportunities for historical exploration of dominant assumptions and practices that are simply too important to be neglected.

Behavioral history coins a new approach, but it depends on the work of countless scholars in social and cultural history over the past generation and more, and it invites a new commitment, from history training programs on up, to widen history's utility just as its field of inquiry has expanded.

Introduction

Peter N. Stearns

Over the past thirty years, many Americans have developed not only a healthy fear of tobacco smoke, but an eager disapproval of smokers. Only slightly deflected by criticisms of the ploys of Big Tobacco or possible genetic proclivities on the part of smokers, Americans have turned against smokers not only as threats to health but as creatures of bad character. As one expert put it in 1991, smoking constitutes "some element of human frailty or incompleteness in the smoker" deserving of every reproof both because smokers were nothing more than "merchants of death" and because cessation was simply a matter of self-discipline, "readily mastered with learning and practice."[1] Harsh beliefs translate into rigorous laws and also into the shamed ghettoization of smokers as they cower in building entrances, weathering the glares of self-righteous passers-by. The whole phenomenon is a not inconsiderable passage in recent American history, as both behaviors and attitudes reversed trends of the mid-20th-century decades. But it is not recent history alone. The unusual fierceness and moralism of the American response—quite different from reactions in other industrial countries, despite the same health data—derive from an association of health and good character that took shape in the 19th and early 20th centuries, and with an American delight in castigating sinners—albeit, now, secular sinners—that blended Puritanism with Victorian values even earlier. Our antismoking stance, though partly derived from rational health campaigns that gradually won through, can only fully be understood through a richer history.

This, in turn, is behavioral history in a nutshell: the capacity to understand ourselves, including depths of feeling and differences from other societies and subgroups, through the use of historical explanation. There is no way to grasp why many Americans react to smokers as they do without looking at some deep features of our history, not only the health campaigns that led up to the reversals of policy in the 1970s, but also the older moralism and its transitions from sin to issues of health and character.

Behavioral history rests on two assumptions. The first involves the conviction that substantial components of beliefs and actions, even in very personal areas, are shaped by developments in the past. They cannot be fully understood without examining their origins and the factors that shaped and sustained them. The second assumption embraces the wide range of behaviors that historians are now capable of probing, well beyond conventional textbook staples of wars and presidents, and even beyond the newer trinity of class, race, and gender. While gaps remain, including some that probably can never be filled for lack of adequate data, an explosion of historical knowledge has occurred in the past quarter-century that greatly improves our capacity to understand ourselves. Behavioral history, as a label, seeks to use this capacity for exactly that purpose, building on but surpassing the historian's delight in adding to the richness of the past.

The idea of using history to understand the present is hardly new, of course. No one would pretend to convey some key aspects of American politics—like the difficulty of forming a significant third party or the aversion to socialism—without significant recourse to historical analysis. The American approach to war, including the delight in highest-possible technology, or the continuing reluctance to abridge national sovereignty even in an age of globalization, are other clear products of an interaction between present and past. Only the most superficial presentation would ignore the historical overlays that help determine contemporary responses in political structure or diplomacy. Behavioral history simply but vastly extends the range of historical application.

The major barriers to this kind of explicit historical understanding of ourselves come from a combination of historians' frequent hesitations (read, sometimes, obscurantism) and a related public impatience with serious analysis of any sort. Many historians, quite sincerely, are reluctant to move into direct connections with the present, because these involve more potential controversy, less certain judgments, than does a more remote past. There's no question that behavioral history is deliberately presentist, in focusing on using the past to explain contemporary patterns. It is important to insist that present-focused history is not the only kind of history that should be done by historians, though it needs more attention than it sometimes receives—as in survey history courses that somehow never get past World War II. Less excusably, some historians think of the past so completely in terms of discrete stories and factoids that they are really incapable of using it to explain much of anything—it is just a list of things to be memorized. For their part, many Americans who are open to history think of it, somewhat similarly, as an entertaining hobby, full of juicy anecdotes (preferably about past wars), or museum visits stressing the distant quaintness of the past, but not really a serious tool for contemporary explanation.

Behavioral history must overcome these barriers, by arguing, indeed, by demonstrating, that many of our most cherished or ingrained reactions are really constructed by developments in the past—that, once again, we need history to understand ourselves. There are some nice stories attached—who can write about the construction of present grief in contrast to past grief without noting how, 130 years ago, girls were encouraged to buy coffins and black dresses for their dolls, to train themselves in proper mourning?[2] Analysis of contemporary revulsion against smoking can recall the too-easily-forgotten array of legal prohibitions that greeted the rise of the cigarette and that only began to yield in the early 20th century—another good set of stories, but with a bit of a message about our moral proclivities to boot. But it's analysis—explaining ourselves to ourselves through examination of the origins and historical causes of our behaviors—that forms the main point. We deprive ourselves of vital insight if we look primarily to the past for dramatic anecdotes rather than explanation. But we need a good bit of work, from historians and the consuming public alike, to complete the necessary conversion.

Behavioral history faces additional obstacles. Many of the topics discussed in this book are not commonly seen as part of history at all, but rather the province of fields such as psychology, sociology, even genetics. Discussions of the family might offer a historian the chance to write a background chapter, for a bit of cachet, on past patterns before turning to the latest analysis of the impact of the divorce rate or why American parents have become overly anxious.[3] Behavioral historians will insist, of course, that historical analysis is an explicit component of explaining both divorce rates and parental anxieties. But what about really personal stuff such as experiencing or reacting to jealousy? Clearly this is the province of psychology, but it also requires behavioral history to show how current patterns of jealousy emerged from rather different past forms and to explain why Americans react differently to jealousy from the French or the

Dutch (a comparison that psychological findings establish but cannot by themselves account for). (The French, by the way, get mad when they are jealous, the Dutch tend to get sad, while Americans rush around checking with their friends to see if they've behaved inappropriately; and, truly, the history of jealousy can show why.)[4] Behavioral historians deliberately intrude on domains where other explanations are more common, not to displace these explanations entirely but to demonstrate that historical construction must be part of the diagnosis.

There is more to this than disciplinary quibbling. Some of the most ambitious reaches of behavioral history take us into areas where, until recently, we might have assumed considerable constancy in human experience—like the senses, for example, or dreams. But it turns out that the senses aren't just part of human nature; they can vary and change, not just on an individual basis but societally as well. And when they change, they become part of an analyzable past, which is where behavioral history comes in. As an essay in this volume demonstrates, we can't understand why we smell as we do or think about smell as we do without knowing the modern history of smell. This isn't to deny some constant features for the senses, best captured by psychological or physiological studies; behavioral history, in emphasizing the importance of change, inevitably involves dealing with the complex boundaries between nature and nurture. But the elements constructed through historical processes play serious roles, well in front of the background scenery of human affairs. Need and opportunity combine for behavioral history, where the goal is improving our understanding.

And this is where the real excitement comes in. The redefinition of the past to include more than politics, the idea that any significant human behavior, from sex to death, has the potential for change and therefore for history, opens an additional avenue, sometimes a major highway, to self-appraisal. To be sure, there are still some tentative topics. The history of sleep is not yet advanced enough to shed abundant light on contemporary patterns—though it is clear that we worry about sleep more than our ancestors did and that we nap less, and both anxiety and distinctive behavior can be researched.[5] Boredom is a modern term, suggesting the capacity to define a state that has become much more important in modern than it was in premodern life; and it has changed, interestingly, from being something that well-bred people should learn to avoid causing to an experience that can legitimately be complained about as someone else's fault. But though there's a glimmer of analysis here, it has yet to be rounded out into something that can and must be known if boredom is to be comprehended.[6] Another case, even less developed, involves loneliness. We are sometimes told, probably correctly, that more people are lonely now than was true in the past, which is an open invitation to serious historical analysis, but I have not seen significant work in this direction. Another intriguing instance: despite significant work on emotion, efforts to deal historically with joy are surprisingly limited.[7] Tragically, to take a final example, no one has yet tried a serious historical explanation of modern rates of psychological depression at all—granting that it would be a challenging task.

But the gaps pale before the accomplishments, which is why the definition of behavioral history is overdue. Anyone who wants to know about eating patterns, death, child rearing, emotion, aging, walking, body types, intelligence or retardation, even certain kinds of diseases, needs serious history, well beyond introductory prologue, as a key component in explaining why we do as we do and think as we think. The opportunities are fascinating.

This book is designed to offer a number of case studies in behavioral history. Authors have been asked to identify a contemporary phenomenon, in patterns of action and/or in attendant beliefs and values, that must be, and can be, historically explained at least in part. The phenomenon is a significant part of the way we live, and the historical analysis is intended to be interesting and useful in itself as well as illustrative of the broader case for behavioral history. There is no effort to be comprehensive, either in the list of contents or in individual articles. In terms of overall contents, lots of productive topic areas were omitted simply in the interests of keeping the book manageable (thus, despite the initial example above, no history of smoking habits). And the same selectivity applies to the individual essays. The focus, therefore, is on a particular emotion that can be better understood through history, not on emotions history in general—though it is a rich field; or on one aspect of the history of sexuality, or the history of leisure. The goal is to help people—both historians and others interested in better understanding—become accustomed to doing and using behavioral history.

We're still in a discovery period. Several essays in this book feature research that is just beginning to produce results—the "aha" phase of behavioral history that involves the first serious attempts to show that a familiar phenomenon, such as homesickness, really has a history worth knowing and capable of being known. Others are drawn from well-established work that still deserves a wider audience. For though behavioral history still has its new frontiers, it has raced ahead of public usage, which still looks to history for less than it can deliver. It is this kind of discovery, of a kind of analysis that provides a new mirror on the present, that is most compelling.

While specific methods in behavioral history will vary with the project, in part because of variations in the types of data involved, there is a common set of requirements that should show up in most explicit efforts.

Hypotheses begin with the identification of the contemporary behavior worth investigating—not always an easy task and one that may sometimes emerge from a more general historical inquiry, sometimes from other social science findings. The next step involves identifying the point of origin of the behavior—not to indulge in a mindless debate about the exact month or year, but because pinpointing in time is essential to the next two stages of analysis.

And these entail, first, an explicit contrast with the ways the phenomenon played out prior to the onset of the contemporary trend or pattern. There needs to be a baseline, in other words, along with the identification of origins. Only with this is it possible to discuss real change and novelty.

This in turn leads to the determination of the causes of the shift from precontemporary to contemporary pattern. Obviously, historians cannot deal with causation through experimentation, and their efforts are always open to some debate. But probable attributions of cause add to the meaning of the contemporary trend. It is fine, for example, to know that a modern concern about dieting and hostility to fat began in the United States around 1900, and that it contrasted with a previous tendency to welcome plumpness as a sign of health. Without moving to an assessment of why this change occurred, the opportunity for a full historical understanding of this important aspect of contemporary life will be missed.

With origins established, contrasted with a prechange baseline, and causation assessed, the remaining task involves tracing the phenomenon, along with any adjustments in course, to current manifestations. This process need not involve detailed narrative. It should allow for the addition of other supporting factors. Modern anorexia nervosa, for example, seems to have originated in the mid-19th century for one set of reasons but then greatly gained momentum when the implications of newly slender body imagery were added in the early 20th century.[8]

Behavioral history, in sum, relies on carefully honed historical analysis, whether the practitioner is a professional historian or another social scientist willing to take on the responsibility of converting, at least in part, to this approach to identification and explanation. (A number of social science efforts falter, in fact, because they don't go to the trouble of really identifying origins and establishing contrast with prior patterns.) Of course, methodologies cannot always be as tidy as suggested here. A clear transition from prior status to new trend—as in the conversion, within two decades, from esteeming plumpness to expressing disgust at human fat—does not always emerge, which means that establishing starting points and before-and-after contrast becomes more complex. It is far easier to evoke the need for assessing causation than to produce clear results. But, pending further experience, there are standards in behavioral history that invite emulation and are open to evaluation.

The behavioral history illustrated in this book, in various topic areas, has a few other general features and issues best highlighted in advance. Without getting mired in complexity, there are four principal items of orientation: where to look, chronologically, for the causes of contemporary American behavior; what kinds of causes to seek or expect; what is American about American behavior; and how American is American. We also need to say a word about what is meant by "behaviors," though the assumptions here are more straightforward than those that frame the historical analysis.

On issue 1: there is no set script in terms of chronology for behavioral history. Some developments—such as the 1970s turning point for attitudes toward smokers—may well be quite recent. But in many cases, essentially contemporary behaviors, or key components of them, go farther back in time. Some may have been imported from Europe or Africa during colonial times or have taken root with the colonies themselves. There is an important argument, for example, that colonial Americans developed an unusual degree of attachment to children because of the importance of child labor and the possibility of flight to the frontier and that elements of these attitudes persist in American reactions to their children even today. Significant changes occurred in the United States around 1800 as a result of the formation of a new nation but particularly because of growing commercialization of the economy. So some behavioral history may cast back to the early 19th century, if not for literally contemporary behaviors, at least for elements thereof.

Another significant set of shifts occurred in the second decade of the 20th century, associated with fuller urbanization, the rise of a corporate and service economy, and the advent of big government. But again, there is no set periodization, and depending on what kind of behavior is involved, explanations may begin at quite different points in time, and some will accumulate as a result of several chronological phases of development. For example, while inquiry into contemporary concern about fat has to begin around 1900, when body fashions first started to shift to the still current direction, a larger explanation of our contemporary obesity problems needs to go back to the earlier 19th century when some characteristic and durable American eating patterns initially began to draw comment.[9] Behavioral historians promise (against some of the canons of the mother discipline) that details of the past will not be explored for their own sake but rather pruned for their analytical value; they do not and should not promise that their purview is confined to recent history alone.

The same variety applies to causation, issue number 2. Significant contemporary behaviors may be shaped by prior changes in values and beliefs. Historians have recently come through a strong emphasis on what is often called the "cultural turn," in which attitudes and values gained primary attention as the essential historical reality and the best single guide to actions and policies. We have already referred to durable facets of American culture, such as the tendency toward moralism, as part of the explanation for behaviors current today. But other behaviors have been shaped by changes in economic organization, such as growing commercialism, a corporate environment, and consumerism—in other words, by developments in material standards and institutions. Technologies can loom large, along with scientific discoveries. Shifts in the birthrate have a prominent role in the formation of contemporary attitudes toward children. Strictly political causation may have less to do with behavioral history, at least in the United States, than might be imagined. But even here historians have noted a significant shift in the relationships between families and the elderly once the advent of social security placed primary responsibility for elderly upkeep on the government—a key, if now increasingly vulnerable, aspect of contemporary intergenerational relationships and policy considerations alike.[10] And of course many current behaviors result from combinations of factors: contemporary approaches to death, for example, have something to do with prior cultures juxtaposed with medical and institutional developments and even with consumerism and a corporate economy.

The types of causes relevant to behavioral history also promise considerable mixture in types of sources. The cultural turn has placed substantial emphasis on prescriptive materials—materials that offer implicit or explicit recommendations about child rearing, emotional behavior, the treatment of criminals, and the like—and on qualitative analysis. But there are limitations here, as in the often-discussed gap between prescriptions and actual values and behaviors on the part of those to whom the guidelines are directed. And cultural explanations do not always suffice, in any event. So analysis of causation may turn also to quite different kinds of evidence, such as changes in death rates or disease incidence, where quantification plays a substantial role. Often, finally, an eclectic analysis will prove essential, mixing qualitative and quantitative factors.

Issue number 3 is comparative. Behavioral history readily applies to issues such as Americans' unusually limited vacations (compared to those in Europe and now even Japan) or their unusually extensive weight gains in recent decades. Several of the essays that follow at least briefly evoke some comparisons designed to show distinctively American features of the behavior in question. Given length limitations, however, the comparative elements are often suggested at best. But behavioral history needs geographical as well as chronological parameters. Some important contemporary behaviors may be shared with other countries, or at least with countries that are also Western and/or industrial. Explanations, in these instances, will not rest in the United States alone. But behavioral historians are also interested—sometimes, probably particularly interested—in behaviors that differ from those found in other modern, Western, or industrial settings, where an American twist applies both to the description of behaviors and, as a result, to their analysis. It has already been noted that American jealousy seems a bit different from French or Dutch, so an analysis of the emotion, in terms of behavioral history, must look to what the particular sources of the American variant are. And all this must be established in terms of some explicit comparative effort.

Many significant behaviors that occur in the United States are not generically American—and this is the fourth issue: coherence. The United States, we are often and correctly reminded, is a diverse place. While behavioral history does not focus on class, race, gender, or region alone, as noted, it must take these factors into account. Many excursions in behavioral history to date have focused disproportionately on the American middle class, with at most some allowance for gender differences. There is nothing wrong with this, in that the middle class is quite important. But sometimes explicit definitions have been missing, leaving the impression that the middle class is in fact the whole of the national experience—that it is possible to talk about coherent national patterns of behavior, without actually testing the proposition against the nation's various subgroups. Sometimes also, the effort to establish behavioral history for largely non-middle-class groups, such as African Americans, has not received adequate attention, if only because the sources are more difficult. So behavioral history must be tested not only through comparisons with other societies but also through explicit attention to internal variations within the nation itself.

Here too, the essays that follow recognize this issue. A number of essays deal explicitly with gender and with race, treating both variables as factors in behavioral history that require attention. (Social class is also noted, but taken up in less detail.) It is both possible and desirable to deal with these factors carefully but without confining the results to separate subfields such as African American or women's history.

More generally, as behavioral history gains ground, clarity of definition of the interaction between "national" standards or patterns and the experiences of more specific groups will constitute an essential guideline, as against facile generalizations about undifferentiated national character or behavior. Along with explicit justification of chronology, in terms of definable starting points for the identification and analysis of contemporary behaviors, and appropriate range in terms of the combination of causal factors involved, these features must characterize the best efforts of behavioral historians now and in the future.

Behavioral history assumes some agreement on what behaviors involve, and, without belaboring this definitional issue, a brief explanation is warranted. With varying emphases, most of the articles in this book see behaviors as a mixture of attitudes about actions and actions themselves: what people do as they or others die and how they think about death, to take one example. This approach differs somewhat from the more conventional history of death, which may focus more on mortality statistics, objective causes of death, or formal mourning practices; but all these topics, particularly the last, may be part of an explanation of how people react to death and how they contemplate their own demise. Manners, an aspect of human behavior much explored in the past decade, similarly involve reactions to others and to particular social situations, plus the actions that result from these values and assumptions.

· · ·

The essays in this book are divided into five kinds of behaviors, though overlaps occur. The first part deals with aspects of the family, with particular focus on relationships with children, currently a rising field in historical research more generally. Family history has moved increasingly from an initial interest in structural matters such as household size or marriage age to relationships and emotional connections, and behavioral history benefits greatly from this expansion. Part II deals with consumer behaviors—behaviors that change and those that revealingly remain stable despite surrounding change. Consumerism is another area of recently advancing knowledge, and behavioral history will contribute to these gains. Changes in emotional life are factored in as well, another expansion of behavioral history's range. Part III covers manners and rituals, the latter particularly focused on American approaches to death. Finally, parts IV (on the senses) and V (on sexuality) deal again both with vital contemporary behaviors and with important extensions of historical analysis. In both cases, behavioral history explicitly takes on any assumptions that innate human qualities preclude a significant past, with current patterns emerging from the familiar but challenging historical mixture of continuity and change. Here is where, correspondingly, some of the most strikingly historical findings have emerged over the past decade or so.

The overall intent of all these sections is to represent exciting findings and the ongoing potential in behavioral history through a sampling of a much wider potential array. All five topical categories involve important recent findings, and all involve basic tensions between qualities inherent in the human species, whether for buying things or for dealing with children or with death, and the actual experience of significant historical change and construction. Emotions, the senses, and the interactions between intimacy and a wider society play out in all the categories, which in turn display the basic apparatus of behavioral history in challenging domains.

Behavioral history is a new term, though it refers to some well-established research in social and cultural history as well as pointing to a new frontier. Both the existing qualities and the need for innovation deserve some final comment.

Innovation must embrace historians and their audience alike, if behavioral history is to realize its promise. Interested historians—and again, this neither can nor should include the whole discipline—need to become more comfortable with topics derived explicitly from current behavioral issues. History has always taken cues from the present in deciding what aspects of the past to look at, so the idea of a connection is not new at all. But explicitly using history to explain a current pattern is less common than it should be, particularly outside the arena of politics and diplomacy. For their part, other disciplines devoted to accounting for human behavior need to create a much larger window for historical analysis—for the inclusion of factors of change, and of historically derived explanation.

Happily, some connections have already been made. A number of sociologists and anthropologists, and an occasional psychologist, contribute directly to behavioral history by adding serious historical research—and, equally important, historical thinking—to their repertoire. Even aside from these individual conversions, research conferences in the applied social sciences, on subjects such as addiction, drinking, or crime, now often include historians as central players. Addiction is a particularly interesting case in point. Most addiction researchers battle to demonstrate that their subject is a legitimately scientific-medical topic, that addiction is really a disease worthy of (funded) study. The task is particularly challenging when not only substance abuse, but also behaviors such as gambling, are drawn into the mix. But, as several addiction authorities have recognized, the drive for scientific legitimacy need not preclude serious inquiry into how addiction emerged in modern American culture and into the needs the concept serves in addition to designating a disease entity. For a society eager to identify individual responsibility, the addiction concept, from its inception in the early 19th century, played a significant cultural role in calling attention to the individual but with possibilities of exculpation and treatment. It continues to serve this role in contemporary America, though the range has expanded from initial concerns with alcohol to drugs (late 19th century) and gambling (1920s).[11] Science and historical analysis can conjoin in showing both how addiction works and how its exploration can help individuals and society at large.

What is needed now is an amplification of this kind of connection between history and behavioral inquiry, considering three specific steps beyond simply more examples of the same.

First, we need more historians willing to accept the challenges of behavioral history, from initially defining their topics to setting their research agendas in terms of explanatory analysis.

Second, there must be a willingness on the part of those disciplines most commonly devoted to seeking changeless aspects of the human condition—through the psychology of human nature, for example, or genetics or neuroscience—to allow for a creative tension with explorations of historical change. Behavioral history does not require either/or di-chotomies, such that behaviors are entirely historically constructed or not at all. It is quite possible to allow for significant genetic or psychological components while noting that they work out somewhat differently de-pending on historical context and interaction with historical variables. Historians have sometimes been guilty of overkill, claiming that people "back then" were entirely different from what they are now, incapable, for example, of the kind of familial love that was discovered in the 18th cen-tury.[12] Scientific experts even more often make overstatements by arguing that the past and change can be ignored in the excitement of pinning one more marker on the genome project. In fact, against both extremes, inter-action and debate are essential, as behavioral historians make their case.

And further, of course, we need to enlarge the audience for behavioral history as one way to gain understanding of why people act and think as they do. This means more explicit efforts, by behavioral historians, to use their work to this end; it means educating the public to expect new gains from historical research; and it means fostering the wider collaborations among disciplines, history now included, that have assessments of human behavior as their preserve as they address a wider public.

Behavioral history may lead, finally, to suggestions for change. Like any examination of current values and actions, behavioral history may illumi-nate patterns we find desirable and wish to keep. There is no inherent re-form agenda, but behavioral history may also be employed to help explain behaviors that are undesirable, such as the rapid increase in obesity, to take one example where historians have been asked for guidance. Behav-ioral history faces two obstacles in this connection.[13] First, historians are not usually accustomed to offering explicit advice about how people should behave, unless they follow an older fashion of suggesting past ac-tions or characters that might be usefully emulated in the present—an in-teresting kind of historical exercise but rather different from behavioral history. It's one thing to show how the past leads to the present, another to say how this analysis in turn might guide conduct. Some behavioral histo-rians, comfortable with their pretentious focus, may nevertheless shy away from the advice column.

Second, behavioral history lessons are likely to be complicated. As a so-ciety, we have become accustomed to a quest for dramatic remedy: this bit of psychological advice will help reduce the divorce rates; that medicine will definitely treat our children's Attention Deficit Disorder; this bit of ge-netic tinkering will lead us to the conquest of psychological depression.

Behavior history, even if we grant its utility in improving understanding, is not so snappy. But, in showing how behaviors emerge as part of past change, it is intrinsically optimistic about the possibility of further change—more optimistic than approaches that emphasize the human condition as a set of natural constants. Knowing that Americans became committed to rapid eating over 150 years ago, and that in a contemporary context rapid eating contributes to obesity, suggests a complex connection that is not likely to be easily broken. But it does suggest a pattern that emerged from specific causes and that can be changed in turn, and it provides a definite target for remedial measures in case the quicker fixes don't work. Learning to use behavioral history as a source of constructive change is not the least of the challenges the field has to offer.

Understanding comes first, however, and that is what behavioral history puts front and center. Identifying distinctive features of the present—with the help of many disciplines—but then using a focused approach to the past to explain when and why these features took shape provides a fascinating window on the human panorama. Even when the result does not yield a clear prescription for change, it will provide the kind of perspective that enables people to think through the behaviors they see around them, free from any sense that they are merely natural or inevitable. And this result of behavioral history, in encouraging personal inquiry, may be far more valuable than the more common how-to approach. A new chapter is opening for one of the oldest disciplines in the book.

NOTES

1. David Keogh, *Smoking: The Artificial Passion* (New York, 1991), 15, 18, 97, 141, 155; Barbara Lyrich and R. J. Bonnie, eds., *Growing Up Tobacco Free* (Washington, 1994), 77, 98; Robert Tollison, ed., *Smoking and Society* (Lexington, MA, 1984); John Burnham, *Bad Habits: Drinking, Smoking, Taking Drugs, Gambling, Sexual Misbehavior, and Swearing in American History* (New York, 1994), ch. 4.

2. Peter N. Stearns, *American Cool: Constructing a Twentieth-Century Emotional Style* (New York, 1994); Paul Rosenblatt, *Bitter, Bitter Tears: Nineteenth-Century Diarists and Twentieth-Century Grief Theories* (Minneapolis, 1983); Jeffrey Steele, "The Gender and Racial Politics of Mourning," in Peter N. Stearns and Jan Lewis, eds., *An Emotional History of the United States* (New York, 1998), 91–108.

3. John Demos, *Past, Present and Personal: The Family and The Life Course in American History* (New York, 1986).

4. Edmund Zilner, *Jealousy in Children: A Guide for Parents* (New York, 1949);

Gordon Clanton and Lynn Smith, eds., *Jealousy* (Englewood Cliffs, NJ, 1978); Peter N. Stearns, *Jealousy: The Evolution of an Emotion in American History* (New York, 1989); Peter Salovey, ed., *The Psychology of Jealousy and Envy* (New York, 1991).

5. Peter N. Stearns, Perrin Rowland, and Lori Giarnella, "Children's Sleep: Sketching Historical Change," *Journal of Social History* 30 (1996): 345–66; Roger Ekrich, "The Sleep We Have Lost: Pre-Industrial Slumber in the British Isles," *American Historical Review* 106 (2001).

6. Patricia Spacks, *Boredom: The Literary History of a State of Mind* (Chicago, 1995); Richard P. Smith, "Boredom: A Review," *Human Factors* 23 (1981): 325–40; Peter N. Stearns, *Anxious Parents: A History of Modern Childrearing in America* (New York, 2003), ch. 6.

7. R. Marie Griffith, "Joy Unspeakable and Full of Glory: The Vocabulary of Pious Emotion in the Narratives of American Pentecostal Women, 1910–1945," in Stearns and Lewis, eds., *Emotional History*, 218–40.

8. Joan Jacob Brumberg, *Fasting Girls: The Emergence of Anorexia Nervosa as a Modern Disease* (Cambridge, MA, 1988).

9. Hillel Schwartz, *Never Satisfied: A Cultural History of Diets, Fantasies and Fat* (New York, 1983); Marcia Millman, *Such a Pretty Face: Being Fat in America* (New York, 1980); Roberta Seid, *Never Too Thin: Why Women Are at War with Their Bodies* (New York, 1989); Peter N. Stearns, *Fat History: Bodies and Beauty in the Modern West* (New York, 1997).

10. Tamara Hareven, "Life-Course Transitions and Kin Assistance in Old Age: A Cohort Comparison," in David Van Tassel and Peter N. Stearns, eds., *Old Age in Bureaucratic Society* (Westport, CT, 1986), 110–26.

11. Harry Levine, "The Discovery of Addiction: Changing, Conceptions of Habitual Drunkenness in America," *Journal of Studies on Alcohol* 39 (1978): 143–69; Stanton Peele, "Addiction as a Cultural Concept," *Psychology: Perspectives and Practice. Annals of the New York Academy of Science* 602 (1990): 205–20.

12. Edward Shorter, *The Making of the Modern Family* (New York, 1975): Lawrence Stone, *Family, Sex and Marriage in England, 1500–1800* (New York, 1979). It was Stone who opined that in premodern families one would find as much love as one would expect in a bird's nest, in contrast to the emotional intensity of modern family life.

13. It is important to be candid here. Behavioral history, as a new endeavor, needs some time to develop its potential for lesson drawing. Many historians, willing to offer historically derived advice, don't quite know how to do it without seeming presumptuous. They are much more comfortable pointing out erroneous historical references by other kinds of advice givers, as in the family realm where prescriptions routinely oversimplify past family forms and bathe them in a kind of false nostalgia that can actually impede a sensible take on current issues. For their part, audiences frequently crave a specific applicability to which few if any disciplines, history included, really lend themselves without serious distortion. What

we need, beyond greater experience, is some mutual accommodation, with historians willing to think about what behavioral changes might follow from their findings and how these can be framed, while audiences learn to take greater pleasure in analysis and understanding, realizing that much of the responsibility for applying behavioral history lies with individuals themselves.

Part I

Family and Childhood

The Cute Child and
Modern American Parenting

Gary Cross

Few would immediately think of the "cute" as shaping modern parent-child relations and behavior. But the "cute"—defined as particular ways that children interact with adults, suggesting at once dependence and vulnerability as well as vitality, innocent charm, and impishness—has for a century been central to modern American child rearing. Of course, children, because they are new to most experiences and have few strong learned responses to these encounters, quite naturally behave similarly over time and place. To a degree, three-year-olds have always been "cute." But until the twentieth century, they have seldom been represented as such in literature or visual arts. Even more, adults did not cultivate the "cute" in the young; instead, they seem to have punished or ignored it. A marker of modern child-adult relations is the adult expectation that children should be "cute." Modern adults not only look for the "look" of the cute and encourage cute behavior in children, but, in many cases, cultivate cuteness in themselves and in their relationships with other adults. The cute challenges other behavioral modes, with important social and personal consequences. This is a behavior that cannot easily be explained by psychology but is instead a response that is rooted in social and cultural changes that appear only in the twentieth century.

Evidence for the historically recent emergence of the cute is everywhere. Today we pose children for photographs (with about half of amateur photos featuring children), dress up toddler girls for beauty pageants, and are attracted to images of desiring and desirable children in about a third of advertisements, no matter the subject. We buy in the millions photos of babies and toddlers dressed as bunnies or gazing out at the sea with outstretched arms in sheer delight. A century ago all this would have been considered strange, if not perverse and immoral. These images suggest that children are capable of wide-eyed wonder at what jaded adults no longer see or of blank-eyed indifference at what frightens, obsesses, or disgusts the experienced. Grownups often love the way that children look and respond, even though adults feel superior to their naiveté.

The cute is far more than a curious obsession of modern Americans. It shapes family life, gender development of children, and even the identities of adults. The longing for "cuteness" permeates the life-changing decision to bear or adopt children. Having a child is so important that Americans spend two billion dollars a year on fertility drugs and test-tube fertilization. Childlessness is, for many, a tragedy, not for the traditional reasons—desire for an heir or for economic assistance—but because of the longing for the emotional satisfaction of evoking a child's delight. Adoptions have steadily shifted since the 1930s, from the practical choice of the older productive child to the charming infant. A major part of adults' relations with children is the attempt to evoke cute responses by giving children toys, dolls, and even Disney vacations. The longing for that look has helped to create mass demand for consumer goods and the transformation of holidays into rituals of giving to children.

The cute also is expressed differently by gender. In boys, the "naughty" side of the cute is often a naive rebellion from domesticity and responsibility, while in girls that side is often coquettish, an innocent or unintended sensuality, and even sexuality. This contrast not only contributes to later gender identity but also explains why adults may respond to the cute in boys differently (often with great toleration) than the cute in girls. Cute behaviors often reappear in adults both as ways of winning positive responses from others (especially the opposite sex in courtship games), but also as a personal identity with appeals of its own. Sometimes called the Peter Pan Syndrome in popular psychology, the cute takes both adult male and female forms and contributes to a contemporary tendency to discount behavioral markers of maturity (responsibility, muted emotions, and deferred gratification).

The adult longing for the cute in children seems to have led those children as they grew older to reject the cute for a rebellious culture of the cool. The cool today may mean simply a kind of cutting-edge fashion or, more subtly, emotional restraint. But here I am using it in the sense of the opposite of the parent's cute, often a challenge to middle-class sensibilities.

It is frequently associated with "dangerous" behaviors—playing violent video games and premature and overt sexuality, for example—and, in response, adult "moral panics" that lead to demands for control and repression. This pattern of rebelling from the cute in favor of the cool contributes to adult preferences for small over older children and perpetuates generational conflict. The phenomenon of older children seeking autonomy that elicits negative parental response is, of course, not new. But its intensity is often greater than in the distant past, and it is fueled by very different issues in the ever-changing consumer culture.

Finally, the cult of the cute child has come into regular conflict with other models of parent-child relations, especially as expressed in the child-rearing manuals that appeared after 1900. Conservatives, especially those inspired by traditional religious belief, have insisted that parents dominate the process of shaping the child and denounce the "permissiveness" at least partially created by the cult of the cute. Modernist child rearing has argued that the child must be systematically nurtured in an orderly process to meet that world. It too has rejected the cute as an indulgence of adults that interfered with the developmental needs of the child. Despite opposition of conservative moralists and modernizing experts, the language of the cute gradually seeped so deeply into family culture that many experts compromised with it, allowing a more tolerant, even playful child-parent relationship.

The cult of the cute has often been ignored by scholars because it appears trivial, but it offers a radically different understanding of childhood, rooting it not in the youth's potential (and need for a formal, detailed scheme of child rearing) but in the child's natural and positive wonderment that age destroys and adults find rejuvenating. The cute was obscured by the fact that it was not celebrated, much less promoted in the pulpit and child-rearing manuals, but rather in magazine covers and advertising, shop windows, comic strips, new holiday rituals, and toys and novelty goods. The cute has distant origins in the romantic ideas of the late 18th and early 19th centuries, but it emerges as a defining ideal of childhood only in the first decade of 20th-century consumer culture. The cult of the cute implies a less moralistic and more expressive approach to child rearing but also endows the child with desires that increasingly have melded child rearing with consumer culture.

Origins of the Cult of the Cute

This essay is not making the argument that love of children is essentially a modern idea, nor even that children were bereft of articles of pleasure and delight before the 20th century. Authors such as Linda Pollock have decisively shown the folly of such extreme views. But something surely changed in how children were imagined around 1900. In some ways, both the developmentalist view of child-rearing experts and the popular cult of the cute were effects of similar causes. Sharp decreases in child mortality produced more optimistic attitudes toward the survivability of the young. Beginning in the 1870s, when infant mortality in Massachusetts was still almost 16 percent, that rate dropped, especially sharply after 1900. While American parents had a 62 percent probability that one of their children would die before adulthood in 1900, that rate dropped to 16 percent by 1940 and to 4 percent by 1976.[1] This decline in death rates was both the effect and cause of new practices and attitudes: improved sanitation and better obstetrics improved survival, and because this impact was widely understood, parents embraced new scientific child-care practices promoted by physicians such as E. L. Holt, further lowering death rates.[2] In turn, the apparent possibility that parental action could improve children's life chances made parents, and especially mothers, more responsible for improved care, allowing advertisers of antiseptics to appeal to parental anxiety. Peter Stearns notes that 20th-century parents learned to see children as "more fragile, readily overburdened, requiring careful handling," even if they had a better chance of surviving than in the past.[3] At the same time, this improvement in infant morality rates and children's health contributed to a shift in the image of the child, from a frail innocent to a vital and all-desiring being—that is, cute. Equally important was the decrease in family size: there were 40 percent fewer children per American family in 1940 than 1900. Smaller families provided more time and energy for parents to follow the message of the developmental child-rearing experts. Fewer children also made it possible for parents to lavish more attention on the delight of and in the child and to be more tolerant of naughty (if nice or innocent) behavior.

    The declining economic utility of the child in the early 20th century increased the psychological investment in the young, leading to more deliberate child care. At the same time, the affluence that made possible the withdrawal of children from the labor market also fostered a merchandis-

ing revolution that encouraged adults to buy symbolic goods (toys, li-
censed apparel, games, etc.) for children. The same prosperity also
brought adult frustrations with modern economic and cultural changes
that led to nostalgia for childlike wonder and freedom.

All of this led to surprisingly complex parental behavior. Despite the
impact of the cult of the cute, it hardly displaced protection and prudence
in child rearing. Rather, there emerged a "new dualism" in the words of
Peter Stearns, where "adult constraints on children became more detailed
and demanding even as children's outlets through consumerism expanded."[4] Consumerism produced contradictory anxieties: that children
were being corrupted by entertainment and that they were not being entertained enough, leading to dreaded "boredom." And, with the advent of
commercial fads and the threat of entertainments that prematurely introduced children to the world of adults (especially lower-class adult taste),
the only solution was an alternative consumer culture—for example, the
hyperactivity of music lessons, Little League, exclusive summer camps, and
"educational toys." In effect, the two understandings of the child fed off
each other, reinforcing each other as well as producing perpetual conflict.

The cult of the cute shared its origins in new demographic and economic conditions with the child-rearing experts. Yet images of the cute
child emerged out of a very different culture—a fantasy, largely commercial world—separate from the educational and scientific worlds of the experts that both emerged roughly around 1900. Down this distinct path, the
cult of the cute became as important in shaping modern childhood as did
the contents of the experts' manuals.

The old images of the child as an innocent (and even an angelic one) in
need of moral protection, or alternatively as a creature born to sin, are
very different from the cute child. As a source of spontaneity and wonder
(even if that meant toleration of mischief), the cute child was hardly fragile or heavenly. The cute suggests that the attractive, bubbling enthusiasm
of the child is no longer seen as "manipulative" or devil-like but charming
and even desirable. The cute child is naturally a little naughty but always
nice. What made cute children "nice" was that they responded to adult
affection with affection—that they needed adult emotional, if not so obviously as in the past, moral care—and that their vitality was ultimately domesticated. This complex image reflected both the adult's greater understanding and toleration of the foibles of the child but also the adult's un-
fulfilled emotional needs projected onto the child. Moreover, the cute
child expressed the presumably natural desires of the boy and girl but re-

mained the object of possession and giving and thus was integrated into a culture of expanding consumption.

The idea of the child as "cute" as opposed to angelic or devilish appears only in the 20th century. One way of showing this is by considering the changing meaning of the word "cute" and its shifting association from the adult to the child. Cute is a shortened form of "acute," signifying "sharp, quick witted," and shrewd in an "underhanded manner" (first noted in 1731, according to the Merriam Webster Dictionary). In American slang (Oxford University Dictionary), it came also to be "attractive, pretty, charming" or "attractive in a mannered way" around 1834 but only in reference to things (for example, socks in 1857 and a tidy room in 1868). In a digital word search of *Harper's Weekly* from 1857 to 1913, "cute" appeared repeatedly to refer to the clever, as in a sneaky "cute Yankee landlord" (1857), "cute miser" (1867), or even a "cute lass, who can understand" (1858) and "a cuteness for which widow mothers are proverbial" (1875). Animals could be "cute," too (pug dogs and kittens in the late 1880s and 1890s). An ad for a watercolor picture of a "cute Chinese kid" appeared in 1900. But it was only in 1909 that the word ever applied to the American child in *Harper's:* "I like cute little girls that look up at you and take your hands and cuddle right up to you—they are so much sweeter than the other kind." A final article in 1910 insists that a "thirteen month old baby is expected to be . . . a cute mischief maker."[5]

By the 1900s, the word "cute" was interchangeable with "cunning," a word that also meant "clever"—a corruption of "can" and used as an adjective for "crafty" but also "insightful." The sliding meaning of both words from a manipulative intelligence to a naive charm suggests a new tolerance for the willful, even exploitative child. While "cunning" lost this positive connotation in the 20th century, the little girl who bats her eyes to win favor and little boy who steals cookies from the cookie jar remain "cute."

Other evidence confirming this new openness to cuteness involves the change in the portrayal of children in the commercial art of the late 19th and early 20th centuries. Despite a growing sentimentality toward children, in the 1880s they rarely appeared in advertising and magazine illustrations. Pear's soap (later famous for its child icons) featured endorsements from a countess and a professor in 1885. In magazines, children appeared in stock settings: the sad child street musician (1870); shoeless, but clean, street kids given ice cream by charitable uptown New Yorkers; cautionary images of devilish newsboys frightening the respectable excursionist at the seashore; poor, faceless youngsters dragged to the Bowery "dime museum" by thoughtless parents; or alternatively well-dressed Sunday schoolers on parade. These were scenes evoking pity, moral outrage, and uplift, but children were not particularly associated with delight or pleasure. They were not even shown laughing or smiling in pleasant scenes such as picnics.[6]

In a familiar scene, a *Harper's Weekly* cover illustration of 1870 displays a father frightening a child with a Jack-in-the-box; toys and fairy tales of this era were not supposed to amuse and delight children but to educate and frighten them. At the same time, St. Nicholas as well as the Easter Hare and the Birthday Man were as much boogeymen as gift givers (and the anxiety that this caused children seems to have amused adults). Even when artists tried to create an image of the naughty innocent, as in *Frank Leslie's Illustrated Magazine*'s (1885) "The Little Mischief Maker," the result was not a cute but an angelic, almost devoted girl as she takes eggs from a bird's nest.[7]

A dramatically new image of the child (and with it new imputed behaviors between adults and children) emerged slowly from about 1870. Literary historian Jackie Wullschlaeger notes a shift "from an emphasis on the child as a moral icon, emblem of purity, to a craze for the child as fun-loving playboy hero."[8] We can see this in Thomas Aldrich's *The Story of a Bad Boy* (1869) and especially in Mark Twain's *Tom Sawyer* (1876) and *Huckleberry Finn* (1884). Another marker of this change is the contrast of two Thomas Nast images of children interacting with Santa Claus between 1870 and 1879. For decades prior to 1879, Santa, portrayed as an essentially benevolent figure who showers children with gifts, had been displacing the old judge St. Nicholas, who had been paired sometimes with the boogeyman figure of Black Peter. As late as December 1870, Nast presented Santa as a scary figure in the form of a Jack-in-the-box threatening two very anxious children with switches. But by 1879, Nast pictured Santa as a kindly grandfatherly figure with happy children on his knee, surrounding him in delight with the gifts that he provided.[9] These contrasting images mark important steps in the origins of the cult of the cute.

This transition also can be subtly seen in advertising "trade cards," colorful images that were produced by manufacturers and retailers in great number between the 1860s and 1900.[10] In many of the earlier cards, sentimental images of children predominated. Still, there was another side to the trade card that showed it to be a transition to a new image and understanding of the child as innocent rule breaker. Many show children in comical situations (e.g., a humorous image of two boys sewing the tails of a cat and dog together with a new sewing machine). The naughty-boy theme became even more prominent at the end of the century. Another curious trend was illustrated in card series that showed the child transformed into an animal, anticipating the portrayal of animals as children by Disney and others in contemporary cartoons; others featured images of Japanese and Dutch children (foreshadowing the association of the word "cute" with "exotic" Asians and perky and vital Dutch, as is particularly evident in the popular Disneyland attraction, "It's a Small World"). Even more common were representations of children transcending their dependent status when dressed and playing adult roles: wearing top hats, bedecked in gowns for an elegant 18th-century French banquet, or dueling for a "lady." These images celebrated the child not as an angelic innocent but as being spunky, willfully assuming adult roles, and even naughty (if nice).

By the last decade of the trade card's prominence, we begin to see a change as the child became the avatar of desire. For example, in an 1896 card for a cocoa drink, a sweet, pensive girl notices a toddler sipping from a cup. In frustration at being left out, she shouts, "I want a cup of Huyler's cocoa too!" The sentimentalized child is given a will, even a desire that might have earlier been seen as rude or wicked.[11] The child's longings were no longer dangerous, but natural, even normative. This became another element in the cute theme that would soon permeate ad images.

In the opening decade of the 20th century, the trade card gave way to colorful cover art and display ads in new mass-circulation magazines, especially the *Saturday Evening Post, Colliers*, and *Ladies' Home Journal*, all of which often borrowed child themes from the trade cards.[12] From 1904 to 1915, images of impish boys became common—like the lad who sets off a firecracker under a standing policeman, or boys going skinnydipping in a forbidden swimming hole. This type of image was particularly common in the emerging art of the comic strip. The earliest example (1895) was the street child, Richard Outcault's "Yellow Kid." Here was a streetwise urchin, parentless child, vaguely Asian in appearance (as other images of the cute), but Irish by intent, who lived in Hogan's Alley, where he created mischief at every opportunity. This urchin appealed to a popular audience as a protest against the stuffy, "improving" genteel tone and culture of the major newspapers of the time.

However, popular middle-class sensibilities required that a more domesticated image of the urchin prevail: the willful child, even selfish and devious at times, who was ultimately good at heart when cared for and controlled by the loving parent. Outcault himself accommodated this apparent demand with a new comic strip, "Buster Brown," in 1902. Buster was a mischievous lad but well protected from corruption by a bourgeois home. Portrayed in the familiar image of innocence in a Little Lord Fauntleroy costume and haircut, he played tricks on his dog and family. The strip repeated this theme over and over, ending with a spanking and a moral lesson given by a contrite Buster. This naughty-but-nice boy was ultimately a domesticated urchin.[13]

The cultural power of this image of the naughty but nice child is shown by its many imitations in the United States and Britain (Mischievous Willie, The Kid, Funny Side Gang, Little Jimmy, Little Annie Rooney, Skippy, and Little Lulu). By the 1910s, the punishment for naughtiness in the comics declined, disappearing altogether with Skippy (featured in newspapers from 1926 to 1945). Even the residual hint of the child of original sin had vanished and was replaced by the suggestion of merely a natural inquisitiveness. By 1951, Hank Ketcham's comic strip "Dennis the Menace" culminated the trend. Dennis was "cute" because he was merely "curious" when he got into trouble. It was usually only the adult's fussiness (especially that of neighbor Mr. Wilson) that was the problem. This was equally true of H. A. Rey's storybook figure, *Curious George* (1940), the childlike monkey who got into trouble but, in the end, saved the day. All this points to a more tolerant attitude toward children: they were often innocently and ignorantly naughty, and even their antisocial behavior was naturally adventuresome. Through the evolution of popular representations of the child, adults seem to have worked out complex feelings about their offspring, gradually replacing older, often religiously inspired emotions and reactions to children's behavior with new ones based on "nature."

This new celebration of the natural was embodied in the "cute" boy portrayed as the magical, diminutive, and "good-natured" animal. Instead of advocating that parents beat the "animal" out of the child, popular commercial culture suggested that the wild, even grotesque, could be cute because it is willful (impish) and yet harmless. The childlike animal was also pitiful and evoked a sense of superiority and protectiveness in adults (as powerful today as in the early 20th century, with adult collections of Beanie Babies, Cabbage Patch Kid dolls, and Trolls). The teddy bear is only one of many possible examples of this curious affection for the wild animal. In the 19th century, the bear was a frightening image and used in toys to scare children (similar to the Jack-in-the-box). But in the form of the "baby" bear (spared, according to a popular newspaper story, by Teddy

Roosevelt on a hunt in 1902), the "teddy" bear soon became a plush doll (made from "huggable" material similar to modern upholstery). The bear had become the embodiment of the cute child, especially when it was associated with boys, who were first given teddy bears on the boardwalk of the New Jersey shore in the summer of 1906. When photographed hugging the bear, adults found endearing the transformation of the beast into a love object held close by their "brave" boys.

Like the urchin, the childlike animal gradually became cute through domestication. Note the change from Ignatz the Mouse, a comic strip character in the 1910s and 1920s, who regularly hit Krazy Kat (Ignatz's admirer) with a brick, to the loveable homebody, the Mickey Mouse of the 1930s. Ignatius was very much in the tradition of the European Punch and Judy puppet shows where children were entertained with the story of an enraged Punch killing a policeman. Even though middle-class parents willingly embraced the naughty but nice child, they rejected what they saw as a thoughtless introduction of children to a violent world. Mickey Mouse fit that need, especially after Disney abandoned his early portrayal as an anarchic figure (as in *Steamboat Willie* of 1928, striking a parrot). By 1934, Mickey was transformed to conform to this new sensibility, becoming the bashful, clean-cut, small-town "All-American" boy with his own dog.[14]

The female form of the cute also appeared in film (most obviously with Shirley Temple in the 1930s), but its origins were certainly in the transformation of the doll in the first decade of the twentieth century. While Victorian-era dolls possessed adult bodies and faces (with pursed lips, high cheeks, and small straight eyes), German and then American doll makers introduced dolls that presumably looked like the girls who played with them—with childlike body proportions and faces featuring large, round, wide-open eyes, "full of childlike humor." The doll now mirrored a new adult image of the natural child but invited girls to abandon the traditional function of doll play—imitation of adulthood—for contentment in a world of the innocent cute.[15] More important, these dolls often had a slightly impish, even coquettish look to them. Dolls' names ("Miss Mischief," "Naughty Marietta," "Miss Coquette," or "Flossie Flirt") openly appealed to a strange adult admiration for the spunky, even slightly manipulative and self-centered child. The visual clues were the eyes askance or even eyes that "naughtily roll from side to side in that delightful flirting way."[16] The Kewpie doll of Rose O'Neill (1909) recalled the impish cupid: shy and lovable with a baby's top knot, wide eyes, snub nose, outstretched arms, round belly, and sexless; yet also a fun-loving urchin with the authenticity absent in the formality and dullness of adults, especially those from the genteel class. Kewpie was the "vital and honest waif against the jaded bourgeoisie" and a model for a long succession of dolls and lovable images of the cute and coquettish girl.[17]

Shirley Temple films in the early 1930s followed this tradition: Shirley was dependent (often portrayed as an orphan), evoking affection, but she was also a nymphet, an innocent that curiously imitated the sensuous woman in one of her earliest roles at three years of age in a series of *Baby Burlesks*. Temple impersonated the sexy Marlene Dietrich to the amusement of adults, just as children dressed up for baby beauty pageants do today. The cute as the combination of the needy and coquettish appealed to adults, but it also created tensions that have been passed down to the present, as Anne Higonnet has shown in the confusion between the innocent "cute" and child pornography.

Magazine advertising became another site for the cultivation of the cute. Picking up where the trade cards left off, the desiring and desirable child became a trademark image to spark interest in new products that were emerging at the beginning of the 20th century. Grace Drayton's Campbell Soup Kids (1905), those pudgy, red-apple-cheeked "Dutch" youngsters in overalls, conveyed health and vitality in an era of concern about food purity and good nutrition, but they also expressed a spunky willfulness that was soon associated with many new products. Especially common were foods and cleaners purchased by women ("Uneeda" biscuits, "Spic and Span," and "Fairy Soap," for example).

These images of the child suggested the natural desire as well as desirability of the "cute." A 1911 Kellogg's Corn Flakes ad featured a sweet, seemingly angelic child in glowing light cradling a box of cereal in her arms for herself. The caption reads, "You'd be selfish too." A pure, even "selfish" desire for corn flakes and much else was no longer something to control and discourage; it had become natural and, in an increasingly secular culture, good. In fact, ads for new products promised to let children's desires coexist with family harmony. Wesson Oil boldly asserted: "We hope you have a fussy family" because this product could help mothers cope with demanding offspring and, even more, because those desires should be accommodated.[18] In this commercial context, the cute was cultivated to sell goods by convincing adults that children's desires were natural and that accommodating them could both meet their needs and resolve family conflicts. But the cute was far more than a sales trick.

The cute was a way of working out many cultural tensions emerging around 1900, as adults projected onto children their conflicting embrace of change and nostalgia for "timeless tradition." A major shift in the representation of children involved associating the young with the "new." Although children by definition have always been "new," adults had seldom linked children with novelty until the 20th century. After all, childbearing was a timeless process, and the perpetuation of civilization required that the young be repositories of received learning and tradition. This may help explain that, while adults adopted fashion in the Renaissance, children were still dressed in archaic costumes and would be for centuries. This association of children with timeless nature and tradition remained strong at the end of the 19th century when the young were still dressed in old-style "sailor suits," given traditional toys (such as Noah's arks), and told ancient fairy tales. Around 1900, Americans extended this principle when they made their children repositories of the festivals that they had abandoned (May Day, Halloween, July Fourth parades, and, in modified form, Christmas). Traditional, often violent rituals full of social tension were bowdlerized and "cutesified" when passed down to children (e.g., the transformation of mumming into trick-or-treating).

Yet, by the 1890s children were also associated with the new and novel (especially in the marketing of continuously changing board games and toys). While adults had, since the 18th century, passed on their fads to children (balloons, miniature houses, even automata) and continued to do so into the 20th, by 1900 we see signs of a reversal. Adults began to embrace children's fads and fantasies. The teddy bear was an object of children's endearment before it was embraced by adults. This sentiment was certainly exploited by advertisers and continues to be so, but the central point is that adults accepted change by giving novelty to their offspring and, in effect, basked in the reflected glory of cuteness by adopting the fads of their children.

The "cute" child signaled another important cultural change by imparting new meaning to the ritual of gifting. Increasingly, after 1900 parents saw children not as burdens or assets to train and exploit (or, at least, they no longer openly admitted such views). Rather, adults found children to be natural recipients of delightful things, not merely on holidays but eventually on almost a daily basis. This reminds us again that the "cute" child was needful and that fulfilling its desires gave delight not only to the child but to adults. Children gave parents pleasure through the "sacrifice" of giving. This was a particular form of vicarious consumption (applying to children Veblen's concept originally linked to wives): adults enjoyed spending by spending on their offspring. But what was being conveyed in gifts was more than adult status display through the child. It was the "look" of the child (either of happiness or disappointment) upon receiving the gift. A favorite setting for evoking this "look" was, not surprisingly, the entry of the delight-seeking child on Christmas morning to see the presents under the tree (which in ads became occasions for selling everything from boxed raisins to central heating).[19] This pattern, fully developed by the 1920s, was the culmination of the urge to gift the child—a custom progressively more elaborate at Christmas from the 1820s and Hanukkah from the 1910s.

It is not surprising that commercial culture nurtured and expanded the cult of the cute, giving adults permission to spend on children and affirm children's desires. But consumerism largely picked a bud already there. Adults longed for ways to connect to or "re-create" their own childhood emotions through the young and to affirm a positive feeling about the future through gifting children with novelty. The cute child eased complex and contradictory feelings about the emergence of consumer culture and the economic changes behind it, offering in fantasy an escape from uncontrolled change (in associating the child with timelessness) but also an embrace of the excitement of novelty. Even more, through the gifting of the wondrous child and enjoying the delight in the child's eye, adults renewed feelings of discovery in a consumer culture that by its sheer repetitiveness produced feelings of satiation and even boredom in many adults. The pleasure of the "innocent" consumption in the child brought adults back to their own Edenic state as consumers.

Links to the Present

The cult of the cute was well established in American consumer and family culture by the 1930s. It would be renewed and even extended thereafter in a wide range of children's commercial fantasies (from Public Television's *Sesame Street*, Muppets, Teletubbies, and Barney to fad characters and toy lines such as Care Bears, Cabbage Patch Kids, Beanie Babies, and, recently, SpongeBob SquarePants). A key linkage, from the 1930s to the present, was the way that Disney drew upon and solidified that cult in his movies and amusement parks. Disney's transformation of Mickey Mouse into a "neotenic" figure described by Stephen Jay Gould as "small, soft, infantile, mammalian, round, without bodily orifices, and nonsexual" made Disney the premier proponent of the cult of the cute.[20] Mickey not only evoked protective feelings in adults, but made Disney's animal characters appear innocent and thereby less threatening in their desires and behavior (even Donald Duck's tantrums became less problematic). Moreover, this Disney look replaced the natural, sometimes dangerous animals at the circus. The ominous elephant had become the childlike Dumbo with big floppy ears that could "fly" while children and their parents rode on his back at Disneyland. In effect, Disney cutesified the freak show by transforming these "oddities" into cartoon characters who appealed to the wonder of children rather than the morbid curiosity of adults. A root of this connection can be seen in the Coney Island exhibit Lilliputia (1904–1911), a "city" of midgets that was supposed to attract families with small children. This presumed affinity between Little People and children was exploited in Disney's *Snow White and the Seven Dwarfs*, the 1938 feature cartoon. The dwarfs, like so many of Disney's cartoon characters, were often feisty, sometimes rebellious, but always "nice" like small "innocent" children.

Disneyland (near Los Angeles, 1955) and its successor, Walt Disney World in Florida (especially the Magic Kingdom, opened in 1971) made the movie world of the cute three-dimensional. Especially at Fantasyland (and more recently, Critter Country and Toontown) within Disney parks, adults were encouraged to delight small children by introducing them to people-sized Mickeys, Minnies, and Goofys and to delight themselves by regressing to their own childhoods. One way that Disney evoked this nostalgia is Main Street U.S.A., a romantic reconstruction of the 1900s American small town. Not only is this site a highly idealized version of the middle-American business district and a mood funnel that all must walk through to get to the rest of Disneyland, but it was designed to evoke the feel of a play set or toy, being constructed on a five-eights scale of real-life buildings. "Memory" and the childlike were evoked simultaneously.

The core reason for Disney's success may be in the bonding of nostalgia and "timeless" cuteness across the generations. Rides and other attractions did not get "old" because oldsters expected to return to the past at Disneyland. At the same time, adults "passed" on to the next generation these same sites and experiences, which, for the very young, were truly new. Their "newness" was supposed to be enjoyed not simply as novelty but as a "timeless" wonder, with that same look and feeling of delight shown on the five-year-old's face in 2000 that had suffused the face of her parents twenty-five years before. This may explain why core attractions in Fantasy-land remained for decades: Peter Pan's Flight, Mr. Toad's Wild Ride, Dumbo Flying Elephants, and the Mad Tea Party—staples from the mid-1950s that lasted into the 21st century. Visits to Disney are today almost obligatory rites of childhood and for many define a minimal requirement for parenting.

Cuteness was of course extended in family rituals, especially in ever more elaborate celebrations of children's imagination and desire (for example, in the 1930s, the elevation of the Happy Birthday song to virtual liturgical status, and in the 1940s making trick-or-treating into a national Halloween rite). Vacations became increasingly family affairs, built, at least in part, around the celebration of children's delight. Sites of traditional reverence and patriotic commemoration such as the Gettysburg battlefield in the 1950s were dotted with child-oriented motels and mini-amusement parks. But the greatest evidence for the survival of the cult of the cute and its impact on contemporary child-parent relations is the many ways that we have reacted to it.

Reactions to the Cute

The cute challenged the child-rearing experts' advice at every turn. These child-development authorities called for the withdrawal of young people from the labor market but also resisted their introduction to the consumer market and tried to teach youngsters to be rational and adaptive within the laboratory settings of schools, professionally managed playgrounds, and properly equipped homes led by trained parents. The hard-headed behaviorist John Watson demanded that desired behavior be methodically reinforced, and he sharply rebuked any signs of maternal sentimentality; even the "gentle" pioneer of the modern kindergarten movement, Patty Smith Hill, warned parents in 1914 to dole out playthings to meet changing developmental needs throughout the year, not to lavish children with gifts at Christmas or birthdays. Holiday extravagance only served parents' longing for festive delight through their children, not the youth's need for scientifically timed play tools. Despite differences, all of these experts adhered to the notion that childhood was a stage that adults had to expertly transcend, leading the young into mature adulthood. They could agree with Dr. Douglas Thom's claim: "The home is a workshop which, unfortunately, often spoils much good material."[21] Giving in to children's unceasing desire led only to uncontrolled desire (conforming to the traditional religious doctrine of concupiscence).

Over time, the attack on the cult of the cute was forced into retreat. Despite gallant efforts, the inherent asceticism and elitism of early 20th century child-rearing experts gradually lost its hold on its middle-class audience. This was in part because economically secure parents wanted more than rationally reared offspring prepared for the rigors of competition. They wanted to join in childhood fantasy and to enjoy the emotional relationship with their children that the culture of the cute provided. The same middle-class parents who bought *Parents' Magazine* (from 1926) for expert advice also read the *Saturday Evening Post* with its charming covers of children by Norman Rockwell. Equally important, most of the experts were themselves torn between rational goals of their Victorian predecessors and the values of spontaneity and vitality emerging in the 20th century. By the late 1930s, they were beginning to "succumb" to the cute. Manuals no longer demanded a strict regimen of feeding, early toilet training, selective response to crying, and a limit on emotional attachments to babies.

Instead, they expressed far more tolerant and responsive approaches to child rearing. The view that children's desires were insatiable and antisocial and must be controlled gave way to a "permissiveness" promoted by Benjamin Spock's *Baby and Child Care* (1946). Freudian child psychologists assured parents that "fixations" could only result from rigid toilet training and harsh repression of desires, and some experts even insisted that parents could not spoil a baby. These messages were repeated over and over in the 1950s and 1960s, culminating with the arch-permissive expert, Haim Ginott. Probably even more to the point is the simple fact that advertising and other commercial images taught parents that children had the right to have their desires fulfilled and that it was the parents' job to make them happy.

None of this, however, stopped a reaction to the cute that in part led some adults to decide to be child free. Despite the permissive messages embedded in ads from the 1910s and much child-rearing advice from the 1940s, Americans never felt entirely comfortable with the celebration of children's desires. The American George Boas spearheaded an attack on the cult of the cute in 1938 when he complained that the modern rule of the child has made youth not only the "focus of all our thought but also the model for our behavior." He lamented that "our women dress and act like girls, our men like undergraduates. . . . Hence the passion for 'cute-

ness' in our houses [and] pets." Children who were taught that "their desires and personalities are sacred" inevitably suffer false expectations as
adults.[22] This was a rare opinion, certainly from the 1940s to 1960s, but it
gained ground after a generation of child-focused baby-boom families in
the 1970s when some young women rejected their mothers' sacrifices for
their children. These attitudes corresponded with a sharp drop in childbearing (a 51 percent decrease in the total fertility rate from 1960 to 1964 to
1975 to 1979).[23]

More common were attacks on the rites of cuteness from the 1970s.
While many condemned the commercialized sentimentalism of Christmas, it was the more recent and vulnerable rituals of Halloween and Disney that met the greatest criticism. Unlike Christmas, where gift giving to
children let adults abandon community exchanges and focus without guilt
on the family, Halloween trick-or-treating was always suspect because it
invited children to be cute in costume to neighbors (who increasingly
were becoming strangers in the ever more anonymous communities of
America). Halloween also retained associations with the violent and irrational traditions of mumming and the pagan occult that could not be as
easily tamed and disguised as they had been in Christmas and other holidays. Both of these factors made trick-or-treating questionable. Panics
about pins, razor blades, or poison in Halloween apples and candy appeared as early as 1971 and escalated in the 1980s. In 1984, hospitals even
offered to X-ray children's candy bags for dangerous objects, and many
towns and cities shifted trick-or-treating to a Saturday afternoon.[24] Although these panics abated by the late 1980s, they remain today just under
the surface.

Another assault on Halloween rituals of the cute came from the religious right. Rejecting the long-established practice of passing on to children sanitized versions of old community and even pagan traditions in
cutesified forms, from the 1970s religious literalists claimed that, because
of the pagan origins of Halloween, trick-or-treating was a form of devil
worship, and they organized successfully to ban Halloween parties and parades from schools. Finally, the bowdlerization of Halloween was challenged by adults who wanted to "get back" their Saturnalian holiday. By
the 1980s, adult Halloween costume parties had become common, and
crowds of 100,000 thronged the streets of Georgetown or New Orleans on
Halloween night. Today, Halloween parades, parties, and even concerts attract millions of young adults.[25] Of course, the "charm" of greeting the
neighbor's kids dressed as bunnies or ghosts and stuffing suspect candy

into their bags survives. Yet Halloween is no longer so cute, nor are children's delighted responses as central to its celebration as they were a generation ago.

Inevitably, if the cult of the cute appealed to many Americans, it also repulsed others, especially in its commercial form. The most obvious example is the hostility of many to Disney. This has been true since Disneyland first opened in 1955. Today, there is even a Society of Disney Haters on line (www.sodh.org) that gives vent to people "forced" to go to Disneyland or Disney World with spouses and kids. These naysayers share with a whole industry of cultural criticism that attacks Disney for its celebration of the puerile and regressive. Inevitably, a trip to Disneyland/Disney World is portrayed as an "inauthentic experience."[26] At least a part of this critique is resentment against the child-centered culture of Disney and its perpetuation of the cult of the cute.

Even more important than adult rejection of the wondrous child was the revolt of children themselves against the image of the cute imposed on them by adults. A common expression of this rebellion is the older child's cult of the cool, a look and behavioral patterns that constitutes a mirror opposite of the cute and that frees the child from parents' possessive needs. The cool is the "aesthetic of the streets," a thorough rejection of domesticity, notes Daniel Harris. Signs of the cool are the child's "emphatic rejection of the smile" and of "rosy-cheeked good looks" for the "cult of the grotesque."[27] To be cool, a posture, attitude, or response has to be the opposite of wondrous, spunky, sweet, and dependent; it has to be jaded, emotionally reserved, independent, and, in some cases, deliberately unattractive. The quest for autonomy and deliberate rejection of markers of dependence are hardly unique to the age of the cute, but their expression in the cool is new and represents a direct response to the adult's imposition of cuteness on children.

The first clear signs of the cool appeared among older boys in the 1930s and 1940s, with the hard mechanical stories of Buck Rogers and Dick Tracy and in the 1950s, with the dark, violent worlds of horror and crime comics. In the 1960s and 1970s, rebellious fantasy extended to girls and small children when the cool look of Barbie and grimacing action-figure toys partially displaced Tiny Tear baby dolls and electric trains. What ties all these examples together is the absence of the bond between parent and child. The science fiction hero Buck Rogers has no father and is no son. The cool is often adapted from the world of the working class or minority, allowing the middle-class child to break from the parent's domesticating cult of the cute. Today, we may recognize all this in the loose-fitting clothes of ten-year- olds, the tattoos and pierced body parts of teens, and the long-lasting popularity of horror videos and violent video games among older children.

The cool in children has also arisen from the logic of the cute. The cool is a distinct form of escape that is not built on explicit models of realistic adulthood (as was the case in earlier juvenile literature) but on an ever-changing fantasy world that adults encouraged in the "cute" child. Increasingly after 1900, adults met deep-seated needs by giving their children unexpected excitement and relief from today's reality and tomorrow's uncertainty. By their very nature, these gifts of fun connected children neither to a live heritage nor to a responsible future. The cute provided no cues for growing up and, because the cult of the cute required parents' acceptance of children's self-expressiveness, even a measure of naughtiness, children quite naturally transformed adult-imposed fantasies into dreamworlds of their own that became the cool. Media and fantasy toy makers provided the material by marketing directly to children since the 1930s, especially with the appearance of children's radio, Saturday film matinees, and the comic book. From the mid-1950s, Saturday morning TV cartoons and ads designed specifically for children greatly accelerated this process. Movies such as *Star Wars* (1977) and video games from the mid-1970s produced the autonomous culture of the cool that we know today. A powerful mark of its hold on older children's imaginations is the fact that even the Disney Company has had to modify its old formula and to adapt to the thrill-ride amusement parks that sprang up in the late 1970s. Since then, Disney's parks have abandoned quasi-educational exhibits and built gut-wrenching rides, not abandoning the "cute" but relegating it to very young audiences and their parents.

Contradictions of the Cult of the Cute

The ongoing tension between the cute and its enemies has produced many curious behaviors. While children fled the cute, some adults embraced it in their own culture. Adult women took up the teddy bear and other plush figures in the early 20th century almost immediately after they entered children's commercial culture. Recently, young Japanese women have cultivated cuteness by wearing childlike hairstyles and clothes and adopting an argot of "baby talk" in order to cope with the stresses of late marriage and motherhood. Many adults admire the freedom of youth and turn it into a lifestyle rather than a life stage (with some, especially men, preferring the child's cool to the cute). Adults have found in the delights of the child refuge from modernity and its demands. In many ways this has led to the disappearance not so much of childhood, as others have lamented, but of adulthood, reducing the cultural distance between the adolescent and adult. Put another way, the cute represents for adults the "virtual child" (in the language of John Gillis), combining in a complex image the contradictory longings of adults even as real children decrease or even disappear from the lives of adults. The idea that children's "natural" needs should be satisfied led adults to assume to have the right to indulge their "inner child" without guilt or compromise. As Henry Jenkins put it, by the 1950s, parents "desired their children's desires."[28]

Ironically, the adult's expectation of the cute child on Christmas morning or even on the shopping trip to the mall may have made for a greater tolerance of innocent desire or even naughtiness, but it also made the chronically troublesome, demanding, and whiny child even more unacceptable. One way that this was expressed was in the parents' desire to control but, even more, to displace, children's "uncute" negative emotions of fear, jealousy, and envy (some emanating from the cute itself). Of course, this effort to reduce children's negative emotions had many causes, ranging from the rise of the helping professions and the smaller family to discoveries about the deep fears and jealousies experienced by many children. But parents' efforts to reduce negative encounters with children was a necessary part of their desire to maximize the "cute." It is no surprise that Shirley Temple was "America's Sweetheart" in the 1930s: behind that smile was a little girl very closely disciplined by a hard-handed mother.

Moreover, adults' longing for the cute has contributed to a relative disaffection for the older child, jaded by parental indulgence perhaps in years of trying to evoke childlike delight, or simply no longer possessing that unique combination of dependence and spunkiness that makes the young cute. It is not surprising that parents and grandparents feature photos of babies and toddlers who are all potential and no accomplishment while neglecting to capture images of teenagers who often have real achievements and developed personalities.

An even more frustrating problem was that the wondrous child slipped out of the control of parents. The images, goods, and rituals of commercialized childhood led very subtly to a fantasy culture of the cool from which, as we have seen, parents were excluded. In effect, kids took over the secret garden and, with the help of fantasy merchants, largely locked their parents out. Adults responded to this apparent subversion of the cute by attempting to draw a line between permissible and dangerous fantasy and pleasure. Across the 20th century, this attack on the cool took many forms, from regulating movies and video games to attempting to ban comic books and toy guns. Often these "moral panics" were directed against minority or working-class "threats" to middle-class white youth with the former's presumed taste for violent comic books and sensual rock music.

Child-rearing experts and parents for decades have been searching for an elusive middle path: rejecting the excesses of "permissiveness" and adult self-indulgence in the cult of the cute while not imposing on children an austere culture of improvement that denies them access to the fun and social world of contemporary commercial fantasy. The problem has been that the cult of the cute has been in symbiotic conflict with the child-rearing ethos of the developmental expert for a century. Simply put, adults have long been caught between their desire to worship the child and attempt to mold the child. The culture seemed to demand that children be divided into idealized states of present perfection and future possibility with no easy way to resolve the conflict.

More subtly still, adults seem to use the contrast between the cute and the improving child to cope with the contradictions of modernity in their own lives and willingly to split the child's world to meet these needs. They insist that children be protected from premature contact with the worlds of work and business by confining them to schools designed to prepare them for the market. This leads to ever greater reliance on standardized testing, academic tracking, and summer educational enrichment, especially among middle-class parents. At the same time, these same adults impose on children a culture of cuteness, especially when they are very young, that celebrates desire and consumption (leading to unwanted consequences). They project onto the achieving child their hope for success and power while seeking in the cute child the delight they have lost in their own experiences as affluent consumers. Even more, they project onto the young their own segmented lives—between rationalist work and playful consumption—creating numerous frustrations on the part of children, many of whom find solace in the world of the cool. Any solution is elusive, but it surely must involve adults taking seriously their duty to meet the needs of children rather than of themselves. Here is an important case where behavioral history can help.

NOTES

1. Samuel Peterson and Michael Haines, *Fatal Years: Child Mortality in Late Nineteenth-Century America* (Princeton, 1991), 3–5, 51.

2. Beginning with Holt, experts systematically debunked the often sentimental styles of Victorian mothering and justified their child-rearing advice with claims of professional status and hard data. This reassured modern parents and provided mothers with a new rationale for their nurturing roles (making them, in effect, part of a new managerial culture, preparing children for their formal school training). Holt sought to eliminate the emotional (both positive and negative) from the process. Luther Emmett Holt, *Care and Feeding of Children* (New York, 1894–1943 multiple editions).

3. Peter Stearns, *Anxious Parents: A History of Modern Child-Rearing in America* (New York, 2003), 3.

4. Peter Stearns, "Historical Perspectives on Twentieth-Century American Childhood," in William Koops and Michael Zuckerman, eds., *Beyond the Century of the Child* (Philadelphia, 2003), 96.

5. "Cute," in Merriam Collegiate Dictionary on-line: http://search.eb.com/dictionary. Oxford University Dictionary on-line: http://dictionary.oed.com, accessed 21 Apr. 2004; Word search in the on-line collection of *Harper's Weekly* (1857–1912) at http://app.harpweek.com. Quotations from *Harper's Weekly*, 13 Jan. 1909, 13, and 14 Apr. 1910, 10.

6. Pear's soap ad, *Frank Leslie's Illustrated Weekly*, 14 Feb. 1885, 432; images from *Harper's Weekly*, 26 Feb. 1881, 149; 3 Sept. 1881, 596; and 1 Jan. 1881, 4; *Frank Leslie's Illustrated Weekly*, 13 Jan. 1885, 396; 29 Aug. 1885, 29; 7 Nov. 1885, 88; 12 Mar. 1996, cover. Anita Schorsche, *Images of Childhood: An Illustrated Social History* (New York, 1979), 30–31.

7. Images from *Harper's Weekly*, 9 Jan. 1870, cover, and 21 May 1879, 328; *Frank Leslie's Illustrated Weekly*, 12 Dec. 1885, 261.

8. Jackie Wullschlaeger, *Inventing Wonderland: The Lives and Fantasies of Lewis Carroll, Edward Lear, J. M. Barrie, Kenneth Grahame, and A. A. Milne* (New York, 1994), 109.

9. Thomas Nast, *Christmas Drawings for the Human Race* (New York, 1971; reprint of 1890 ed.), n.p.

10. Bancroft Library Special Collection (University of California), Charles Lathrop, "Scrapbook of American Trade Cards, 1881–ca. 1900"; "Trade Cards of San Francisco Businesses, 1881–1883."

11 "Trade Cards of San Francisco"; Lathrop, "Scrapbook"; "Scrapbooks of American Trade Cards," vols. 3, 4; Alice Muncaster, *The Baby Made Me Buy It* (New York, 1991), 12.

12. Weekly cover art in the *Saturday Evening Post* that featured children at play and in cute poses peaked at twenty-four in 1915 and averaged sixteen per year in

the 1910s. Jan Cohn, *Covers of the Saturday Evening Post* (New York, 1995), x–xii, covers by year, n.p.

13. The Yellow Kid shared much with other early comics. In early 1907, five of seven strips in the *New York World* featured children, most in these naughty roles. Richard Outcault, *Outcault's Buster Brown and Company, Including Mary Jane* (New York, 1907).

14. Norman Kline, *Seven Minutes: The Life and Death of the American Animated Cartoon* (London, 1993), 30–31.

15. *Playthings,* June 1919, 74, and Bye Bye Kids ad, *Playthings,* June 1908, 102.

16. Flossie Flirt ad, *Sears and Roebuck Catalogue,* 1931, 669.

17. Shelley Armitage, *Kewpies and Beyond: The World of Rose O'Neill* (Jackson, MS, 1994), 112.

18. Kellogg ad, *Ladies' Home Journal,* Aug. 1913, back cover; Wesson Oil ad, *Ladies' Home Journal* Jan 1934, back cover.

19. Sun Maid ad, *Saturday Evening Post,* 17 Oct. 1914, 32, and 16 Dec. 1922; Spencer ad, *Saturday Evening Post,* 7 Dec. 1929, 131.

20. Stephen Jay Gould, "Mickey Mouse Meets Konrad Lorenz," *Natural History,* 88, 5 (1979): 30–36.

21. John Watson, *Psychological Care of the Infant and Child* (New York, 1928), 136, 257; Patty Smith Hill, "Avoid the Gifts That Overstimulate," *The Delineator,* Dec. 1914, 22–23; Douglas Thom, *Child Management* (Washington, DC, 1924), 100.

22. George Boas, "Century of the Child," *American Scholar,* July 1938, 268–76. Note also his *The Cult of Childhood* (London, 1966).

23. U.S. Census Bureau, *Statistical Abstract of the United States* (2000), 68.

24. "Halloween Safety Guide," *Parents',* Oct. 1971, 20; *Newsweek,* 11 Nov. 1982.

25. "Halloween, an Adult Treat," *Time,* 31 Oct. 1983, 110; *Washington Post,* 30 Oct. 1987; 1; *Wall Street Journal,* 22 Oct. 1999, 1.

26. "America Loves to Hate the Mouse: Behind the Fantasy Walt Disney Built Looms a Dark Reality," *Washington Post,* 5 Dec. 2001, C1.

27. Daniel Harris, *Cute, Quaint, Hungry, and Romantic: The Aesthetics of Consumerism* (New York, 2000), 52–74.

28. H. Jenkins, *The Children's Culture Reader* (New York, 1998), 227.

3

Abduction Stories That Changed Our Lives
From Charley Ross to Modern Behavior

Paula S. Fass

When parents take their children to the local police to have them fingerprinted in response to fears about child kidnapping, they are acting in
ways that stem from a long history about which most Americans are to-
tally unaware. While few Americans today will do something so extreme as
preemptive fingerprinting, most parents in this country and increasingly
in Europe as well, in the beginning of the 21st century have become more
and more reluctant to let their children play alone in the streets or even
unattended in their own front yards. The growing restrictions placed on
children's activities and the pains that parents take to chaperone and carefully organize their children's lives are all significant changes in contemporary behavior that are based in historical events and precedents. Ask most
parents today how their children's lives differ from their own, and they
will tell you that their own childhood, thirty or forty years ago, was freer
and much less hindered by parental supervision.

These perceptions, the important attendant behavioral changes and
their consequences for today's generation of children, are embedded in a
broad landscape of historical events as well as demographic, residential,
and employment patterns. The shrinking size of the American and European family is well known, and the new prominence of mothers' employment and suburban isolation have been widely studied and discussed at a
time when "soccer moms" are a political phenomenon. These contemporary social changes are often invoked to explain growing parental anxiety,
guilt, and activities aimed at shielding children from harms of many
kinds. And some historians and social scientists have learned to talk about

cycles of panics—accelerating media alarms—from which parents learn to fear for their children but whose real anxieties are lodged in perceptions about changes in gender and sex norms.[1] Far less attention has been paid to the specific history that not only frames contemporary parental fears about child safety generally, but which, I would argue, forms the basis for quite specific fears about child abduction. It is that history that I propose to examine in this essay since it is essential to understanding contemporary behavior and especially the pronounced tendency in our society to move away from once informal and unsupervised children's play activities to the much more organized patterns of the present.

Peter Stearns has written recently and pointedly about "anxious parents" in the 20th-century United States who try to shield their children from pain, stress, and excessive schoolwork.[2] This middle-class urge to control the details of the self and household was understood by both Max Weber and Sigmund Freud in psychological terms. In a recent *New Yorker* magazine piece, Margaret Talbott described it as follows: "Middle-class parents tend to be exquisitely aware of health and safety issues and often micromanage their children's lives in order to fend off a buzzing pack of threats."[3] Stearns provides real insight into the forms these efforts have taken as well as the family developments and social and emotional changes that have accompanied this drive in the 20th century. This general anxiety about children's welfare, and the drive to control that often accompanies it, certainly underlies the history I am eager to describe. But the origin of the specific fears about child abduction, whatever its psychological base, can be more precisely dated in time and place. Indeed, to understand the shape that general psychological drives take requires that we understand very specific historical developments.

Fears about children taken away or substituted for are manifested in a wide variety of tales about fairies, elves, and changelings and date back for centuries. Anthropologists have located them in so many varied cultures that they may have some primal quality. In the West, real people such as gypsies, American Indians, or others perceived as uncivilized and marauding outsiders have also been associated with and accused at regular intervals of similar depredations. But the first historically potent modern American story about child kidnapping takes shape around a real incident. In 1874 Charley Ross was abducted from the front lawn of his family's house in Germantown, Pennsylvania.[4] After that event, his story and parental fears about child abduction became deeply inscribed in American culture. This is the necessary beginning to our own examination.

The Story of Charley Ross

Charles Brewster Ross, always known as "Charley," was a solidly middle-class child, and his story became widely known because his parents were respectable people and locally well connected. Other children who had been abducted before this time did not have these advantages. Charley was not the first child to be abducted, but his was the very first widely known story about child abduction. Its circulation in the United States and around the world became the touchstone for knowledge about child kidnapping for decades afterward. It also served as the basis for imitation by subsequent child abductors, as well as a cautionary tale for police and parents. As such it served as the historical origin of parental fears about losing children to kidnappers. When Charley was taken on July 1, 1874, the historical imprint of that event would be long lasting and deep.

As a foundation story for child abduction, the story of Charley Ross—an adorable, blond, curly haired, sweet-tempered four-year-old—also had other advantages. The story had the advantage of specificity: his abduction was not only witnessed by his six-year-old brother, but the brazen demand by his kidnappers for a $20,000 ransom was presented in a series of concrete and threatening ransom notes. This left a paper trail that made clear that the child had not simply wandered away or fallen off a cliff, as many children previously described as "lost" were assumed to have done. This also made it evident that children could now be held hostage as part of an attempted extortion. In creating a new crime, the Charley Ross abduction became a subject of widespread publicity as well as the basis for a horrified public reaction. At a time when concerns about the welfare of children were prominently publicized in the creation of a variety of organizations devoted to child saving, Charley's story resonated with the American public as evidence of new threats to children as well as signs of declining community stability and neighborly trust. Thus, the Ross case came at a point when modern life seemed to be becoming more menacing and when children were perceived as newly vulnerable. Community organizations were formed whose aim it was to see to their welfare.

Just as important for our purposes were the specific responses that the experience created in laying the foundations for how parents would respond to this kind of incident and how it was portrayed in the press. Child ransom abduction was certainly a new and sinister crime, but its potential for generating knowledge about the crime and fear was not simply the result of a new general threat to society and its children, and publicity about it was not preordained and inevitable. Rather, the way Christian Ross, Charley's father, responded to his child's abduction, his actions and inactions, helped to determine subsequent parental responses and responsibilities.

After Christian received his first ransom demand on July 4, 1874, he decided to act cautiously and responsibly and not to pay without also devising some means to trap the abductors. In concert with the Philadelphia police and other city officials (who helped him raise the huge ransom as a subscription), Christian's response was aimed at defending public safety. He had been advised by the police that "any arrangements made with the kidnappers for the restoration of the child would be a public calamity; no child would be safe hereafter if it had parents or friends who could raise money."[5] And the *New York Times* noted that many thought that paying the ransom "was an act of weakness,"[6] although the paper voiced its own disagreement with this position. In his own words, Christian had decided to "wait and suffer in the hope of securing the criminals with the child."[7] And suffer he did. The cost of public courage turned out to be an astonishing personal grief and despair as Christian was forced to negotiate for months with kidnappers whose blood-chilling threats to his child were embedded in a series of barely literate but very vivid notes. As a result, Christian experienced the terrible fears and imaginings about the fate and experiences of his son that would subsequently define parental anxieties as future parents anticipated the possibility of similar crimes against their own children.

The strategy also backfired, since it generated a long-drawn-out and ultimately unsuccessful trail of attempts to find the child and the abductors, and the delay put Christian's motives and his sensibility as a parent under scrutiny. The public was hardly impressed by Christian's actions as a good citizen. Why, the public wanted to know after several weeks—and then several months—of negotiation had taken place without Charley's return had the father not simply redeemed his child?

As wild rumors about his complicity in the crime or mean-spirited speculations about his wife's (possible) infidelity began to spread as an explanation for Ross's inaction and the events even took shape in a Broadway play, Christian not only lost control of the investigation but suffered a complete personal breakdown. Almost two years later, after more fruitless searches, Christian finally wrote a memoir about his experiences in an attempt to clear his name and also to reclaim control over the search for his son. That memoir, *The Father's Story of Charley Ross,* was published in 1876 and became a best seller. It registers the parental despair that would become familiar to all subsequent victims of child abduction and charts the path that most would thereafter *not* take in their attempts to reclaim their children. Christian's memoir rings with emotional pain and truth: "Five long months a constant dread possessed us that the threats they [the ransom notes] contained would be literally executed; and though our hearts yearned to hear something of our suffering stolen one, yet each letter was opened with fear and trembling . . . none but ourselves can ever know how bitter the draught in the chalice."[8]

Christian had made a lasting mistake. In relying on the advice of others he had not followed the promptings of his own heart to a simple and direct means to be reunited with his son. In telling his tale of sorrow, regret, and expiation, Christian charts new emotional and behavioral territory, a territory that parents could subsequently anticipate in their own experiences with or fears about kidnapping. Christian's memoir is an extraordinary testament to a particular turning point in behavioral history as it charts a new guidebook for parental action.

Christian's memoir is also more, since he claims that it does not mark the end of his search but a vital step in its continuation:

> The publication of the narrative at this time might assist in explaining the mystery which is still connected with the concealment of the child, or that possibly, through the perusal of the book, someone not familiar with the circumstances might be enabled to give a new and fortunate direction to the search, or perhaps that the child himself, seeing the illustrations of once familiar scenes, or learning from some incident herein related something to suggest early recollections, might be led to his home. Another object in issuing the book now is that of obtaining the money to enable me to continue a search that cannot be abandoned until the child is found alive, or his death is certainly proven to us.

Christian tells his readers that he has dedicated his life to one purpose after his loss—to finding his son or at least "some definite information . . . as to whether the child was living or dead."[9]

Knowing today what we do about the parents of victims of contemporary child abduction, of parents like Patty Wetterling, David Walsh, and Marc Klaas, and their ceaseless strain to recover their children, the missing-children foundations they have established, and the careers they have rerouted to devote themselves to finding other missing children, one looks back in amazement at Christian's memoirs to realize how it had all been anticipated 130 years ago. Ross, too, could not give up the hope of retrieving his son; Ross, too, wanted some closure through knowledge about the whereabouts or death of his child; Ross, too, gives up the rest of his life to finding his son. In the process he, too, finds other missing children. Ross fends off personal feelings of guilt and inadequacy as the parent of a lost child by devoting himself to publicizing the terrible crime of which he has been a victim, and to urging legal action; "No laws are found in the books of any State which anticipated the commission of so unnatural an offense, nor was any punishment provided commensurate with its heinousness."[10] In the wake of the Ross case, Pennsylvania became the first state to make child kidnapping a felony. Thereafter, Pennsylvania's actions would be quickly imitated in other states where parents and police were now put on notice about a new danger to their children. Over the course of the next 130 years, new laws would almost inevitably follow on the heels of widely publicized child kidnappings, as grieving parents and other citizens have sought legal means to punish criminals as a means to define the society's commitments to its children.

Finally, Ross's reflections and his actions inflamed public apprehensions about children lost to evildoers. "This book," the introduction by Charles P. Krauth, a professor of theology and vice provost at the University of Pennsylvania, tells readers, "is a picture of contrasts—the lamb in the talons of the vulture—the innocence of childhood in the iron grasp of calculating murder."[11] The case of Charley Ross enshrines a particular portrait of childhood innocence and vulnerability that is the ground from which all future pictures of the crime would grow. As a story, Christian's tale of grief touches the deepest feelings of injustice and ignites a sense of vulnerability that fashions the archetypal story of a kidnapped child.

None of today's parents of kidnapped children are familiar with this story, but all of them have followed in its footsteps. In its time, the trials and tribulations of Christian Ross were so widely known, and so often invoked after 1874, that even subsequent ransom notes included allusions to the case in their demands. Thus, when Eddy Cudahy's kidnappers wanted to spur a positive response to their note in 1900, they included the following: "If you remember, some twenty years ago, Charley Ross was kidnapped in New York City and $20,000 ransom asked. Old man Ross was willing to give up the money, but Byrnes, the great detective, with others, persuaded the old man not to give up the money, assuring him that the

thieves would be captured. Ross died of a broken heart, sorry that he allowed the detectives to dictate to him." Eddy's father, who was a rich Ne-
braska meatpacker, turned over $25,000 on the same day and his son was
returned the next. "What is $25,000 compared to my boy?" he observed in
what had become a lesson well learned by parents.[12] The specific details of
the Ross kidnapping and the kidnapper's communications were imitated
by a young Richard Loeb and Nathan Leopold when they sought to create
a spectacular kidnapping. The particulars of the Ross case also lingered in
the minds of lawyers and prosecuting attorneys for years. In the final arguments in the kidnap-murder case against Leopold and Loeb in 1924, Illinois state's attorney Robert Crowe noted, "Fifty years ago Charlie [sic]
Ross was kidnapped. . . . He was never found and yet we all, even those of
us born many years after, still talk about the case of Charlie Ross. There is
something in the nature of the crime itself that arrests the attention of
every person in the land. . . . The *heart* of every father, the *heart* of every
mother, the *heart* of every man who has a heart, goes out to the parents of
the child."[13] Because Christian had not found his son, the heart of his
story—that parents' love for their children required that they do everything in their power to save them from the threat posed by strangers—had
been deeply lodged throughout the country.

The publicity surrounding the Ross case spread information about it
far and wide: through word of mouth as Charley's name became synonymous with lost children and became part of the popular culture; through
hundreds of thousands of missing children's posters distributed everywhere in the United States by Pinkerton detectives and by P. T. Barnum,
who could not resist getting involved in so obvious a publicity magnet; by
Christian Ross's memoirs.[14] And by the press. Then as now, the press was
active in seeking out sensation, and it both spread rumors about Ross and
sought to touch as many hearts as possible with the story of his loss. Because the case was so drawn out and eventually involved the police in New
York (where the abductors, but not the child, were found but killed as they
were being captured), and because Ross went all over the East and Mid-
west following leads on his son's possible whereabouts, newspapers everywhere became alert to the story's potential as a carrier of an astonishing
new form of human interest news. The papers could believe that they were
advancing Christian's cause as they stirred up the hearts and fears of their
readers.

Before the Ross case, parents whose children had been stolen could not
stimulate an interest in the police or the press and were accustomed to

placing personal ads in the "lost and found" column of the local paper. After the Ross case, a child abduction almost automatically became news. It also became the occasion for reinvoking all the sentiments about parenthood and all the fears about loss that the case had inspired and dramatized. Indeed, a new case gave papers the opportunity to remind their readers about Charley, who had become a fixture of American popular culture. By the late 19th century, the need to find sensational and personally interesting news and the very wide familiarity with the Charley Ross case meant that it soon served as the model for other stories about abduction. And because Charley was never found, any possible new sighting of the child or claimants to that identity rekindled all the heart-wrenching possibilities of the story. Thus, the case lasted long after Christian's search for his son had expired. In 1924, the *Ladies' Home Journal* printed a commemorative fiftieth anniversary article about the "Lost Boy" to remind its enormous audience of middle-class women about the fears that still attached to modern parenting. In 1927, an experienced newspaper man, Edward H. Smith, observed that "any kind of an item suggesting the discovery of Charlie [*sic*] Ross is always good copy and will be telegraphed about the country from end to end, and printed at greater or lesser length."[15] Charley Ross was still news.

Of course, also telegraphed across the country with any news about an abduction were the specific grounds for parental fears. As Christian had warned in his memoir, "Well may parents be struck with terror in realizing this peril, and in feeling that their children are no longer safe upon the lawns or lanes which were once thought as safe as the nursery or schoolroom. Well may they shudder at the bare possibility of one of their offspring being snatched from them by miscreants for vile traffic." "Any one of us," the *New York Times* concluded, "is liable to such a loss.[16] But the fear was also accompanied by a particular kind of relief that Christian articulated first and most fully: "Children never seemed half so precious as now. . . . A new reason for thankfulness was found that the kidnappers had not invaded the family circle in their absence. Men awoke to the existence of a danger to which their children were exposed of which before they had no suspicion, and the grateful acknowledgment of a protecting Providence in a direction in which before they had no fears."[17] The kidnappers of Charley had indeed created a new crime, and the publicity about the crime had created a new public psychology.

Only in 1932, when America's internationally acclaimed "hero" Charles A. Lindbergh became the victim of a ransom abduction, did the image of

Charley Ross recede from the public mind as the avalanche of publicity about another blond, curly-haired Charlie literally buried it deep in the nation's unconscious. By then, as news about the Lindbergh abduction convulsed the nation, lasting long after the child's body was found, through a publicity orgy unprecedented in modern history that followed Richard Bruno Hauptmann through his trial and to the electric chair, America's hunger for stories about stolen children became a permanent fixation.[18]

In sum, the Ross case provided press, parents, and future kidnappers what turned out to be a durable template. The story itself endured, and specific references to it helped fuel later crimes and abductions that themselves maintained fears that easily outlasted knowledge of the Ross experience. Finally, the breadth of press coverage and the intensity of the reactions it conveyed made abductions a seeming threat well beyond the specific places where they occurred. Local fears resulting from abduction were not historically new; national anxieties were, however, novel, but they quickly became commonplace.

From a Father's Loss to Public Fear

While the carriers of news learned to follow kidnappings closely and to envelop them in an irresistible story form, they have over the course of 130 years also depended heavily on provoking certain emotions and enshrining particular parental obligations. In so doing they relied on and helped to create large-scale behavioral responses. The *New Republic* predicted such behavior on the occasion of the Lindbergh abduction: "The men and women who were children in the days of the Charlie [*sic*] Ross kidnapping can remember how their mothers warned them to stay in the house, never talk to strangers, and regard every old clothes man as a potential ogre who would carry them off and strangle them and cut them into little pieces. The Lindbergh case is likely to produce an even wider reaction. One can hardly estimate its effect on popular psychology."[19] The Lindbergh case, like Charley Ross before it, helped to create a public sense of threat and vulnerability that inspired a protective response. But while these abductions created a real sense of generalized alarm, and many parents undoubtedly warned their children to be wary of strangers, the parents who needed to worry the most were those who had reason to fear a ransom demand. And in the 1930s, many of these hired private guards for their chil-

dren. People without wealth could also be targeted, but most ransom kidnappings were aimed at people who had something to lose other than
their children. Parents with little money could still feel for the Rosses, the
Cudahys, and the Lindberghs, but they could hardly feel full solidarity.
After the 1950s, however, the crime of kidnapping was democratized and
parents could easily be made to identify with the losses of the much more
ordinary people who were suddenly pressed into the limelight. The ransom abduction that the Ross case defined and the Lindbergh case embodied was replaced later in the century by abductions which could now be
even more widely feared because sex, not money, appeared to be their objective.

The shift in public perceptions about kidnapping, from money ex-
changed for children to the sexual exploitation of children, is not a simple
one, and even before the 1950s, cases like Leopold and Loeb created public
awareness of the possibilities of sexual kidnapping and perverse murder.
Part of the explanation lies in 20th-century culture's increasing frankness
about sex and its habitual use of sex to excite attention. By the late 19th
century the Ross case, as we have seen, had allowed the drive to rouse public interest to incorporate children into its widening circle. As the drive to
excite became more and more blatantly sexual in the 20th century, the
turn to sexually motivated abductions was natural. But the shift is more
emotionally complex than this. As the publicity surrounding kidnappings
became staples of newspaper copy and as public attention to such cases
became assured, the very nature of the excited response became heavy
with sexual overtones. In the 19th century, Ross had spoken about "the
thrill of horror" that the new crime had evoked in the public, and voiced
his deep apprehensions about the possible abuses that his respectable son
had to endure and other children might expect in this "vile traffic." In
vividly covering the mysterious loss of children to strangers whose motives were foul and unknown, and in exciting speculation about just what
was happening to these children, the newspaper-stimulated thrill of horror was from the beginning eroticized. By the 1950s, when fears about the
abduction and abuse of teenage girls became the subject of widespread
newspaper coverage and FBI alerts,[20] explicit sexual connections became
increasingly commonplace.

In one such case, the abduction of Stephanie Bryan in Berkeley, California, in 1955, the body of the fourteen-year-old girl could not be made to
yield any evidence of sexual abuse. Yet the much publicized trial of her ab-
ductor, Burton Abbott, was steeped in sexual innuendo. The district attor-

ney in the case, J. Frank Coakley, noted that Abbott had a "sadistic sex urge," and that on the day he killed Stephanie, Abbott "had perhaps the greatest sexual satisfaction of his life." What Abbott had done was never specified, but the imagination of the jury and of the public was certainly set free to contemplate the murder of abducted children "committed by sex maniacs, by perverts, and by psychopathic personalities."[21] Abbott was ultimately executed in 1956 under what was known as California's "Little Lindbergh" law, which made kidnapping with bodily harm a capital offense, in line with the new federal statute created in 1932 after the Lindbergh abduction.[22]

The status of Stephanie Bryan and many of the girl victims in the 1950s as budding adolescents made their sexual victimization part of the very nature of the "horror" of kidnapping. But, when child kidnapping became widely perceived as a pervasive crime in the 1980s, and its toll was (wrongly) calculated as mounting to the hundreds of thousands every year, age no longer determined whether sexual motives were assumed to drive the crime. Neither did gender. By then, the sexual nature of the crime was taken for granted. No longer were kidnappings for ransom considered either typical or likely. Instead, when a child disappeared, parents, police, and the public jumped to sexual conclusions. In spreading the possibilities of child loss ever wider into the general population and making all children vulnerable to the new sexual kidnap threat, stories like Stephanie's, or later Etan Patz's, drew upon earlier kidnap stories and played upon the sure emotions that these had evoked. Just as the sexualization of popular culture is integral to 20th-century history, the sexualization of childhood became part of that story by the 1970s and 1980s. Along with this development, pedophilia, which was a new word and largely a new phenomenon, became a haunting national obsession. Together, the two made the sexual victimization of children the likely contemporary explanation for a child's disappearance. This was first manifested in the case of Etan Patz in 1979 and thereafter became an automatic response when a child disappeared. As the cases were increasingly broadcast by the many new means by which the stories of kidnapping now appeared in public, and as the assumptions about pedophiles permeated the national consciousness, kidnappings, once associated with the drive for money, now became almost inevitably pictured as a drive for perverse sexual gratification with children.

Despite the change in motive for the abduction, perceptions about the crime itself had not changed since the late 19th century. It was still described in the most emotionally gripping terms; it still exploited the most horrific parental fears; it still called for certain behavioral responses. These included extreme forms of protecting children and frequent attempts to change the law. By the end of the 20th century, the forms of protection for children had become more and more elaborate and resourceful, enlisting the aid of modern technologies such as beepers, video cameras, and cell phones. The stories had become much more pervasive and insistent. In addition to newspapers, posters, and word of mouth, there were movies and television stories, real and imagined. There were videos such as *Stranger Danger,* and visits by police to local schools. There were neighborhood and citywide campaigns to have children fingerprinted. And there were constant news alerts beamed into the home on the local news and posted on highways. By the 1990s other intruders also entered the home, in the form of missing children's faces and descriptions on milk cartons and Advo (advertising) cards. The sense of heightened concern resulted now from both a democratization of the victims and a new pervasiveness of publicity.[23]

Underlying it all was a culturally embedded sense that parents could and should be held responsible for ensuring their own children's safety. Indeed, I would argue that all the stories about the kidnapping of other people's children always had this intent and this consequence. Christian Ross's story was about his personal failings as a father; not putting his child first had burdened him severely. It had cost him his son and the anguish of a failed life. Lindbergh's reputation was bruised at the time of the kidnapping and has since been deeply marred by the way he pursued his son's abductors and the many subsequent theories about his role in the child's disappearance. And Stephanie Bryan's father died of a heart attack at the age of forty-seven, just eighteen months after Burton Abbott was executed. He had been so enraged at the time of the trial that he was incapable of being called to the witness stand. Parents of abducted children cannot shake that sense of personal responsibility. And this sense is strongly confirmed by the larger culture. After news of Julie Patz's son Etan's disappearance was widely publicized in New York, she was confronted on the street by sympathetic mothers who made it clear that they thought it had been her fault for losing the child.[24] At best such parents can divert their energies into quests for other children and serve as spokespersons at congressional hearings, on state panels, for foundations, and on television—in the process spreading anxieties more widely.

The consequences for other parents, all those who in the last thirty years have at least periodically imagined themselves potential victims, are also great. A rising sense of dread is one. But so is a sense of relief. Every time a child other than one's own becomes a news story, parents experience a profound sense of relief that the possibility that their own child would be a victim had temporarily passed, that the "chalice" from which Christian had been forced to drink had passed them by. Dread and relief (both experienced by Christian Ross each time a ransom note arrived) have become regular parts of an emotional cycle connected to child abduction that parents experience again and again when a child abduction is publicized. This is not to deny either the sympathy that Americans feel for the loss of other people's children or their anger. Hundreds, sometimes thousands, of Americans become actively involved in the hunt for lost children, as they did in the search for Jacob Wetterling, and as they do when they respond to features on *America's Most Wanted* or Amber Alerts. And many more campaign for or vote to tighten the law. Most will tell you that they do this because the child could have been their own, expressing once again their behavioral response to the perception that the danger has temporarily been averted. Christian Ross was quite aware of this response when he noted the relief that parents felt to find their own children unharmed and thanked a "protecting Providence."[25] This in turn suggests that child abduction in the late 20th and early 21st centuries has taken a particular path that can be understood only once we are fully familiar with its origins and its particular historical evolution.

In this regard, it is worth emphasizing how regularly the community response to abductions has taken the form of a turn to law. This was first manifested in the Ross case when what had previously been a misdemeanor in law became a felony, and where every state followed in Pennsylvania's wake. After the Lindbergh case, because of Lindbergh's fame, the Federal Bureau of Investigation became a far more active force and was reorganized, and the federal government took the lead in making kidnapping a capital offense. In the 1970s and 1980s, the FBI became for the first time involved in ordinary cases as the heightened alarm over missing children required central monitoring. At the same time, states beefed up their sexual offender laws. In some states, including Kansas, those laws now permit sex offenders to be held in some kind of custody after the expiration of their sentences, a move the Supreme Court has recently judged to be constitutional. The abduction of Polly Klaas in 1993 in California is the direct basis on which the passage of that state's three-strikes law was passed, while another California kidnap victim, Amber Garcia, serves as the name bearer for its most recent law concerning the immediate posting of highway alerts when an abduction is suspected. This is meant to encourage the highway patrol and citizens to pursue possible abductors whose license plate numbers and car descriptions are prominently posted on the roads. Every state now also has some form of community notification law that requires public access to lists of sex offenders as a result of public outrage at the abduction, sexual abuse, and murder of a little girl named Megan Kanga in New Jersey in 1994. By the beginning of the 21st century, every level of government, as well as our homes, communities, highways, and streets have been enlisted in our obsession with child abduction. And it has left a deep imprint on our national and state laws.

If our emotions have followed a path organized by the stories of abduction in the past (and our laws now inscribe them), so have our children's. In his usual prescient way, Christian noted in 1876, "Even little children themselves realized the danger to which they were exposed, and would shudder and cry out with alarm upon the approach of suspicious-looking persons."[26] Today's children are ever more alarmed. They discuss abduction formally in school and informally among themselves. They respond to their parents' fears and to their own. An ad for the television program *Stranger Danger* (also available on video) notes, "Kids tell us that today, few things are quite as scary as their fears of abduction," and a Roper poll in 1994 found that American children feared kidnapping as their "number one concern." Actress Wynona Ryder testified, "From the time I was really little, I knew what kidnapping was and it was always my worst fear."[27] Why should this be the case? Stranger abductions are relatively rare, almost certainly no more than two hundred a year, while far more children are killed by cars and household hazards such as fires and swimming pools. Children's well-being is endangered by bad schools and lack of health care. Why then should kidnapping have such power to frame the fears of children and of their parents? Why have we altered our behaviors and our laws in response to our perceptions about the pervasiveness of the danger? Why do our perceptions, for example of the rate of sexual offenses against children, so massively outstrip reality (and is this an issue, from either the personal or policy standpoint, that we should reevaluate through, among other things, a better grasp of the historical factors involved)? The answers lie embedded in a long history that began when a sweet four-year-old was lured into a wagon by two strange men who offered him candy on a hot July afternoon in 1874.

NOTES

1. Philip Jenkins, *Moral Panic: Changing Concepts of the Child Molester in Modern America* (New Haven, 1998).

2. Peter N. Stearns, *Anxious Parents: A History of Modern Childrearing in America* (New York, 2003).

3. Margaret Talbot, "The Bad Mother," *New Yorker*, August 9 and 16, 2004, 67.

4. For the full story, see Paula S. Fass, *Kidnapped: Child Abduction in America* (New York, 1997), chap. 1.

5. Christian Ross, *The Father's Story of Charley Ross, the Kidnapped Child Containing a Full and Complete Account of the Abduction of Charles Brewster Ross from the Home of His Parents in Germantown, with the Pursuit of the Abductors and Their Tragic Death; The Various Incidents Connected with the Search for the Lost Boy; The Discovery of Other Lost Children, Etc. Etc. with Facsimiles of Letters from the Abductors* (Philadelphia, 1876), 229.

6. *New York Times*, July 14, 1874, 4.

7. Ross, *The Father's Story of Charley Ross*, 20.

8. Ibid., 243.

9. Ibid., 18.

10. Ibid., 19–20.

11. Charles P. Krauth, Introduction to Ross, *The Father's Story of Charley Ross*, 11.

12. *New York Times*, December 21, 1900, 1; December 20, 1900, 1.

13. *Chicago Herald and Examiner*, June 1, 1924, 4, 5.

14. See Fass, *Kidnapped*, 48–51, for the details.

15. Clarence Edward Macartney, "Charley Ross, the Unforgotten Lost Boy," *Ladies' Home Journal* 41 (July 1924): 7, 75–78; Edward H. Smith, *Mysteries of the Missing* (New York, 1927), xv.

16. Ross, *The Father's Story of Charley Ross*, 419; *New York Times*, July 14, 1874, 4.

17. Ross, *The Father's Story of Charley Ross*, 90.

18. For a discussion of the Lindbergh case in the larger history of child abduction, see Fass, *Kidnapped*, chap. 3.

19. *New Republic* 70 (March 16, 1932): 110.

20. See Estelle B. Freedman, "'Uncontrolled Desires': The Response to the Sexual Psychopath, 1920–1960," *Journal of American History* 74 (June 1987): 83–106.

21. *San Francisco Examiner*, July 22, 1955, 1, 2.

22. The case became a worldwide cause célèbre against capital punishment. For some of the details of the case and its international reputation, see Fass, *Kidnapped*, chap. 4.

23. For a discussion of the developments in the 1980s, see Fass, *Kidnapped*, chap. 6.

24. Phyllis Battelle, "Help Find Etan Patz," *Good Housekeeping* 190 (February 1980): 71.

25. Ross, *The Father's Story of Charley Ross*, 146, 90.

26. Ibid., 90.

27. Ernie Allen, "Missing Children: A Fearful Epidemic," *USA Today* 123 (July 1994): 47; *New York Times*, May 16, 1994, A7.

4

"If They Have Any Orders, I Am Theirs to Command"

Indulgent Middle-Class Grandparents in American Society

Linda W. Rosenzweig

When Helen Lehman Buttenwieser celebrated her eightieth birthday in 1985, she received a book of letters from family members, including her nine grandchildren, in honor of the occasion. Mrs. Buttenwieser's twenty-year-old grandson thanked her "for letting me be a part of your life these past 20 years." He remembered that she always let him choose between three different bedrooms when he visited, and that she served "vanilla ice cream with *hot* chocolate sauce." Her twenty-four-year-old granddaughter recalled "how you let me order escargot and milk together in Paris." This same young woman hoped to be able to emulate her grandmother: "I realize how lucky I am to have you, to look up to and set my standards by," she wrote. Another adult granddaughter noted that during visits to her grandparents, "I felt that grandparents were people who loved and delighted in their grandchildren, and were more forgiving of the children's shortcomings than the parents. I was sure that being a grandparent was a lot of fun. I knew that being a grandchild was a lot of fun—and still is!" A younger granddaughter wrote, "You are always very generous, and you spoil me rotten whenever I visit (Who wouldn't love that?!)." She too aspired to be like her grandmother and hoped that she had "picked up" some of her "traits" in her genes.[1]

These letters describe happy memories and express love, admiration, and appreciation for a generous, capable, and accomplished woman. They also highlight a key component of grandparental behavior in contemporary American society. If Mrs. Buttenwieser indulged her grandchildren and made them feel that they were important and special, she was far from unusual in the late 20th century. The image of grandparents as affectionate, indulgent companions represents a familiar aspect of contemporary middle-class family life. We are not surprised when grandparents claim the right to "spoil" their grandchildren—indeed, we expect this behavior, and we tend to view it as a phenomenon unique to the current cultural moment.

Recent empirical research focusing on various aspects of grandparenting over the past fifty years appears to support the argument that indulgence represents a major change from earlier patterns of intergenerational interactions. For example, the results of the first national survey of American grandparenting, published in 1986, suggest that contemporary grandparenthood differs significantly from that of earlier periods. More than half of the 510 survey participants reported strong emotional bonds with their grandchildren and described their grandparental roles as those of affectionate, indulgent companions, often contrasting their own behavior with that of the distant, authoritarian figures they remembered from their own childhoods. "It's different," one woman stated, "My grandma never gave us any love . . . never took us anyplace, just sat there and yelled at you all the time." Another grandparent offered a similar response: "Things are different today. Grandparents are more indulgent because they don't want to lose their grandchildren's love."[2]

Personal documents and popular periodicals and advice literature also highlight the prevalence of grandparental permissiveness in the second half of the 20th century. Letters, diaries, and memoirs indicate that both grandparents and grandchildren considered indulgent behavior as fundamental to the grandparental role. At the same time, a critical tone in the periodical and prescriptive literature during this period identified grandparental indulgence as an area of cultural concern and implied that it represented something new in family relationships.

It would be easy to conclude, then, that grandparental indulgence was a novel phenomenon that epitomized the sort of behavior that would naturally emerge in the milieu of an affluent, consumer society—though also a society unusually anxious about the stability of family ties—like that of post–World War II America. Indeed, the experience of grandparenthood in American history reflects the influence of a variety of changing social, economic, and cultural factors situated in particular historical contexts. Such factors include demographic variables; social and economic structures and norms; cultural attitudes about the family and about aging; gender, class, ethnicity, and location.

Like all other aspects of family life, however, grandparenthood also involves emotional experiences. Research in emotions history has documented change over time in emotional standards and in emotional expression; some studies also link changes in these areas with alterations in the ways people in the past actually experienced emotions like anger, sadness, and joy. Alterations in the latter category are more difficult to ascertain, however, because emotional experience involves intrinsic psychological as well as cultural components.[3] Family relationships—including those of grandparents and grandchildren—reflect the social, economic, and cultural factors, including emotional standards, that define a specific time period, but they also reflect the universality of biologically based, affective human experiences.

Given the role of changing historical factors in the construction of grandparenthood, evidence of an apparently new 20th-century grandparental behavior is hardly surprising. Indeed, the degree of indulgence and the range of such behavior clearly represent a 20th-century development. But the roots of this phenomenon can be traced as far back as the colonial period. A nuanced approach is essential in this facet of behavioral history. The extent to which grandchildren have been spoiled over the last fifty years, and the specific ways in which they have been spoiled, illustrate a significant change over time, but this behavior also reflects a core of continuity in relationships between grandparents and grandchildren. While social, economic, and cultural factors have influenced styles of grandparenting, tendencies toward indulgence also manifest the influence of intrinsic emotional inclinations. Earlier factors that discouraged indulgent behavior declined over time, to be replaced by new social, economic, and cultural developments that allowed the incidence and scope of such behavior to grow. The incorporation of indulgence as integral to the grandparental role and the prevalence of indulgent behavior in contemporary society reflect these changes and the enduring, intrinsic (or at least, long-standing American) aspect of emotional experience.

Indulgence did not, to be sure, define typical grandparenting in colonial and early American society, which essentially offered no encouragement for such behavior. The hierarchical structure of society in Puritan New England fostered respect for the elderly and stressed intergenerational familial obligations as opposed to relationships governed by affection. Grandparents, particularly grandfathers, exercised economic and social control primarily through the ownership of land in an agricultural society. Even when offspring married and established their own households, as long as they remained dependent on their parents' assets, grandfathers maintained authority in the family. Only a small minority of the elderly actually lived with adult children and grandchildren. These factors and other features of 17th- and 18th-century life discouraged the development of close, indulgent relationships between grandchildren and grandparents. The characteristic western demographic pattern of high mortality, high fertility, and late marriage age meant that unlike their 20th-century counterparts, few adults in early America experienced grandparenthood as a separate stage of life. Few survived to experience the maturity and marriage of all their children. Grandparents were particularly rare in regions like the Chesapeake, where environmental conditions created short life expectancies, although the situation would change in the following century. Moreover, even when generational overlap did occur, the birth of a first grandchild often coincided with the arrival of a last child. Almost certainly, grandparents with ongoing responsibilities for young children of their own had little time or inclination to indulge their grandchildren.

Demographic records from early New England present a somewhat different picture. Here, first- or second-born children were likely to know all of their grandparents in early childhood and possibly have two or three surviving grandparents in adolescence. Life expectancy was relatively long, and New Englanders survived in larger numbers than elsewhere in the colonies or in England.[4] No full picture of grandparent-grandchild relationships can be constructed because little direct evidence exists regarding the behavior of the elderly in early New England. But wills, probate records, and other documents suggest that longer life expectancy facilitated frequent contact and the development of affectionate ties between grandparents and grandchildren even in the 17th century. Grandparents often left property and money to their grandchildren and frequently cared for them in childhood. In turn, older grandchildren helped and cared for frail grandmothers and grandfathers. Letters to grandchildren express love and affection along with a sense of obligation to provide moral and religious guidance, but they offer little specific information about indulgent behavior.[5] The evidence suggests an indulgent element, but it also indicates that this behavior was not a prominent part of grandparent-grandchild interactions.

By the 18th century, moderate Protestants sought and welcomed the influence and assistance of grandparents in child rearing, and this brought

them closer to their grandchildren. Grandparents during this period articulated their concerns about the well-being of grandchildren, their hopes
for the future of their grandchildren, and their views about the importance of proper religious and moral training.[6] In contrast to those in New
England, "genteel" Southern parents appear to have been reluctant to discipline their own children, leaving the duty to servants, nurses, slaves, and
so on. In some cases, grandparents objected strongly to this; at least one
grandfather attempted to keep an unruly grandchild from being "ruined"
by insisting on whipping the boy himself. As life expectancy in the South
improved in the 18th century, grandparents there developed strong attachments to their grandchildren, along with a greater tendency toward indulgence. Charles Carroll of Annapolis eagerly anticipated his granddaughter's birth and regularly sent gifts to her. His letters to her parents often included statements such as, "I long to kiss my little Granddaughter." Her
long and frequent visits to his plantation increased his fondness: "It is no
Compliment to you & Molly [his daughter-in-law] when I tell you that it
seems to me I long more to see my Dear little Granddaughter than either
of you," he admitted to his son on one occasion.[7]

The potentially negative influence of indulgent grandparental behavior
concerned evangelical Protestant writers as early as the 17th century, when
the Pilgrim pastor John Robinson expressed his views on the subject.
"Grandfathers are more affectionate towards their children's children, than
to their immediates, as seeing themselves further propagated in them, and
by their means proceeding on to a further degree of eternity," Reverend
Robinson observed, "and hence it is, that children brought up with their
grandfathers or grandmothers, seldom do well, but are usually corrupted
by their too great indulgence." In the 18th century, John Wesley urged
women to show "all possible respect" for their mothers and mothers-in-
law but not to allow them to take part in the rearing of their grandchildren. "She would undo all that you have done; she would give them her
own will in all things," he warned, "She would humour them to the de-
struction of their souls, if not their bodies too. In four-score years, I have
not met with one woman that knew how to manage grand-children." In
short, grandparents could corrupt the character of children through indulgence and should be kept at a distance emotionally, if not spatially.[8]
Advice of this sort articulates the dominant religious and cultural hostility
toward indulgence, but it also indicates that this behavior occurred often
enough for clergymen to address it formally.

In a religious culture that defined children as greedy and intrinsically sinful and stressed "breaking the will" as a major component of child rearing, such threats could be disquieting. Puritan New England grandparents who accepted this point of view may have felt compelled to suppress any impulse to indulge their grandchildren. Yet expressions of cultural concern about such behavior, along with indirect evidence of indulgent grandparenting, imply that it was present to some extent in 17th- and 18th-century New England families as well as in Southern families. At least for some grandparents, the power of intrinsic affective inclinations apparently outweighed the impact of the economic structure and the dominant social and cultural restraints in colonial and early American society.

Many examples of grandparental behavior over the course of the 19th century demonstrate an increasing tendency toward indulgence among middle-class white families. Others show that some grandparents preferred and practiced earlier, more authoritarian patterns of interaction with grandchildren. Over the course of the century, emerging structural, demographic, and cultural changes produced a different environment for intergenerational relationships from that of the preceding centuries. A significantly larger proportion of the population survived into old age. People married younger, bore children earlier, and had smaller families. These changes increased the likelihood of three-generational families, decreased the possibility that the birth of a youngest child would coincide with the arrival of a first grandchild, and made coresidence progressively more likely. Because trigenerational households still remained the exception, however, most grandparent-grandchild interactions, like those in earlier centuries, still did not take place in households, where intergenerational domestic friction would prevent or discourage grandparental indulgence.[9]

As birthrates declined and life expectancy rose, grandparenting clearly represented a separate stage of life. Older people had more time and more physical and emotional energy to devote to grandchildren. Because they were no longer responsible for their own children, they could focus more fully on intergenerational relationships. Falling birthrates eventually produced fewer grandchildren, which made it easier for grandparents to know and appreciate each child as an individual. Victorian emotional culture stressed the importance of loving family relationships and supported intense expressions of emotion, while urging proper restraints on negative feelings such anger and jealousy. This culture, and the presence of fewer grandchildren, promoted emotional investment in grandchildren.

Nineteenth-century industrialization and urbanization further altered family interactions in several ways that eventually fostered affectionate, indulgent grandparental behavior. The separation of home and work triggered a transition in the function of the family from its preindustrial role as an economic unit in which all members worked to an affective unit of support and refuge from the outside world. As this transition took place, a new cultural stress on children as precious and emotionally valuable replaced the earlier emphasis on their economic worth. Moreover, the gradual movement away from family farms to towns and cities meant that proximity to, and thus close contact with, grandchildren could not be assumed. Thus, at the same time as children became more important to adults, grandparent-grandchild relationships required more effort. Part of that effort could include more explicit expressions of affection and indulgent behavior.

An increasingly mechanized work environment required new skills that the older generation, formerly valued for its experience and expertise, did not have. This development generated revised images of the elderly as nonproductive and superfluous in an increasingly industrially and technically sophisticated society, and thus fostered a growing perception of older parents and grandparents as a burden to the family and to society. New medical interpretations of aging as a disease, as opposed to a dignified status, also supported the construction of negative cultural representations of older Americans.[10]

While the proliferation of negative images of aging individuals during this period might have been expected to impede efforts to establish close, loving relationships with their grandchildren, 19th-century grandparents, and especially grandmothers, frequently enjoyed relationships of this type. Indeed, the desirability of countering the larger imagery with positive family relationships may have provided an active spur, in a period in which family warmth was used to counter a number of less favorable trends in the social environment. The separation of home and work, the concomitant cultural construction of women's domesticity, and the emergence of Victorian emotional standards undoubtedly contributed to the central role middle-class women played in the lives of their grandchildren.

Grandmothers were often accused of spoiling their grandchildren, though evidence illustrates that they also disciplined and corrected them. In accordance with contemporary cultural images of women's roles and attributes, they cared for young children in times of illness or family crisis. In return, adult granddaughters supplied companionship and assistance for frail grandmothers. Many adult women stressed the influence of grandmothers as models when they looked back over their earlier lives, while older women saw reflections of themselves in young granddaughters. "That bad Jane is like a piece of myself," one woman wrote to her son, the child's father. Some women found visits with granddaughters therapeutic as well as enjoyable. Deborah Logan's favorite granddaughter was "a cordial in the Cup of Life, to delight and exhilerate [*sic*] my Old Age."[11] While these expressions of regard do not document specific instances of grandparental indulgence, they do connote the influence of intrinsic affectionate inclinations. Moreover, experiencing a powerful sense of identity with a granddaughter or a strong feeling about her contribution to her grandmother's well-being would certainly be conducive to indulgent behavior.

Grandmothers' involvement with grandchildren and their special empathy for granddaughters fit 19th-century images of the "true" woman as pure, pious, domestic, and submissive, but grandfathers also participated actively in intergenerational interactions. Grandparents of both genders enthusiastically followed their grandchildren's progress and corresponded with granddaughters and grandsons on a regular basis, while letters from both young women and young men document enduring ties between the generations. Two poems for children, published respectively in 1817 and 1818, depicted gendered images of affectionate, and to some degree, indulgent grandparental behavior. "My grandfather a poem" describes a grandfather who built a toy boat, told stories, played with a small child, rescued him from a dog, and let the child use his cane for a horse. "My grandmother a poem" portrays a grandmother who soothed a child's pain, gave her a "pretty Doll," and consoled her when her mother was ill—an individual to whom her granddaughter would show throughout life "the debt of gratitude I owe."[12] While the poems also allude to grandparental standards and expectations for proper conduct, these lines indicate that both adults and children in the early 19th century recognized indulgence as part of the role of a grandparent.

Other early 19th-century examples address indulgent behavior more directly. In her memoirs, Eliza Cabot Perkins compared her lenient maternal grandmother "who was always bent upon making you happy" and her stern paternal grandmother who "seemed rather awful." She respected Grandma Perkins for her dignity and strength of character; however, she was not as "fond" of her as she was of Grandma Elliot, and she considered it "the greatest privilege" to visit the latter.[13] Letters from Eleanor Parke

Custis Lewis, a grandmother who resembled Grandma Elliot rather than Grandma Perkins, reveal that indulgent grandparenthood was central to her happiness. After the birth of a grandson, Mrs. Lewis, whose own grandparents, George and Martha Washington, had played a vital role in her life, wrote to a close friend, Elizabeth Bordley Gibson: "You will readily suppose that my Grandchild is the object of my devoted affection. The *Child of My Child*, it excites even more interest than I should perhaps feel for my own, at its present age. . . . It is certain that the title of *Grandmother* is most dear to me & excites the most anxious & affecte [*sic*] feelings." Her letters continued to reflect such sentiments. Following a visit to her daughter's family, Mrs. Lewis extravagantly praised her two-year-old granddaughter's physical and intellectual attributes and her engaging personality traits. "She is so small, her form is so perfect, so ladylike, she is so graceful, so engaging, & so very intelligent. . . . I know not how to leave her when I am obliged to go," she confided to Mrs. Gibson. As subsequent grandchildren appeared, Eleanor Lewis sent news of their health, their progress, descriptions of the "worsted work" she embroidered for two granddaughters, and even a "specimen" of her youngest granddaughter's "handy work."[14]

In this period, indulgence was often balanced by grandmothers' efforts to modify the behavior of grandchildren in accordance with proper conduct. One grandmother enclosed the following note when she sent a fan and a thimble to her granddaughter in 1822: "If she does not spit on the floor, she will find them very pretty indeed." This message suggests that indulgent behavior, in this case sending "very pretty" gifts, did not imply the absence of any disapproval or criticism of a grandchild's conduct or demeanor. Grandmothers also complained when their expectations for care and companionship from older grandchildren remained unmet; such complaints often targeted grandsons rather than granddaughters, whose socialization to the domestic sphere undoubtedly made them less inclined to neglect such duties.[15] A series of letters from a Virginia grandfather clearly illustrates a strong tendency to judge and instruct rather than to indulge. Although Peter Lyons assured her of his regard, he criticized his granddaughter's negligence as a correspondent. He urged her to concentrate on her studies, to make her handwriting larger, and to "quit the giddy idle girl and emulate the industrious." In addition, he reminded her that her father had spared no expense to provide her with tutors, and that he expected to be able to rely on her companionship and assistance when he became too infirm to handle his affairs. To this end, he urged her to "make yourself perfect in arithmetic."[16]

While indulgent grandparental behavior was not unusual in the first decades of the century, it increased noticeably after about 1830. As social, economic, and cultural change gained momentum in succeeding decades, these factors constructed a context in which indulgent grandparenting expanded and flourished. Post-1830 examples clearly document this expansion. For instance, when sixteen-year-old Agnes Lee recorded the loss of her beloved grandfather in her journal in 1857, she remembered him as an affectionate and caring companion: "So kind he was, so indulgent, loving us so fondly, humouring our childish caprices, grateful for our little kindnesses," she mourned.[17] Letters from Abigail Hopper Gibbons to her granddaughter, Bonnie Morse, and to other family members reveal a similarly devoted grandparent. "As for Bonnie," Mrs. Gibbons wrote to the child's aunt, "she grows more and more to us [*sic*] each day of her sweet life." On one occasion, she quickly acknowledged the arrival of Bonnie's "dear letter," pronouncing it "a *very* VERY nice one" that merited an immediate reply. In another letter, she reported that the "children," Bonnie's dolls, were in good condition and that "their clothes are all clean and ready for thee when thee comes home." She also enclosed "a sack, hoping it will fit 'Violet Blue-eyes,'" Bonnie's newest acquisition: "I am glad thy father bought thee a doll, for what is a child to do without one?" she declared. Although she loved all her "children" equally, Mrs. Gibbons admitted, "Bonnie is a little nearest my heart." Despite this expression of explicit preference, which may reflect a sense of shared gender, she corresponded regularly and affectionately with her grandsons, and eagerly anticipated spending time with them. "Say to the little brothers we will have lively times, and if they have any orders, I am theirs to command," she told Bonnie in preparation for a forthcoming visit.[18]

Such expressions of fondness were not the exclusive province of grandmothers in the second half of the 19th century. Dwight Moody, an evangelical minister, wrote affectionate letters to his granddaughter, Emma, almost from the moment of her birth. He looked forward to assuming the role of a loving grandfather and indulgent companion. "I wanted to get a letter to you before you got your first tooth," an early letter stated. "Hurry up and get them all before the hot weather comes on, for I will get you some candy and you will want teeth to eat it." In another letter, he urged his infant granddaughter to "hurry up and grow, so I can come early mornings and take you out riding when your mother and father are fast asleep. We will slip over the river to see Irene [Emma's cousin] and have some good times." In anticipation of Emma's first birthday, he wrote, "You will never know how much your grandfather thinks of you and I shall be glad to get you in my arms again." A birthday telegram reiterated her importance to him: "My dear Emma we all praise god [sic] for what you have been to us this first year on earth may you live for ever is the prayer of your Grand Father." A few weeks later, Mr. Moody mentioned taking Emma riding again. At the same time, he observed, "I do not often write letters on the Sabbath, but thought I must write you this morning and tell you that I was thinking of you." Occasionally he revealed a tendency to advise and instruct rather than indulge, as in letters that contained warnings against the habit of thumb sucking or listed his expectations for her future education.[19] Because Dwight Moody died when Emma was only four years old, it is impossible to know how this relationship would have developed as she grew up. Nevertheless, it is clear that, like many of his contemporaries, he regarded affectionate indulgence as central to the role of a grandfather.

So did Louise Dew's grandmother, who allowed visiting grandchildren to stay up much later than they were permitted to do at home and provided other treats as well. Unlike Dwight Moody's granddaughter, who probably remembered very little about her devoted grandfather, Louise Dew's memories of her indulgent grandmother endured. In an article written as a mature adult, Ms. Dew described the happiness she and her brother experienced during their visits with her. She recalled that they enjoyed swinging on their grandmother's front gate and often refused to stop, despite "many kindly admonitions." She remembered too that when they were punished for this behavior, usually by their parents, these situations were "abbreviated and alleviated by the angel we called Grandmother."[20]

When post-1830 grandparents found themselves directly responsible for raising their grandchildren, indulgence had a lower priority. In such cases, it was not the proximity of three generations in a household that discouraged indulgent grandparental behavior, but rather a sense of responsibility for the welfare of grandchildren, and for teaching them good religious and moral values and proper conduct. Caroline Cowles Clarke and her sister, Anna, who lived with their grandparents after their mother's death, seldom encountered grandparental permissiveness. Their grandmother could be very stern: "We asked Grandmother if we could have some hoop skirts like the seminary girls and she said no, we were not old enough," Caroline confided to her diary on one occasion. About two years later, she described an experience playing "mumble te peg [*sic*]" with a friend. "It is fun, but rather dangerous. I am afraid Grandmother won't give me a knife to play with," she concluded. Another diary entry reported that Anna had not been allowed to have a special dress when she sang in a children's concert: "She [Anna] ought to have worn a white dress as the others did, but Grandmother said her new pink barege [*sic*] would do." Nor was Anna successful in persuading their grandmother to let them finish a game they were playing on the backyard swings one evening at dinner time. "Grandmother called us in to dinner, but Anna said we could not go until we 'let the old cat die.' Grandmother said it was more important that we should come when we are called," Caroline recounted.

The duties of substitute parenthood apparently took precedence over indulgent grandparenting in this family. This suggests that even in a social, economic, and cultural context that was conducive to indulgence, special or unusual factors sometimes produced more authoritarian behavior even where love and affection were present. Yet even in the distinctive circumstances of custodial grandparenthood, some evidence of indulgence can be discerned. Diary references to riding excursions and other recreational activities with their grandfather indicate that he provided companionship to Caroline and Anna and let his wife serve as the family disciplinarian. Other examples also evoke this tendency toward lenience. Although Caroline hesitated to tell her grandfather when she lost her thimble and scissors on the way to school and had no money to replace them, she felt sure that he would just say "Accidents will happen." She was delighted when he gave her fabric for a new calico dress: "It is white with pink spots in it and Grandfather bought it in New York," she wrote, "It is very nice indeed and I think Grandfather was very kind to get it for me." Caroline and Anna might have wished that their grandmother had been more permissive, but they apparently understood and accepted her behavior. As Caroline put it at the age of seventeen, "Grandmother knows that we think she is a perfect angel even if she does seem rather strict sometimes."[21]

Mary Ezit Bulkley would not have understood Caroline Cowles Clarke's assessment of her grandmother's behavior. Miss Bulkley's grandmother, a stern Baptist with strict ideas, was "never the cuddly kind," and her granddaughter "was never fond of her." As an adult, she attributed her grandmother's ideas to her upbringing in Somerset, England, where "she had no diversions." Miss Bulkley also thought that her grandmother's behavior represented an effort "to point [out] the outrageous way in which children of later generations were being spoiled." This observation itself actually offers interesting evidence that 19th-century observers realized that grandparental indulgence was growing. While many grandchildren were aware of their grandparents' love and admiration during this period, Mary Ezit Bulkley had no idea that her grandmother thought highly of her: "I was never more stunned in my life than when I heard someone tell my mother that grandmother had said that in spite of the way my parents spoiled me she thought I might grow up to do them credit," she recalled. But even this difficult relationship offers a hint of grandparental indulgence. Although they seldom agreed, Miss Bulkley remembered that she had thoroughly approved of her grandmother's "attitude on surreptitious feedings of milk and gingerbread." Still, her dominant memories of this formidable woman remained negative—many years later, as she wrote her memoirs, she could "still hear the stridencies of [her] Somerset Grandmother's voice: 'What be 'ee a-doing' of? Why be 'ee a-sittin' here?'"[22] As her granddaughter surmised, the behavior of Mary Ezit Bulkley's grandmother undoubtedly reflected the continuing influence of her early life in a different society and culture. Like those of Caroline Cowles Clarke's grandmother, her personal circumstances apparently overshadowed the 19th-century influences that encouraged both explicit expressions of grandparental affection and indulgent treatment of grandchildren.

The preceding examples of the impact of particular individual experiences and special circumstances on grandparental indulgence remind us that diversity and heterogeneity have characterized family relationships in all historical periods. Thus, while 19th-century social, economic, and cultural factors, in conjunction with intrinsic emotional components, promoted the growth of indulgent behavior, other factors—individual personalities and preferences, plus the effects of ethnicity or class, for example—had an impact on grandparent-grandchild relationships.

Intergenerational relationships in enslaved families offer an important case in point. It is especially difficult to document family interactions in American slave society, but clear evidence of efforts to preserve a sense of lineage, both symbolically and in practice, can be cited. A study of child-naming patterns among Thomas Jefferson's slaves indicates that in the second half of the 18th century, black families in Virginia named their offspring for grandparents more often than was the case in white New England families. Slaves on plantations in Louisiana, North Carolina, and South Carolina used similar naming practices in the late 18th and early

19th centuries. This custom suggests the influence of at least two West African cultural traditions—a view of kinship networks as central to social relationships and a family custom that has been described "the merging of alternate generations." In contrast to parent-child relationships of authority and "essential inequality," West African grandparent-grandchildren relations reflected "friendly familiarity and near equality."[23]

This heritage, along with the disruption of nuclear family life under slavery, contributed to the development of strong affective ties between grandparents and grandchildren. Grandparents played a central role in the enculturation of grandchildren, and grandmothers in particular participated extensively in their upbringing. Grandmothers also provided a wide range of other assistance to grandchildren of all ages—hiding fugitives, taking food to jailed offspring, and even saving enough money to purchase their freedom.[24] Obviously, relationships between enslaved grandparents and grandchildren involved more serious issues than fun and companionship; slave children had to be taught that their safety and well-being might well depend on obedient and respectful behavior toward white adults. But evidence of close intergenerational ties in slave families raises the possibility that a combination of West African traditions and intrinsic affective inclinations, along with observations of spoiled white grandchildren, may have inclined African American grandparents toward indulging their own grandchildren in whatever ways they could manage.

The case of immigration, like that of slavery, illustrates both diversity and consistency in grandparental behavior. Many immigrant families brought European traditions of respect for the elderly to the United States. The Italian American community in particular maintained these traditions diligently and continued to honor the older generation as late as the 1920s. Because age and poverty often prevented older adults from emigrating, numerous first-generation American grandchildren knew their European grandparents only at a distance. This changed quickly; subsequent generations of grandparents and grandchildren experienced frequent opportunities for interaction, either in coresident households or as nearby neighbors. Despite growing perceptions of the elderly as potential if not actual burdens, grandmothers who helped in the house and provided child care were highly valued. Even when geographic distance no longer separated grandparents from their grandchildren, cultural differences and linguistic barriers could still impede the development of close relationships. In cases like this, and when grandparents stayed behind in Europe, evidence of grandparental indulgence is difficult to uncover. As communication barriers in white, ethnic families declined, close intergenerational relationships increased significantly, especially between grandmothers and granddaughters. Diverse ethnic values continued to influence the nature of intergenerational interactions, but by the late 20th century, affectionate companionship, presumably accompanied by some form of indulgence, had become the norm for most ethnic families.[25]

Increasing evidence of middle-class grandparental indulgence across ethnicities and hints of its presence even where diversity structured grand-parent-grandchild relationships in particular ways attest to the spread of this style of grandparenting over the course of the 19th century. Pre-1830 manifestations of indulgence constrained by their combination with efforts to instruct and discipline grandchildren gave way to the unambiguous advocacy and practice of this behavior. The growth and development of indulgent grandparenthood would continue into the next century. Eventually it would become the defining characteristic of grandparenting in American society.

At the beginning of the 20th century, cultural images continued to portray the elderly in negative terms. Nineteenth-century culture had depicted aging individuals as obsolete and irrelevant in a modern technological society. Now they were represented as interfering nuisances who lived with their offspring and threatened family peace and stability. Although 70 percent of Americans who were sixty or older in 1900 did not live with their children, the adverse effects of coresidency were perceived as a real issue that triggered intergenerational discord. Middle-class commentators complained about the problems of living with aging parents and stressed the frequency of conflict over child-rearing issues. At the same time, dislocated parents objected to the constraints imposed by coresidence and what they perceived as ungracious treatment.[26]

In response to such concerns, grandparents who actually lived in three-generational households may have resisted any desire to spoil their grandchildren. Alternatively, conflicts with grandchildren and/or their parents may have suppressed natural inclinations toward indulgence. This was also a peak period for confusions in multigenerational immigrant households, where grandparents might worry about the more American ways of their grandchildren. However, because coresidence remained an exception, it did not discernibly alter the pattern of grandparental behavior that had emerged in the previous century.

Both younger and older generations espoused the ideal of autonomous households as the 20th century began, but the Depression temporarily disrupted the process of achieving this goal. Nevertheless, by the middle of the century, Social Security benefits, private pensions, and growing prosperity among older people enabled most grandparents to live independently. Revised cultural images depicting the elderly as busy, active, independent individuals rather than as burdens accompanied this development. Advice about intergenerational relations reflected this reevaluation of older people: an increasing emphasis on love, affection, and companionship as opposed to discipline and authority now officially defined grandparenthood; in this milieu, indulging and spoiling grand-children officially represented appropriate behavior.[27] Indeed, it had become the only job assigned specifically to independent, financially secure grandparents.

This clearly was the most obvious change: a far more complete authorization to indulge, though as we will see, some newly worried commentary inevitably responded. The level of social approval for indulgent grandparents, and their own willingness to proclaim their impulses, differed considerably from the past. To an extent, as we have seen, this simply reified tendencies that had been building for several decades, around an even older, possibly intrinsic inclination. But this is an example of behavioral history where real continuity must be combined with explanations for additional change. In this case, the pronounced tendency for the elderly to move out of children's households contributed to innovation: tensions were reduced but the need to woo grandchildren probably increased as well. The elderly themselves were living more consumerist lifestyles, and this involved both new means to spoil and perhaps a wish to deflect guilt about personal spending. A clear new commitment to children's consumerism, including the desirability to use material goods to motivate and socialize, obviously helped authorize grandparental behavior; child-rearing manuals, for example, began specifically to recommend that grandparents bring toys for siblings when they celebrated the birthday of a particular grandchild, to deflect the potential for jealousy. Finally, new levels of anxiety about parenting itself may have prompted grandparents both to reward grandchildren for enduring novel tensions in the nuclear household and to express their own relief that their own anxious responsibilities were behind them and they could enjoy grandchildren as compensation for their earlier parental struggles. The new environment for indulgence combined past trends with new prosperity, but it also harbored more complex components that help explain the open enthusiasm for the authorization to spoil.

Popular periodical literature showed that, like Helen Lehman Butten-wieser, many grandparents and grandchildren in the second half of the 20th century consciously defined grandparental roles in terms of the pro-vision of indulgent love and companionship. The author of a *Reader's Di-gest* article addressed to expectant grandfathers summarized his new grandparental status succinctly: "I was freed of all responsibilities except to love and indulge her," he observed. Another contributor to the same publication described her upbringing by Welsh grandparents as "the great-est spoiling a child ever had," and emphatically declared, "I'm glad of it." Judith Viorst, a popular writer, celebrated the indulgent treatment and un-conditional love that her own mother offered to her grandsons—Viorst's children—who knew their grandmother as "the lady who thought that whatever they were and whatever they wanted to be was completely great."[28] But some periodicals presented grandparental indulgence as a subject of concern and a trigger of intergenerational conflict. One author characterized the temptation to indulge grandchildren as a way "to win their love and to make sure they like being with you better than with the other grandmother." This author maintained that "to be indulgent with grandchildren is to be *self*-indulgent, to place popularity and love above what one knows is better for their character." Another author also argued that grandparental permissiveness directly reflected an eagerness to be loved. Still other writers lamented the difficulties caused by the fact that "many grandparents see indulging their grandchildren as their right," cited indulgence as the most common complaint made about grandparents, and identified the presence of an overindulgent grandmother as a frequent cause of serious tension in a three-adult home.[29] Articles of this type, rem-iniscent of the statements of 17th- and 18th-century clergymen, indicate that grandparents not only saw indulgence as part of their role, but they practiced this behavior more routinely than ever before.

The 20th-century construction of the role of grandparents evolved in the broader context of a redefinition of middle-class cultural norms for self-control. This process included a reevaluation of emotional intensity, eventually producing a new culture that emphasized emotional manage-ment. A blend of new restrictions and new freedoms concerning personal behavior emerged in response to post–World War II abundance and the expanding consumer culture. Child-rearing trends reflected a similar blend of limits and latitude. In the last quarter of the century, anxiety over permissiveness in society at large generated a spate of child-rearing litera-ture focused on the need for more parental restraint and control of offspring. A variety of books about spoiled children in a self-indulgent world appeared during the 1980s and 1990s.[30]

At the same time, however, guides for grandparents continued to suggest that spoiling grandchildren was both a right and a responsibility. Grandparental spending on toys and other gifts, as well as on more basic items such as clothing, increased. Travel companies now offered organized group trips especially designed for grandparents and grandchildren, thus commercializing and expanding the sort of experience that some prosperous grandparents provided individually.

Cultural anxiety about permissiveness and self-control may have affected the behavior of some grandparents, but indulgence continued to be a grandparental prerogative. Moreover, its manifestations grew more extravagant by the end of the century. This trend reflected both the ability to spoil grandchildren in an affluent society and the 20th-century emphasis on emotional management. In a culture that no longer valued intense, flowery expressions of emotion, indulgent behavior presented an alternative approach through which grandparents could express their love and affection. Rather than articulate these emotions, they acted them out.

Examples of grandparental behavior illustrate the 20th-century evolution of indulgence from expressing affectionate feelings to demonstrating them through explicitly permissive behavior. Letters from Peter Newell to his grandson, Tony, reflect affectionate, comfortable companionship and indulgent love in the first two decades of the century. "I wish you were down here to go a-fishing with me. With lots of love Gran'pa," Mr. Newell wrote in 1916. A year later, Tony wanted his grandfather to come and speak at his school: "Dear Grandpa we invite you to Assembly to give a chock [*sic*] talk," he wrote. Mr. Newell sent a coconut to Tony and his sister, along with helpful instructions about how to open it and drain the milk. Letters to his grandson at camp, and later at boarding school, were enthusiastic and reassuring. Some were accompanied by small drawings; one envelope contained four tiny, round, cut-out faces. He always signed them, "With lots of love."[31]

Alfred Stieglitz's relationship with his grandson, Milton, suggests a different type of indulgence. Milton's letters from the age of seven, in 1930, through, and after, his education at Harvard and his naval service consistently express thanks for the generous checks he received from his grandfather—checks that he saved for "an automobile" that he was able to buy in July 1941. Mr. Stieglitz continued to send regular gifts, even while his grandson was in the navy. They saw each other infrequently, and sometimes Milton worried that his "childish letters" would bore his grandfather. But he also worried about his grandfather's health, looked forward to seeing him, and signed his letters affectionately.[32] These letters document indulgent behavior at a distance rather than in conjunction with affectionate companionship, and they foreshadow the increased spending by grandparents that would occur in succeeding decades.

June Coyne Corotto's experiences during summer and weekend visits with her grandparents in a small town in Pennsylvania in the 1940s anticipate other aspects of late 20th century grandparental behavior, the warm friendship and unqualified indulgence that would define the norm. She and her sister were their grandfather's two most favorite people, along with his wife and his daughter (their mother). On Saturday nights he took his granddaughters to the movies and then to the drugstore, where they looked at comic books and drank sodas. "Nothing was spared when it came to his little girls [sic] wants," she recalled.[33]

Martha Elizabeth Chew also enjoyed being with her grandparents in the late 1940s. "I miss playing cards with you all," she wrote after a visit. On another occasion she told her mother, "Don't worry about me because Granny and I are having a good time." As she grew up, her grandparents were indulgent in other ways. Like Alfred Stieglitz, they regularly sent gifts of money; one particular check funded a trip to Washington, D.C. Ms. Chew especially appreciated her grandmother's "vote of confidence" regarding her plan to attend summer school at the University of Iowa in 1962, and her generosity in "opening [a bank] account" to support the plan. When her parents objected to this idea, she reminded them that her grandmother had originally offered to send her to UCLA "to have just a good time." Later, as Ms. Chew faced marital problems, her grandmother offered to contribute $500 to help her get a divorce.[34]

A round-robin correspondence maintained for over half a century by Radcliffe graduates also illustrates the shaping of grandparent-grandchild interactions in accordance with late 20th century ideas about grandparental indulgence. With one exception, there is no indication that these women were affected by the contemporary cultural anxiety about permissiveness. Letters from the 1970s and beyond describe the joys of grandmotherhood, discuss personal experiences, and contain photographs of beloved grandchildren. "It is such a delight to be able to see Tapley a couple of times a week and have her greet me with such enthusiasm without having the hassle that goes with bringing up your own children," Beatrice Shepherd wrote on April 26, 1978. Just under two years later she reported that her children had moved to Maine: "Tapley is a doll. I don't remember being as impressed with the miracle of a baby growing into a person with my own children. . . . It is probably just as well I am not any closer because I would probably spoil her," she concluded, possibly in response to the contemporary concerns about self-control. One correspondent, who was "ECSTATIC" about her own grandson, advised Mrs. Shepherd, "Bee, your little Tapley *is* a doll; you must enjoy her and go right ahead and spoil her. That's our prerogative as grand!" Later letters that mention a trip to Washington, D.C., for Tapley's spring vacation and a visit to Disneyland in California indicate that Mrs. Shepherd took her friend's advice. Dallas Flinn, another Radcliffe correspondent, admired Mrs. Shepherd's companionate grandparenting style as it appeared in a photograph: "I just hope I can follow in the footsteps (wheel tracks?) of Bee who I see smartly rollerskating with her grandchildren," she observed. Mary Cutting Ivie's note on the back of a photograph of her grandchildren reflects the same late 20th century point of view reflected in the two previous examples: "The girls are *so* much fun," Mrs. Ivie wrote. Another grandmother regretted that remarriage and relocation prevented her from contributing regularly "to the children's lives as a recital, concert, play goer; as a looker-up of important information for projects; as a resource person; as a subject for oral interviews, etcetera."[35]

The grandparenting style of Mildred Levine Albert and her husband epitomizes grandparental indulgence as it looked in the second half of the 20th century. They corresponded regularly with their grandchildren, some of whom lived in London, and their grandchildren reported in detail about school, jobs, future plans, and social life. Their letters reflect both gratitude and appreciation for various forms of grandparental generosity: a gift of ten pounds for one grandson; an "overly generous birthday present" that arrived "on exactly the right day"; a "30th Birthday Present" for a granddaughter who wrote, "Its [*sic*] always so lovely to know that you never ever forget!" and moral and emotional support and professional guidance for another granddaughter who, like Mrs. Albert, worked in the fashion world. "I have so much to thank you for," this young woman wrote, "I am so happy with the work that I am doing and I know that it would not have been possible without you. . . . I feel so incredibly lucky to have two such wonderful and unbelievable people so close to me."[36] The letters also suggest that these young people were not surprised by the behavior of their grandparents, behavior that mirrored the cultural construction of grandparenting to which they had been socialized.

Near the end of her long life, Sarah Bradley Gamble also received grateful letters from grandchildren who acknowledged her companionship, her affection, and the time she had devoted to them. "The warm, ever-interested love you have given me over the years will always stay with me, and I am so very thankful I have been able to know you as a friend," her granddaughter Jenny wrote, "Thank you for that most precious of all gifts, that of your time and your love." Her grandson Miles thanked her "for one hundred memories." Her grandson Benjamin enumerated "all the wonderful things that I have done with you" and offered the following tribute: "I will ever cherish all these memories Nana. I love you very much and will never forget all that you have meant for me and given to me." He ended his letter with the ultimate compliment: "I hope that someday when I am a grand parent [*sic*] I can remember you and be as nice as you have been."[37]

These moments in the lives of two families highlight the key characteristics of indulgent grandparenting in the last decades of the 20th century. As the Albert and Gamble grandchildren observed, middle-class grandparents offered affectionate friendship and companionship to their grandchildren. They indulged granddaughters and grandsons by devoting time and energy to their needs and interests, by providing entertaining experiences for them, and by generously sharing their more tangible resources. This behavior reflected the conditions of life in an affluent consumer culture. Grandparents in this period typically enjoyed financial security and enough leisure time to be indulgent. They lived longer than their predecessors had, and they had no responsibility for young children of their own, nor were they usually the primary caregivers for their grandchildren. Moreover, as birthrates fell, the question of if, rather than when, grandchildren would arrive arose. Uncertainty about the likelihood of having grandchildren made them even more valuable when they appeared. Americans looked forward to the experience of grandparenthood. They relished it, and for many, it became vital to their lives.

In one sense, the development of indulgent behavior as the dominant feature of grandparenting in the late 20th century marked a distinct episode in the history of the relationship between grandparents and grandchildren. The extent to which such behavior was culturally sanctioned and to which it was practiced made it a unique phenomenon. Yet, as we have seen, inclinations to indulge grandchildren were present even in the 17th and 18th centuries, but the influence of the dominant social, economic, and cultural factors of those eras offset their impact. As the weight of these factors declined, other conditions that were more hospitable to indulgent behavior emerged. New social, economic, and cultural developments created an environment and an emotional culture in which affectionate and even permissive treatment of grandchildren became more acceptable. Finally, new 20th-century influences replaced those of the Victorian era, and the historical trend toward more lenient grandparenting reached its peak. Indulgence was now more than appropriate—it was a major component of the job description for grandparenthood, and grandchildren seemed to expect it.

The history of grandparent-grandchild relationships also suggests that indulgence will remain part of the American style of grandparenting because it is linked to the intrinsic, biological component of human emotion. Nevertheless, just as earlier manifestations of indulgent behavior evolved in response to shifting social, economic, and cultural factors over the last three centuries, the current prominence of indulgence will not necessarily endure in the context of new developments. Behavioral historians, even as they explain a contemporary pattern, must be alert to straws in the wind that may suggest novel directions for the future.

Indeed, suggestions of change are already discernible as the new century unfolds. While some new developments have the potential to alter the landscape of grandparent-grandchild relationships significantly, other changes may balance their impact. Thus, for example, increased geographic distance between family members in our highly mobile society would seem likely to produce a shift in the nature of intergenerational relationships. But increased access to communication in the computer age and ease and availability of travel may offset this change. On the other hand, the prevalence of divorce has already created more functional roles, especially for maternal grandparents who have become more directly involved with raising grandchildren. At the same time, contentious divorce battles have distanced many paternal grandparents from their grandchildren. In addition, a range of parental difficulties have produced increasing numbers of older Americans, white and black, who are primary caregivers for their grandchildren. Concurrently, the courts have steadily increased the rights of grandparents to intervene in the lives of grandchildren even when parents oppose such involvement.

Just as the trend toward indulgent grandparenting is rooted in the past, current changes cannot be considered completely new phenomena. African American grandparents have exercised parental authority in the lives of their grandchildren from slavery to the present in ways that distinguish them from their white counterparts. White grandparents too had long-term child-care responsibilities in the past, often for their own children and sometimes for grandchildren whose parents had died as opposed to becoming divorced. Grandparents also frequently took over temporarily as caregivers when children became ill. Whether or not indulgence continues to define American grandparenting in the 21st century will depend on the degree to which increased involvement and coresident caregiving responsibilities, along with other factors—including yet-to-be-determined social, economic, and cultural shifts—will produce a new definition and a new style of grandparenting.

NOTES

1. Peter, n.d.; Jill, October 1985; Sarah, 5 October 1985; and Janet, 24 September 1985, to Helen Lehman Buttenwieser, all in Box 1, Folder 21, Helen Lehman Buttenwieser Papers, Schlesinger Library, Radcliffe Institute, Cambridge, MA.

2. Quoted in Andrew J. Cherlin and Frank F. Furstenberg, Jr., *The New American Grandparent: A Place in the Family, a Life Apart* (New York, 1986), 36, 16.

3. For an overview of the field of emotions history and a relevant bibliography, see Peter N. Stearns, "History of Emotions: The Issue of Change," in Michael Lewis and Jeannette M. Haviland, eds., *Handbook of Emotions* (New York, 1993). See also Peter N. Stearns with Carol Z. Stearns, "Emotionology: Clarifying the History of Emotions and Emotional Standards, *American Historical Review* 90 (October 1985): 813–36, and Peter N. Stearns and Deborah C. Stearns, "Historical Issues in Emotions Research: Causation and Timing," in *Social Perspectives on Emotion*, vol. 2 (Greenwich, CT, 1994), 239–66.

4. John Demos, "Old Age in Early New England," and Daniel Blake Smith, "Autonomy and Affection: Parents and Children in Chesapeake Families," both in Michael Gordon, ed., *The American Family in Social-Historical Perspective*, 3rd ed. (New York, 1983), 269–305, 209–28.

5. See, for example, Josiah Quincy to his grandson, March 16, 1784, Massachusetts Historical Society, Boston; *The Diary of Samuel Sewall, 1674–1729*, vol. 2, ed. M. Halsey Thomas (New York, 1973); Wills of Martha Emons and Thomas Makepeace, in Donald M. Scott and Bernard Wishy, eds., *American Families: A Documentary History* (New York, 1982), 166–69; and Demos's discussion of wills in "Old Age in Early New England."

6. See, for example, Mabel J. Webber, ed., *Extracts from the Journal of Mrs. Ann Manigault, 1754–1781* (Charleston, SC, 1920), and Robert H. Hinckley, ed., *Selections from the Diary of Christina Leach of Kingsessing, 1765–1796* (Philadelphia,

1911), both in North American Women's Letters and Diaries, http://colet.uchicago.edu/cgi-bin/aspa/n.

7. Quoted in Smith, "Autonomy and Affection," 218.

8. Quoted in Philip Greven, *The Protestant Temperament: Patterns of Child-Rearing, Religious Experience, and the Self in Early America* (New York, 1977), 27.

9. Stephen Ruggles, *Prolonged Connections: The Rise of the Extended Family in Nineteenth-Century England and America* (Madison, WI, 1987).

10. Viviana A. Zelizer, *Pricing the Priceless Child: The Changing Social Value of Children* (New York, 1985); Brian Gratton and Carole Haber, "Three Phases in the History of American Grandparents: Authority, Burden, Companion," *Generations* 20 (1996): 7–12; Carole Haber and Brian Gratton, *Old Age and the Search for Security: An American Social History* (Bloomington, IN, 1994); Andrew W. Achenbaum, *Old Age in the New Land* (Baltimore, 1978).

11. Mary Beth Norton, *Liberty's Daughters: The Revolutionary Experience of American Women, 1750–1800* (Boston, 1980), 96; Terri L. Premo, *Winter Friends: Women Growing Old in the New Republic, 1785–1835* (Urbana, 1990), 85–86; Elizabeth Izard to William Shippen III, 1 July 1823 and Deborah Norris Logan, Diary, 20 August 1837, quoted in ibid., 91, 92.

12. Anonymous (Philadelphia: William Charles, 1817, 1818), microform, Massachusetts Historical Society, Boston.

13. Reminiscences of Mrs. Eliza Perkins Cabot, tss, pp. 5–11, Box 1, Folder 9, Cabot Family Papers, Schlesinger Library.

14. Eleanor Parke Custis Lewis to Elizabeth Bordley Gibson, 12 December 1826, 9 February 1834, 10 January 1842, 10 December 1844, and 28 March 1847, in Patricia Brady, ed., *George Washington's Beautiful Nelly: The Letters of Eleanor Parke Custis Lewis to Elizabeth Bordley Gibson, 1794–1851* (Columbia, SC, 1991).

15. Premo, *Winter Friends,* 86–88.

16. Peter Lyons to Lucy Hopkins, 21 June 1805, 1 July 1805, 8 September, 1805, Peter Lyons Papers, #2378z, Southern Historical Collection, University of North Carolina Library, Chapel Hill.

17. 11 October 1857, Journal of Agnes Lee, in Mary Custis Lee deButts, ed., *Growing Up in the 1850s: The Journal of Agnes Lee* (Chapel Hill, NC, 1984).

18. Abigail Hopper Gibbons to Sally Gibbons Emerson, 24 October 1873; to Bonnie Morse, 17 July 1877; to Lucy Gibbons Morse, 9 July 1879; and to Bonnie Morse, 24 June 1882, in *Life of Abby Hopper Gibbons: Told Chiefly through Her Correspondence,* vol. 2, ed. Sarah Hopper Emerson (New York, 1896), in North American Women's Letters and Diaries Database, University of Chicago.

19. Dwight L. Moody to Emma Moody Fitt, 7 January 1896, 10 and 16 December 1896, Box 1, Series 1, Folder 10, Dwight L. Moody Papers, Record Group No. 28, Yale University Library, Divinity Library Special Collections, New Haven, CT.

20. Louise E. Dew, "A Visit to Grandmother's," *New England Magazine* 32 (July 1905): 533–400.

21. Diary of Caroline Cowles Clarke, n.d. November 1852, n.d. 1854, 26 May 1854, 1 September 1854, n.d. May 1854, and n.d. 1860, in *Village Life in America, 1852–1872, Including the Period of the American Civil War as Told in the Diary of a School Girl* (New York, 1913), in North American Women's Letters and Diaries Database, University of Chicago.

22. Mary Ezit Bulkley, *Grandmother, Mother and Me,* tss, 12, 13, 15, 209, Schlesinger Library.

23. Norton, *Liberty's Daughters,* 85–90; Herbert G. Gutman, *The Black Family in Slavery and Freedom, 1750–1925* (New York, 1976); Ira Berlin, *Many Thousands Gone: The First Two Centuries of Slavery in North America* (Cambridge, MA, 1998), 132; A. R. Radcliffe-Brown, Introduction to A. R. Radcliffe-Brown and Daryll Forde, eds., *African Systems of Kinship and Marriage* (1950), 27–30, quoted in Gutman, *Black Family,* 199.

24. Gutman, *Black Family,* 199–200; Harriet A. Jacobs, *Incidents in the Life of a Slave Girl,* ed. Jean Fagan Yellin (Cambridge, MA, 1987).

25. Virginia Yans-McLaughlin, *Family and Community: Italian Immigrants in Buffalo, 1880–1930* (Urbana, 1982), 65–66, 255–56; Corinne Azen Krause, *Grandmothers, Mothers, and Daughters: Oral Histories of Three Generations of Ethnic American Women* (Boston, 1991), 210–11; Carol E. Woehrer, "The Influence of Ethnic Families on Intergenerational Relationships and Later Life Transitions," *Annals of the American Academy of Political Science* 464 (November 1982): 65–78; Cherlin and Furstenberg, *The New American Grandparent,* chapter 3.

26. Samuel Butler, 1885; Anonymous, 1931, quoted in Brian Gratton and Carole Haber, "Three Phases in the History of American Grandparents."

27. Gratton and Haber, "Three Phases in the History of American Grandparents."

28. Floyd Miller, "The Expectant Grandfather's Guide," *Reader's Digest* 92 (April 1963): 153–58; Joyce E. Varney, "How My Grandparents Spoiled Me!" *Reader's Digest* 78 (April 1961): 99–103; Judith Viorst, "My Mother, My Children's Grandmother, My Friend," *Redbook* 153 (May 1979): 58, 61. See also Rolaine Hochstein, "Confessions of a Grandma," *Parents' Magazine* 67 (May 1992): 58, 60, 61.

29. Lucy Worcester, "Am I an Unnatural Grandmother?" *Reader's Digest* 76 (May 1960): 247–50; Carl A. Peterson, "A House Divided Cannot Stand: The Tragedy of the Generation Gap," *Parents' Magazine* 48 (May 1973): 46–47, 80, 82; Veronica McNiff, "The News about Grandparents," *Parents' Magazine* 54 (November 1979): 51–54; Noelle Fintushel, "The Grandparent Bond: Why Kids Need It," *Parents' Magazine* 68 (August 1993): 160–62, 164, 166; Charlotte Curtis, "Third Adult in the Home," *New York Times Magazine,* November 4, 1962, 95.

30. Peter N. Stearns, *Battle Ground of Desire: The Struggle for Self-Control in Modern America* (New York, 1999); Fred Gosman, *Spoiled Rotten: American Chil-*

dren and How to Change Them (Andersen, IN, 1993); H. S. Glenn and Jane Nelsen, *Raising Self-Reliant Children in a Self-Indulgent World* (Rocklink, CA, 1988); Vicki Lansky and Rondi College, *101 Ways to Spoil Your Grandchild* (Chicago, 1996); Christy Fisher, "Grandparents Give of Themselves," *American Demographics* 18, 6 (June 1996): 13–14.

31. Peter Newell to Tony Baker, Jr., 4 March 1916, 14 February 1919, 12 June 1919, 24 September 1920, 9 March 1921, and n.d.; Tony Baker Jr. to Peter Newell, 10 November 1917, all in Series I, Box 6, Folder 87, Peter Newell Papers, YCAL Mss 62, Beinecke Library, Yale University, New Haven, CT.

32. See, for example, Milton Sprague Stearns Jr. to Alfred Stieglitz, n.d. June 1930, 16 June 1931, 2 January 1933, 9 October 1936, 15 June 1938, 13 June 1939, n.d. December 1939, 7 December 1940, n.d. October 1941, 26 December 1943, 23 December 1944, and 8 June 1946, all in Series I, Box 56, Folder 1350, Alfred Stieglitz/Georgia O'Keefe Archive, YCAL Mss 85, Beinecke Library.

33. June Coyne Corotto, Memoir, tss, 1, 11, 34, Schlesinger Library.

34. Martha Elizabeth Chew to her grandparents, n.d. 1940s; to her mother, n.d. 1949; Folder marked 1940s; to her grandparents, 31 August 1958, Folder 7; to her grandmother, postmarked 27 May 1962; to her parents, postmarked 29 May 1962, Folder 10; from her grandmother to her parents, 6 December 1968, Folder 12, all in Martha Elizabeth Chew Papers, Schlesinger Library.

35. Beatrice Wilson Shepherd, 26 April 1978, 5 February 1980, 14 June 1988, 17 April 1992; Helen Lincoln Fowler, 3 March 1980; Dallis Flinn, 21 May 1983; Mary Cutting Ivie, 21 January 1996; Helen Lincoln Fowler, 31 March 1993, all in Cabot Second Floor North, Radcliffe College, Round Robin Letters, 1941–1996, Schlesinger Library.

36. Justin to grandparents, 6 January 1979; Corisande to grandparents, n.d. and 21 May 198l; Tania to grandparents, n.d., all in Box 1, Series I, Folder 6, Mildred Levine Albert Papers, Schlesinger Library.

37. Jenny to Sarah Bradley Gamble, n.d. 1984; Benjamin to Sarah Bradley Gamble, 26 February 1984, Miles to Sarah Bradley Gamble, 28 February 1984, all in Box 11, Folder 198, Sarah Merry Bradley Gamble Papers, MC 368, Schlesinger Library.

Part II

Emotions and Consumer Behavior

5

There's No Place Like Home
Homesickness and Homemaking in America

Susan J. Matt

Each weekend, across the nation, the parking lots of Home Depot are filled. Furniture stores are doing a booming business, and garden stores and nurseries are thriving—all because modern Americans devote an enormous amount of time and energy to building, buying, furnishing, and refurbishing their houses. A recent issue of *Business Week* declared housing to be "an American obsession," and reported that home-building and houseware expenditures accounted for 8.7 percent of the U.S. economy. In fact, since the mid-1990s, Americans have spent more on home furnishings and housewares than on apparel, reversing long-standing spending priorities. The immense popularity of magazines, books, television programs, and Web sites devoted to housing and homemaking testifies to Americans' preoccupation with home, as does the enormous success of several new home-improvement chain stores.[1]

Yet despite the large number of Americans who are engaged in efforts to create the perfect home, there are very few explanations of this behavior. Just why are contemporary Americans so devoted to home?

The homemaking practices of modern Americans are intimately connected to their emotional lives. While emotions are often difficult to disaggregate and consumer motivations difficult to discern, there are many indications that much consumer spending on household goods and furnishings springs from a desire for rootedness in a mobile and transient society. Many Americans are homesick and are actively trying to re-create a sense of home in a new location.

Homes have become meaningful to Americans because they leave them so frequently. As one architect has noted, home does not exist without a journey.[2] And Americans make many journeys. Mobility is the norm in American society, with the average person moving once every five years. While mobility rates have dipped slightly in recent years, Americans of all races, incomes, and education levels still are far more mobile than most other peoples in the world. Between 1995 and 2000, over 120 million people—or roughly 45 percent of the U.S. population over the age of five—changed residences.[3]

While accepted as a fact of modern American life, such mobility carries with it heavy and often hidden psychological costs. Individuals who move frequently find that their social networks are disrupted if not destroyed, their identities are fragmented, and they are depressed, anxious, and preoccupied with the homes they have left behind. In the face of such changes, they suffer grief and homesickness.[4] Yet despite the trauma of moving, few adult Americans openly discuss the emotional pain that accompanies their geographic mobility.

Instead, they channel their feelings into consumer spending, trying to create in their new homes associations and atmospheres that connect them to past homes. Many seem particularly intent on making their 20th and 21st century homes into dwellings reminiscent of the 19th century. Perhaps paradoxically, those most enamored of these traditional-looking houses and furnishings are middle-class baby boomers, who, as young adults, decisively rejected tradition.

To understand why these modern Americans, notoriously restless and forward looking, spend so much time thinking about home and so much energy trying to capture a sense of the past in their houses, one must understand both the history of home and the history of homesickness, for contemporary homemaking behaviors have roots that lie in earlier centuries.

This essay will first examine how the image of home as a cozy, moral, and ideally rural place developed in Europe and America in the 18th and 19th centuries, for this imagery continues to give shape to modern homemaking behaviors. Contemporary Americans who work on their houses often carry in their heads visions of vine-covered trellises, white fences, and gabled roofs, and these visions of what a home is, passed down from generation to generation for two centuries, guide their homemaking and home-building efforts.

The essay then turns to the history of homesickness, a history that runs parallel to the history of home. To understand fully modern homemaking behavior, it is necessary to know not just the visions but the feelings that motivate contemporary Americans. The mental images of home that generations of Americans have harbored have been compelling because so many people so often moved away from their houses and yearned to return to them. Such homesickness has long been a significant if little discussed part of American history. In recent years, as pangs of homesickness have grown even more acute, the idea of home has gained added allure.

Finally, the essay examines the behavior of modern Americans afflicted with homesickness, a condition that has been particularly evident since the 1980s. Over the last twenty-five years, members of the baby boom generation have given voice to their homesickness and their longings for a stable home life steeped in tradition. Their consumer behavior—their spending on housewares and home furnishings, their appreciation of Martha Stewart and *This Old House*—reflects these emotions and has been shaped both by the dramatic changes in domestic life that occurred in the late 20th century and by cultural traditions created two centuries ago. A full explanation of contemporary homemaking behavior must examine both the more distant culture of 18th- and 19th-century America and the more recent and familiar patterns of life during the late 20th century.

The Invention of Home

While dwellings have always existed, homes have not. As architect Witold Rybczynski observes, the notion of home held by modern Americans today is not an ancient ideal; rather, it is an "invented tradition."[5] In Europe, the idea of home as a place that reflected personal identity and enshrined the values of intimacy, privacy, and comfort began to develop in the 17th and 18th centuries. In America, it took root in the late 18th and early 19th centuries. Before this period, dwellings were sparsely furnished, lacked privacy, and made scant accommodations to comfort. Rooms were used for a multitude of purposes, and sanitation was primitive. This changed, however, with the growth of urban capitalism and the emergence of the bourgeoisie. As new economic arrangements took hold in early modern Europe, work and domestic life became increasingly separate, and new ideas about the family gained currency. When this happened, the purpose of houses changed. They went from being places of production to being sites of family intimacy.[6]

This new form of domestic life spread to America in the 18th century, taking firm hold in the 19th. The ideal of home resonated with Americans of this era precisely because so many were leaving their actual homes far behind. As Alexis de Tocqueville noted during the 1830s, "An American will build a house in which to pass his old age and sell it before the roof is on; he will plant a garden and rent it just as the trees are coming into bearing . . . settle in one place and soon go off elsewhere with his changing desires."[7] Antebellum census reports supported Tocqueville's observations. In Boston, nearly a quarter of the city's population moved each year. Other cities had even higher mobility rates—in some growing towns, 50 percent of the population that had been entered in census records in one decade was gone by the next.[8] During the first half of the 19th century, new cities emerged, their entire populations made up of people transplanted from somewhere else. Cincinnati, which had a mere 500 residents in 1795, had over 2500 residents by 1810, and over 8500 by 1816. Lexington, Kentucky, grew from 1,795 people in 1800 to 4,326 in 1810. By 1815, its population was estimated to be between 6000 and 7000.[9]

Not all were sanguine about this restless behavior. In 1838, a Delaware writer lamented the difficulty of finding individuals "occupying the patrimonial estate inherited from his ancestors." He complained that "most of the old and time honored families . . . have been broken up and scattered abroad. And their possessions have fallen into the hands of a few land jobbers; and they are let out to a migratory race, who changing their residence with every revolution of the seasons, form no attachment for their places of abode."[10]

Some writers of the time proposed that in order for a stable society to evolve in the new nation, Americans must self-consciously reverse these trends and cultivate an attachment to home. For instance, Nathaniel Parker Willis, an editor of the 19th-century magazine *Home Journal*, worried that too much moving might create "habits of restlessness" that would prove "*injurious to the important feelings of home.*" To offset such problems, Willis believed that Americans must develop a love of home. In another essay, he explained, "That our plastic and rapidly maturing country would be bettered by a more careful culture of *home associations*, all must feel who see the facility with which families break up, the readiness with which housekeepers 'sell out and furnish new all over,' and the rareness of 'old homesteads'—to which the long absent can joyfully return. . . . It is one of those cultures for which poetry and the pulpit might improvingly and patriotically join, for its popularization and promotion."[11]

Domestic advisers, novelists, painters, and songwriters agreed with Willis and did their best to promote "home culture" and "old homesteads." Many writers who were disconcerted by the restless mobility of Jacksonian America offered sentimentalized visions of cozy homes with white picket fences, green yards, and colorful gardens. They hoped that their readers would build such houses and then remain in them, rather than ceaselessly move from place to place. The attractive portraits of home they painted stood in sharp contrast to the often cramped and frequently dirty dwellings most Americans had hitherto occupied; yet these writers often presented their idealized images of home life as resting on centuries of tradition. Their hope was that stable, rooted home life would become an American tradition, even if it was not one yet. Such mythologizing and tradition making, Witold Rybczynski has noted, "is a modern phenomenon that reflects a desire for custom and routine in a world characterized by constant change and innovation."[12] Hoping to create routine, tradition, and custom where little existed, these writers tried to convince their readers to settle down and put down roots.

Capturing the mood of the era, John Howard Payne, an American living far from home in Paris, penned the lyrics to "Home Sweet Home" in 1823, thereby creating one of the most popular songs of the 19th century. The song reminded Americans that while they might move onward and upward in life, nothing they encountered would equal what they had left behind: "Mid Pleasures and palaces though we may roam,/Be it ever so humble there's no place like home. . . . /An exile from home, splendor dazzles in vain:/O, give me my lowly thatched cottage again./The birds singing gayly that came at my call,/Give me them with the peace of mind dearer than all:/Home Home sweet, sweet Home/There's no place like home/There's no place like home."[13] According to Payne, the losses one incurred by leaving home were substantial, for home, wherever it was, was natural, peaceful, and full of love.

Innumerable homemaking and home-building guides gave concrete shape to this ideal. Domestic advisers such as Catharine Beecher, novelists such as Harriet Beecher Stowe and Lydia Sigourney, and architects and landscape designers such as Alexander Jackson Davis, Andrew Jackson Downing, and Calvert Vaux told readers how to construct a home that would, in the words of Andrew Downing, do more than merely provide "a shelter from the inclemencies of the weather," and that would be more than "an unmeaning pile of wood or stone." Downing, like many of his generation, believed that attractive houses had "moral effects" on those dwelling within them as well as on those who merely saw them.[14]

Architectural drawings, housekeeping advice, and gardening guidelines produced by these antebellum authors depicted the "moral" dwelling as a quaint, often white-washed house, surrounded by flowers and sometimes a fence, and invariably situated in a rural locale.

In *Uncle Tom's Cabin*, the most famous domestic novel of the 19th century, Harriet Beecher Stowe elaborated on this ideal:

> Whoever has traveled in the New England States will remember, in some cool village, the large farm-house, with its clean-swept grassy yard, shaded by the dense and massive foliage of the sugar-maple; and remember the air of order and stillness, of perpetuity and unchanging repose, that seemed to breathe over the whole place. Nothing lost, or out of order; not a picket loose in the fence, not a particle of litter in the turfy yard, with its clumps of

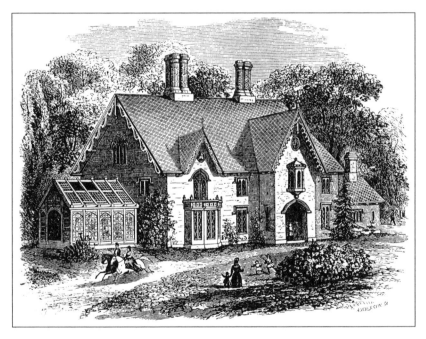

"Design XXIX, Rural Gothic Villa," in A. J. Downing, *The Architecture of Country Houses: Including Designs for Cottages, Farm-Houses, and Villas, with Remarks on Interiors, Furniture, and the Best Modes of Warming and Ventilating* (New York: D. Appleton, 1850), 322.

"Design IX, Regular Bracketed Cottage," in Downing, *The Architecture of Country Houses*, 112.

"Semi-Southern Cottage," in *The House: A Pocket Manual of Rural Architecture: Or, How to Build Country Houses and Outbuildings* (New York: Fowler and Wells, 1859), 71.

lilacbushes growing up under the windows. Within, he will remember wide, clean rooms, where nothing ever seems to be doing or going to be done.[15]

This image of a large, shaded house, in a pastoral setting, where "stillness" and a sense of "perpetuity" were to be found, and "where nothing ever seems to be doing," was relatively novel in the 19th century—an era when household production was for many still a reality, and for others a living memory. Yet while this image of home as a place of calm was newly created, it nevertheless seemed to offer comforting evocations of the past, and these 19th-century authors hoped to make it an accepted part of American tradition. If people began to live up to the domestic imagery presented in novels, architectural guides, and housekeeping books, their restlessness might be quelled, their lives more settled. This was the hope that lurked behind many a floor plan and housekeeping tip.

The authors who celebrated domestic life as having the potential to make American society less restless also often considered it to be a moral counterweight to the marketplace. They saw home as a pure haven where capitalist values such as ambition and competition—so disruptive to settled patterns of domesticity—had no place. In their plans, objects associated with work and moneymaking were banished from the house or tucked away into locations where they would be invisible to visitors. As historian Richard Bushman wrote, "the genteel house" was ideally "oblivious to business and work. The parlor and porch . . . were regions of repose where ease ruled in defiance of the exertions of the economy. The very power of the parlor depended on its naive purity. The walnut chairs and tables, the finished porcelains, the gilt clocks, the carpets, the flowers and shrubs had no functional use in the world of business. Their productive values was nil."[16] It was, in fact, their economic inutility that defined such objects and spaces as domestic. Houses were homes only if they were sheltered (at least superficially) from business concerns.

This noneconomic vision of domesticity was predicated on the idea that those in charge of the home—women—were themselves uninvolved in economic life. As a number of historians have demonstrated, for centuries women had had productive roles, often working alongside their husbands on farms or in shops. It was only during the 19th century that middle-class Americans developed the idea that men and women should occupy separate spheres of life.[17] Men should be engaged in public life, while women should be domestic creatures devoted to raising children and instilling morality in the family. Only by remaining outside economic and political affairs might women retain their purity and goodness. They should use this moral purity to make their houses places that were steeped in love and warmth and that might serve as antidotes to the corrosive acids of capitalist ambition. Such a vision rested on the unspoken assumption that the income of a single breadwinner was sufficient to support the entire family and allow the woman to stay at home. While this was a middle-class ideal and only a portion of the American population could afford such a lifestyle, it was so influential that by the mid-19th century, mother and home had become virtually synonymous.

The ideal of the perfect home—a place steeped in history, full of love, pastoral, feminized, and insulated from economic tumult—was created in the 19th century in reaction to the growth of cities, the expansion of capitalism, and the dramatic increase in residential mobility. Americans found this new image of home compelling precisely because it, and the values it stood for, seemed imperiled and often so out of reach. While later generations of Americans have had slightly different styles of interior decor, furniture, and room layout, their interior dispositions toward home have not been much different from those of antebellum Americans. Middle-class Americans' vision of home—a large house with a green lawn, colorful flowers, a swing hanging from a willow tree, a place offering love and coziness—is one they inherited from the 19th century. And they, like earlier generations, wax poetic about the virtues of home even as they continually move from one residence to another. What has changed over the past two centuries is how people express their pain at leaving home and their longing to return.

The History of Homesickness

At the same time that home was being invented, so was homesickness. While people have expressed pain at being separated from their families throughout history, it was only during the last few centuries that such feelings were deemed serious and given a formal name. In the late 17th century, a Swiss doctor, Johannes Hofer, coined the term "nostalgia" to describe the pain and melancholy experienced by those who had left home. That term came into popular use in 18th-century Europe, when an epidemic of nostalgia swept Swiss troops stationed far from their homes. The English word for nostalgia—homesickness—only entered the language during the 1750s. Those who fell victim to this dreaded disease were frequently bedridden and experienced fever, sleeplessness, loss of appetite, and anxiety. Many reports described those afflicted with nostalgia as gradually wasting away to their deaths.[18]

These dramatic symptoms of homesickness were responses to the changes brought on by modernity. As nation-states were developing and deploying troops to defend and expand their borders, more people were forced to leave home to serve their countries. Similarly, as capitalism grew, it, too, produced new instabilities in daily life, often requiring individuals to roam far from their homes. The movement and change required by modern nations and economies was something profoundly unsettling to the men and women first caught up in these whirlwind transformations, for while populations had migrated in preindustrial Europe, generally these migrations had been local ones. In contrast, by the middle of the 18th century, the mobility of the European population had increased markedly. More people moved, and when they did so, they often traveled greater distances than had earlier generations.[19] Local identities and connections seemed to shatter as individuals developed commitments to far-flung capitals and trade centers. Homesickness represented the tenacious love of the local—of the family, of the home, of the region—and stood in counterpoint to the larger national and international allegiances demanded by the modern order.

It took centuries for people to become accustomed to these new allegiances and, by extension, to the idea of mobility. For a time, as populations in Europe and America became more transient, nostalgia or homesickness became even more prevalent. Colonists in America experienced the emotion as they left Europe to settle in a new country. Settlers moving westward felt it as well. American soldiers certainly were not immune; in fact, homesickness seemed to strike them with particular strength. During the first year of the Civil War, army doctors diagnosed over five thousand Union soldiers as ill with nostalgia, and some army bands were actually forbidden to play "Home Sweet Home" because of the unsettling effects it had on troops.[20] Such restrictions were necessary, given the life-threatening nature of homesickness. In 1863, an American surgeon described the disease as "a species of melancholy or a mild type of insanity," which might have dire consequences for those who fell victim to it. He wrote,

It is frequently aggravated by derangement of the stomach and bowels, and is daily met with in its worst form, in our military hospitals and prisons, and is especially marked in young subjects. The symptoms produced by this

aberration of the mind, are first, great mental dejection, loss of appetite, indifference to external influences, irregular action of the bowels, and slight
hectic fever. As the disease progresses it is attended by hysterical weeping, a
dull pain in the head, throbbing of the temporal arteries, anxious expression of the face, watchfulness, incontinence of urine, spermatorrhoea, increased hectic fever, and a general wasting of all the vital powers. The disease may terminate in resolution, or run on into cerebral derangement, ty-
phoid fever, or any epidemic prevailing in the immediate vicinity, and
frequently with fatal results.[21]

Given such a constellation of dreadful symptoms, doctors and psychologists continued to worry about homesickness and nostalgia well into the
20th century. The surgeon general listed nostalgia as a medical condition
up through World War II and it continued to be used as a diagnosis during the 1950s.[22]

Gradually, however, the belief that homesickness was a physical illness
waned. While some experts continued to speak of it as a psychological
problem, they implied that it was a painful developmental stage that all individuals must pass through rather than a fatal disease. To cope with the
melancholy ache of parting, individuals needed to become accustomed to
leaving home; parents should facilitate this by sending their children away
for short visits so that they might learn to conquer their anxieties early in
life.[23] This new diagnosis and prescription for treatment was consistent
with the behaviorist view of emotions that first gained prominence in the
1920s. Psychologists, convinced that feelings could be shaped through
training and correct child-rearing techniques, believed that individuals
could and should learn to control their emotions. Rather than be subject
to them, they must govern them.[24]

The idea that individuals should be self-controlled meshed well with
many of the demands of modern life. For instance, the corporate culture
of the 20th century required workers to repress their anger and competitive instincts so that business might be transacted smoothly.[25] Similarly,
the economic imperatives to relocate required Americans to master their
homesickness and to repudiate the notion that mobility was inherently
traumatic. Americans gradually came to assume that they would move repeatedly over the course of their lives, leaving childhood homes far behind. They also came to believe that the sadness and anxiety that accompanied such movement should be silently endured and understood as an
unfortunate but unavoidable feature of modern life.

Such beliefs shape the way that homesick individuals act today. While children at camps and schools may still express the pain of homesickness quite overtly, adults are somewhat reluctant to speak openly of such feelings.[26] This reluctance stems from the perception that homesickness is a disease of youth. If adults discuss their homesickness aloud, it is taken as a sign of social maladjustment. As a woman who had recently moved from Minnesota to Manhattan noted, when she mentioned she was "pretty homesick" to her manicurist, a Korean woman who herself was far from home, the manicurist narrowed her eyes, "sucked in some breath and then she barked out an uppercase admonition: 'DON'T BE BIG BABY.'"[27]

In the face of a widespread cultural consensus that it is self-indulgent and childish for grownups to feel homesick, adult Americans have learned to suppress the emotion; however, there is evidence that they still experience its pangs. Recent immigrants often feel homesickness quite acutely.[28] Native-born Americans are not immune to such feelings, either. Psychiatrist Mindy Fullilove, for instance, writes that individuals who have moved recently often experience disorientation, grief, and confusion.[29] Yet today most Americans take these feelings as part and parcel of the modern American condition, a natural feature of adulthood. Consequently, the words "nostalgia" and "homesickness" have come to signify relatively harmless conditions rather than fatal illnesses. Nostalgia, in particular, has lost its connotations of illness and now refers to a general and fairly diffuse longing for the past rather than a painful yearning for a specific place.

In addition to these changes in the meaning of homesickness, there has also been a change in how homesick individuals behave. Because homesickness is no longer seen as the province of adults and no longer considered a serious condition, those who suffer from the pangs of parting have found ways of dealing with their emotions that differ from the approaches of earlier generations. In the past, when homesickness was considered a grave illness, doctors believed that the most effective treatment was to return sufferers to their homes. Today, rather than going back home, many homesick Americans try to re-create their old homes in new locales. They often respond to their homesickness by spending.

Such spending explains the wild success of Martha Stewart, *This Old House*, Restoration Hardware stores, and the proliferation of neo-Victorian home and town designs, and similar "hearth and home" commercial goods. Their broad appeal reflects the persistently felt need among mobile Americans to create a sense of rootedness in an inherently restless society. Often, in fact, it is those who are most mobile who are most concerned with establishing the look and feel of permanence in their houses. These consumers are drawn to objects and designs that hearken back to simpler times and seem to have a patina of age and tradition. Although these Americans do not stay in one place for long, they want their furniture and home facades to imply that they do stay put, that they are settled, and that they have deep roots.[30] A home should look permanent, even if it is, in reality, only a temporary way station. This is the sentiment that drives much of the spending on home. The consumer purchases that homesick Americans make are not empty materialistic gestures: they reflect a deeper longing to regain something that has been lost.

Homesickness and Homemaking in Contemporary Culture

The current consumer obsession with home began in the 1980s and represents a new stage in the history of homesickness and a new form of homesick behavior. A number of demographic and cultural shifts in late 20th century life provoked this wave of homesickness. By the 1980s, members of the baby boom generation, consisting of 78 million people born between 1946 and 1964, were beginning to settle down and have families of their own.[31] They wanted to put down roots but felt they had none themselves. As one baby boomer put it, "We were restless and, for the most part, rootless."[32]

Such restlessness and rootlessness was nothing new to baby boomers. While the imagery of the TV show *Leave It to Beaver* has shaped perceptions of what family life was like in the 1950s and 1960s, historians have demonstrated that there was a yawning chasm between that ideal and the reality of domestic relations during this period.[33] For instance, rather than living in the same houses for their entire childhood, baby boomers experienced high rates of mobility. During the 1950s, an estimated 25 percent of the U.S. population moved each year.[34] Many families were migrating to new suburbs built in the wake of World War II. According to historian Kenneth Jackson, between 1950 and 1970 the suburban population more than doubled—growing from 36 million residents to 74 million. By 1970, more people lived in the suburbs than in cities or in rural areas.[35]

These suburbs, built on cornfields, were brand new and consisted of houses built quickly, using techniques of mass production. Their styles were often repetitive and generic, unconnected to local history or culture.[36] And their residents were, in many ways, equally disconnected from their own histories and cultures. As historians Susan Kellogg and Steven Mintz observed of this generation,

> Transience and isolation were characteristics common to suburban family life. Population turnover in the new suburbs was extremely high, as families relocated as they climbed the corporate ladder, resulting in a lack of stability. In Levittown, one family in every six moved each year, and in the New York metropolitan area, less than 6 percent of the suburban population in 1960 was living in the same house as in 1955. . . . Frequent movement from one house to another accentuated the rootlessness of suburban families, isolating individual families from grandparents and relatives and friendly neighbors; weakening generational continuity; and undermining family networks.[37]

Baby boomers came of age in this era of mobility and flux, and as adults they drove many further changes in modern social life, including the development of new patterns of marriage, home life, and child rearing. For instance, when women in this generation began to have children, many continued to work outside of the home as well: while in 1960, 70 percent of all families had a lone breadwinner and a stay-at-home mother, by the late 1990s only 10 percent of families fit this pattern. In 2001, 69 percent of all married women with children under eighteen worked outside of the home.[38] During this same period, marriages also dissolved more frequently than they had in years past. In the mid-1970s, the divorce rate doubled; overall, since 1970, it has risen 30 percent. Currently, 51 percent of all marriages founder.[39]

The geographical rootlessness many boomers have experienced throughout their lives and the transformations in family life they witnessed as adults created in many an aching hunger for a home life rooted in tradition. As J. Walker Smith of the market research firm Yankelovitch Partners noted, "Boomers are a bit scared of the way things have turned out. . . . There's been a negative fallout to their legacy that they don't feel comfortable with, so we're seeing a return to an interest in stability."[40] Such an interest manifested itself in a variety of ways. For instance, a survey conducted by the American Council of Life Insurance in the 1980s found that 93 percent of baby boomers believed a greater importance should be accorded to traditional family ties.[41]

Another sign of this hunger was the growing preoccupation with home. It was during the 1980s that middle-class consumers—many of them baby boomers—began to express new interest in homemaking and home furnishings. Sales figures reflected this interest. Between 1988 and 1998, consumer spending on such items increased by 50 percent; in contrast, overall personal consumption spending increased by only 29 percent.[42] As shoppers spent on a wide array of home and hearth goods, many seemed to gravitate toward nostalgic objects and furnishings that could be found in a range of prices. A study by Yankelovitch Partners concluded that "boomers want home like it used to be. Not the house itself so much as that sense of security and well-being they remember fondly. They want homes and home products that appeal to this nostalgia."[43]

One sign of this nostalgia was the emergence of the "country style." That style, characterized by "muted checked linens," simple and elegant wooden furniture, and hand-made—rather than factory produced—furnishings gained popularity in the 1980s, promoted by domestic advisers like Mary Emmerling and Martha Stewart. Journalist Deborah Goldman explained the appeal of the country style, writing that "we go home to both a place and an idea. The objects we surround ourselves with put flesh on that idea, on aspirations the outside world not only can't fulfill but seems to thwart. And what more comfortable haven could there be for exhausted, fearful urbanites and suburbanites than a pastoral escape? . . . We want to go home to the Country." But rather than actually moving to the country, Americans chose furnishings they associated with rural places of the past. And these association were often fairly loose. Goldman observed, "If there is anything 'country' in Country style, it's as a code word for already proven fashions[,] for things natural, organic, hand-made, comfortable, well-worn and one-of-a-kind."[44] In sum, it is Mission-style couches, Victorian tables, and antique linens, rather than the modernistic metal furniture that has been filling houses for the last two decades.

Another powerful example of the nostalgic trend in housewares can be found in the enormous success of Restoration Hardware stores. Founded in 1980, the chain offers old-fashioned home furnishings, cleaning products, and other miscellany. Its catalog displays Victorian tin trays, Mission-style chests, zinc window boxes, and stately dining-room tables that, according to the advertising copy, are designed to be passed down from generation to generation. Restoration Hardware caters to the tastes of highly mobile baby boomers—a group one reporter described as being "35–55, educated, and . . . earn[ing] more than $75,000 a year: a group that is increasingly fixated on the idea of traditional home life."[45] The chain's owner, Stephen Gordon, explained his brand's allure in a *New York Times* interview, saying, "We're not 'ye olde,' but I think a lot of us as we get older and have children want to make traditions and keep them, because it seems to add a lot of depth to our lives." The *Times* observed that "Mr. Gordon is inventing history for a suburbia-weaned generation that may feel it has none."[46]

Gordon is not the only one creating a sense of history and home for baby boomers. Other merchandisers, catering to a broader range of incomes, have also capitalized on the longing for home. Perhaps the most famous is Martha Stewart. Stewart gained prominence and fortune in the 1980s and 1990s because of her ability to describe and sell the homemaking traditions of the past. She and her staff (as well as a bevy of imitators) have, in fact, based their entire enterprise on nostalgia. As Stephen Drucker, editor of *Martha Stewart Living,* wrote, one of the goals of the magazine was "to build an archive of American traditions—a record of all the ways that families and regions and cultures set up home, celebrate the milestones of life, and pass along what they've learned to the next generation." This was necessary, he maintained, because "the twentieth century, so eager to get on with the future, hasn't been especially kind to traditions. In fact, much of this century has been dedicated to sweeping them away, which, as it turns out, isn't especially difficult to do. All it takes is one broken link—from mother to daughter, from country to city—and a little bit of hard-earned wisdom valued for hundreds of years is gone." *Martha Stewart Living* promised to reinvigorate these traditions and integrate them into modern life. To that end, the magazine included "timeless quilts in ziggy new patterns; the floorcloths of the American colonists reinvented in chenille; the flavors of Cuban cooking and the sounds of Cuban music living on at a party in Miami."[47] Six years later, a promotional ad for the magazine played on the same theme: "In a world of disposable goods, some things are worth keeping. *Martha Stewart Living* is about timeless pleasures, timeless treasures, things that matter, things that last."[48] *Living* and similar publications promise readers they can create tradition and stability and can build an enduring connection with the past, no matter where they are living or how far they are from family. What is required are the accessories of rooted, traditional family life, even if one lacks the roots. The right things will create a feeling of rootedness.

That belief is widely shared by consumers. A *Martha Stewart Living* reader, Andrea De Fusco of Chestnut Hill, Massachusetts, wrote a letter to the editor in 1996, explaining why the publication held such appeal for her.

First, a confession. Although we're known for juggling superhuman schedules, my generation (the twenty- to thirty-somethings) often lacks the basic skills that our parents and grandparents seemed to have instinctively. I delight in the home- (and life-) enhancing tips you offer: how to make real hot cocoa or glaze a ham; how to improvise a country curtain from linen dishtowels. . . . You lead by example, not only as a guide to old-fashioned, gracious living, but also by showing the virtue of do-it-yourself work—its economical, essential, and good for mind, body, and soul.[49]

De Fusco implied that with Stewart's tips, she was able to create a way of life based on tradition and connected to the past; her letter, however, highlighted just how disconnected modern Americans are from family and traditions, for rather than asking her mother or grandmother how to glaze a ham, she relied on a magazine.

Stewart's *Living* capitalized on the need of readers like De Fusco who longed to recover a connection to the traditions of earlier generations. In countless articles on antique glass, flowers, furniture, old-fashioned recipes, and the like, Stewart created a vision of stable and rooted home life. In her regular feature titled "Remembering," she repeatedly called up the image of golden days in her own childhood home in Nutley, New Jersey. Whether she was recalling her father's flower garden or the way her grandmother preserved fruit, the message was clear: the secret to a happy home life could be found in a return to the past.

The belief that time-honored traditions make for a richer domestic existence is strong and not limited to Stewart and her readers. Participants in a *Better Homes and Gardens* discussion were almost unanimous in their interest in old-fashioned, rustic furnishings. When asked their favorite decorating styles, respondents used words like "romantic cottage," "country," "traditional with an English and French country twist," "rustic country clutter," "cottage/garden style," and "early American attic." One participant expounded in some detail: "I'm aiming for an 18th, early 19th century 'high country' or 'vernacular' look. That is to say, the type of furnishings and decorations a fairly prosperous farmer could afford by buying knock-offs or making imitations of original designer items."[50]

When asked why they liked such styles, respondents offered that the "country look" felt "so cozy and homey," and, in the words of one, gave a house a "relaxed comfy feel. It is also simple and I like that." Another confided,

I do love things and styles from the past. I love things that represent a simpler time . . . things that I remember my mother and grandmother having or using. I love a room now that feels like the quiet living room of my grandma's house that had certain smells and a feeling of safety and serenity. I'm also drawn to my roots which are in England. Country, cottage, Victorian, shabby chic . . . they're all based on the past, and that pleases me.[51]

A woman interviewed by architecture professor Claire Cooper Marcus expressed similar feelings about the antiques and old-fashioned ambience she had created in her rented house. While she lived in Berkeley, California, her decor and possessions made her feel connected to her New England childhood. She reported,

I feel a lot of comfort around me. Harmonious colors. Good feelings under my feet, rugs, pillows, all full of life, warmth. Things that I grew up with as a child, I've brought back with me; I've put them into my nest. Like this lamp and pictures I had a great feeling for. The old chair in the kitchen which I brought back from my mother's house two years ago. I really have a good feeling of continuity. I love having things which have been in the family, which have been used before, and which I can see again in a different light in a different environment, and feel as if they've been around for a long time.[52]

Old chairs, lamps, and pictures might bridge the distance between California and New England, might give a sense of rootedness.

In their search for rootedness, consumers do not limit their spending to items of interior decor. They want the exteriors of their homes to be steeped in nostalgia as well. Whether it's the gingerbread flourishes so commonly put on dwellings in subdivisions or the increasing popularity of neo-Victorian developments, home-building styles that evoke the past sell. As the author of the *Nostalgia Home Plans* noted in the foreword to his collection of floorplans,

It doesn't matter whether we grew up or even lived in a home built long before our time. With a natural instinct, we are drawn to homes seasoned with age and significance. And when we see one—perhaps a boxy Craftsman with its roof bracket and divided-light windows, or one from the Victorian era, adorned with turrets, finials and spiderweb trimwork—we unknowingly stop to admire the beauty of it. We imagine ourselves inside it and with a wistful sigh, dream of living in one that's ideally suited to us. . . . In revealing their timeless craftsmanship to us, we come to understand a little more about who we are and the homes that carry on our legacy. All of us would feel lucky to live in such a home.[53]

Market surveys back up this promotional fluff. In the 1980s, a study of homeowners in and around Buffalo, New York, showed that of those surveyed, 25.6 percent identified a farm house as their favorite style of home, while 23.3 percent named the Tudor style as their favorite. Far less popular was the "modern" style, selected by only 4.7 percent of the homeowners, and the "contemporary" style, chosen by 7.8 percent.[54] Consumer preference for old-fashioned styles has held steady in the intervening years. In 2004, Bill Pisetsky, vice president of sales and marketing for Shea Homes, noted that "it's a growing mindset of authenticity, almost a 'Leave-It-to-Beaver' kind of lifestyle that consumers are interested in."[55]

To satisfy their longings for older-looking homes, consumers are willing to buy completely new houses in towns far from their own place of origin. Many have followed their yearnings to new urbanist communities. The new urbanist movement, which gained popularity in the 1990s, is based on the idea that traditional 19th-century American towns offered sociability, community, and connection, and that these elusive qualities of social life can be regained through good architectural practice. Consequently, new urbanist developments feature traditionally styled houses with front porches, alley ways, sidewalks, and old-fashioned town centers. As one observer noted, "New urbanism is, by definition, nostalgic."[56]

The most famous examples of new urbanist town designs can be found in communities like Seaside, Florida, and the Disney-created town of Celebration, outside of Orlando. Such developments, however, are not limited to Florida; as of the year 2000, more than three hundred new towns were being built according to new urbanist principles, and over one hundred smaller projects were in the works nationwide.[57] Properties in these types of communities have been snatched up by consumers with a deep hunger for the sociability and stability these places promise. According to one reporter, five thousand people entered a lottery that would enable them to buy one of the first 350 houses built in Celebration. Those lucky enough to get the opportunity to buy paid 25 to 40 percent more for their houses than did home buyers in comparable developments in the surrounding area.[58]

People competed for houses in Celebration because they thought such a community might assuage their longings for home. As one baby boomer resident of Celebration noted, the place appealed to her family because, "Like many in our generation, we were always on the lookout for the next great place to live. . . . We were restless and, for the most part, rootless."[59] Another resident of Celebration, Judith Ziffer, a counselor, noted, "The 'Me generation' is a very lonely generation as it grows older." For that reason, Ziffer and her husband had moved to Celebration, hoping to find community and sociability.[60]

That people would move across the country to live among strangers in order to find home is one of the ironies of homesickness in modern society. Americans want their homes and lives to have the appearance of groundedness and permanence even if they are living in a brand-new home far from their families and origins. And the homes consumers choose—built in colonial, Victorian, or plantation styles—while designed to look as though they have remained in one family, handed down from generation to generation, may have few historical or cultural connections to the ways and places in which their ancestors actually lived.

Photos of Celebration, Florida. (By Luke Fernandez, author's collection)

Yet older or even just older-looking houses hold wide appeal. One female consumer explained why:

> I like older homes for many reasons. . . . They're usually in older, well-established neighborhoods with big trees and they have their own personalities. They're not cookie-cutter homes all in a row and down the street there's a strip mall. They help us say that we're individuals, not like all the rest. I like the ones with a lot of architecture. . . . And dining rooms that say let's get the family together for meals. And big kitchens where everyone can cook together. And a yard with a big tree to climb and a garden with lots of sunshine. It's kind of like comfort food.[61]

Such a home was not just space; instead, it represented togetherness, innocence, and close familial bonds. Whether this idealized house actually reflected how earlier generations of the woman's family had lived or how her own family now lived was immaterial. The house had an important symbolic function. It connected the woman to a mythic sense of home and offered comfort. Like the 19th-century writers who "invented" home, she believed that a well-constructed house, steeped in history, could provide stability, unite a family, and offset the pain of mobility.

Many consumers want such houses specifically for these symbolic properties. Yet while home may function as a symbol, the reality it purports to represent frequently does not exist. Today, in fact, home is often what one scholar has called a "conscious fiction."[62] In modern America, the traditional architecture and furnishings of houses serve as stand-ins for traditional values and relationships. Although Americans exert a great deal of energy building and decorating their houses, they do not actually spend much time in them. They may not eat together or cook together but their homes imply that they do, or at least want to. Americans buy old-fashioned-looking houses because they want the lifestyle and values that they believe flourished in such settings in years past, and they carry the stubborn hope that their relationships will be shaped by the architecture that houses them.

Home and Status

If modern American home styles and furnishings do not accurately represent the lives they contain, neither do they always or faithfully represent their owners' pasts. Many consumers admitted that while they wanted the exteriors of their houses to look old and the interiors of their homes to be filled with items from the past, they did not need these styles and items to be from their own pasts. One woman, discussing her tastes with other *Better Homes and Gardens* readers, noted, "I find myself constantly drawn to the things my mom grew up with—the old house, worn fabrics, weathered furniture, milk glass, etc. What's funny is that I didn't grow up with all that stuff because my mom doesn't like it since she DID grow up with it."[63] This homesickness for a home one never actually occupied, filled with old goods unlike those one had as a child, bespeaks a certain blind faith in the redemptive power of the past—anyone's past.

In fact, many consumers who do want to create old-fashioned environments do not seem particularly nostalgic for their own childhood houses, so much as those of other, more affluent people. Even Martha Stewart, who often invoked her childhood home in Nutley, New Jersey, also spoke of its flaws. As an adult, she tried to create a house that had none of the Nutley home's shortcomings. For instance, in an October 1996 column, she recalled that, "in our house in Nutley, New Jersey, there were no fireplaces. The closest thing to an open hearth was the outdoor barbecue." In contrast, the Connecticut farmhouse Stewart currently owns boasts seven fireplaces, and she takes great satisfaction in them. "Fireplaces," she writes, "have become an important part of my home and I now understand their appeal, not only as a source of great comfort and warmth, but also as a symbol of well-being and as a gathering place." Stewart sounded a similar note about antique linens. She had grown up without fine sheets and monogrammed pillowcases; as an adult, she eagerly sought them out and then told people they were family heirlooms.[64]

Stewart is not alone in seeking out the traditional icons of genteel domesticity that she lacked as a child and presenting them to the world as her birthright. Many of those who seek the security and comfort that an oldfashioned house and decorating scheme seem to offer were not brought up in such houses, and it is quite likely that their parents were not, either. In a nation of immigrants, where most people's history is a history of mobility and change, satisfying the need for a home life steeped in tradition is challenging. How can one re-create the Jewish shtetls, the Italian villages, the Chinese hamlets that our ancestors left when they crossed the ocean? The tradition most accessible to contemporary middle-class consumers, even if it is not true to the ways of their own particular ancestors, is the model of domesticity the writers and architects of 19th-century America created. Martha Stewart, nee Kostyra, who was brought up in a Polish-American working-class household and as an adult teaches bourgeois consumers of various ethnicities about the genteel details of Victorian American domestic life, is a powerful illustration of this point. Regardless of consumers' actual backgrounds, the 19th-century American style of genteel living (or some rendition of it) is now available to all who can afford it. And given that Stewart designs goods for K-Mart, such gentility is in the reach of many.

Middle-class consumers of all ethnicities therefore eagerly embrace old-fashioned Americana. Their eagerness is often born of homesickness but is produced by other emotions as well. After all, people buy things for a multitude of reasons, and the older styles of nineteenth-century America satisfy longings for status as much as they fulfill the desire for stability. Home-and-hearth goods offer consumers an opportunity to engage in conspicuous consumption. As Joan Kron noted, often "the past [that] people attempt to link up with is not their own family's but a more illustrious one. Old furnishings give a sense of family genealogy—the illusion of legitimacy."[65] Old-fashioned rustic furnishings, Victorian homes, lush gardens surrounded by picket fences all offer consumers the opportunity to connect themselves to the 19th century and to create the illusion of a long line of genteel, and implicitly WASPy, ancestors.

Such connections between home and social status are nothing new. Those who first created the idealized images of home in antebellum America were quite aware that their model of domesticity was only available to members of some social classes. High status, refinement, and gentility depended on the careful construction of a domestic environment in which labor or any traces of commercial life did not intrude, and this rendered the ideal out of reach for many. Domestic life was supposed to be an antidote to the capitalist forces that were driving people away from home, but its meaning was shaped by capitalism and its pleasures were fully available only to those who could afford them by dint of their market success.[66]

Yet while expenditures on home have long been driven by the desire to show and perhaps raise one's social status as much as they have been by feelings of homesickness, such purchases remain in a category all their own. The fact that shoppers are buying for home and family often makes them regard their purchases in a special light. Since the creation of the idea of home in the 17th and 18th centuries in Europe, and its adoption in

America in the 19th century, domestic goods have been seen as counterposed to public life, to capitalism, to getting and spending, even if they are attained only through considerable expenditure. Yet despite the fact that domesticity has long been commodified, it manages to retain its image of purity. As Marjorie Garber has noted, "The supposed nonmaterialism of the 'home' has become one of its best commercial assets."[67]

When consumers buy objects for the home, or even when they buy new houses, they may well believe that these purchases are, to some extent, noncommercial. They are made to shore up family life, to maintain (or create) tradition, to build community and connection. Bathed in this glow of domestic mythology, home furnishings can be washed clean of their materialism.[68] What David Brooks has written about Restoration Hardware can be applied to the entire hearth-and-home consumer market:

> Restoration evokes the places we have thoughtlessly abandoned: the small communities that ambitious people leave; the downtowns that have been hollowed out by car-friendly shopping malls; the local industrial crafts that are being driven out of business by our global economy; the old-fashioned family traditions we have neglected in the rush to be modern and mobile. Restoration reminds us that it is not too late to avoid the spiritual trap set by our relentless upward mobility. We can rediscover the essential things, and, best of all, we can do so while shopping.[69]

Or as the editor of *House and Garden* magazine put it in 1996, "Sure, shopping and arranging and collecting (or hoarding) are materialistic pursuits, but they are also connnected to deeper passions. . . . They nurture our souls. . . . We burrow into our coziness; we play with the cutting edges of light and metal and glass; we retreat into other centuries. . . . That's materialism in the service of history, a pretty grand idea."[70]

Spending on home fills many emotional needs. It gives Americans a way to feel rooted in a rootless society, and it also allows them to compete for status with other families, but in a guilt-free way. Their spending, cloaked in the sentimentalism associated with home life, seems outside the realm of invidious comparison, purified, and sanctified.

The idea that purchasing home goods is not materialistic behavior is one legacy of the 19th-century culture that "invented" home, and deemed it a noneconomic place. For two centuries, Americans have bought into this ideology as they have bought for home. But modern Americans have inherited other attitudes toward home that continue to shape their behavior as well. The retro styling of American houses, the rustic furnishings, the colorful gardens and flagstone paths, the arbors and pergolas that adorn contemporary residential properties owe their style and meaning to 19th-century traditions that identified such objects as symbols of rootedness and stability, and signs of a commitment to place.

Yet for all of their emotional power, these symbols cannot cover up the fact that American roots are often shallowly planted, nor can they offset the phenomenon of American mobility. For just as common as the old-fashioned touches, the white picket fences, is the "For Sale" sign, planted amid the flowers and the trees.

When 19th-century writers called on Americans to promote and popularize home culture, to celebrate the old homestead, little could they have imagined the extent to which future generations would do just that. While Americans did not stop leaving their homes as these writers had hoped, they did buy into the imagery—if not the reality—of a stable home. In fact, the more they leave their houses, the more important home has become.

Behavioral history helps explain a deep-seated but not really market-rational behavior in the United States, born initially two hundred years ago (though not characteristic of the earlier, colonial experience). Recent intensifications reflect further change, combining a new level of intolerance of overt nostalgia as an adult emotion and the particular living experiences of the baby boom generation and its successors. Behavioral history, in this case capturing changing emotional needs and norms, allows a more profound understanding of activity that might otherwise be dismissed as generic consumerism or affluence.

NOTES

1. James C. Cooper and Kathleen Madigan, "There's No Place Like Home—For Economic Growth," *Business Week,* no. 3785 (June 3, 2002): 31; Melinda Page, "Off the Rack and Into the Home," *HFN* 74, no. 13 (March 27, 2000): 12; Patricia Leigh Brown, "As the Shelter World Turns," *New York Times,* May 13,1993, C1, C8.

2. Kimberly Dovey, "Home and Homelessness," in *Home Environments,* ed. Irwin Altman and Carol M. Werner (New York, 1985), 48.

3. James M. Jasper, *Restless Nation: Starting Over in America* (Chicago, 2000), 71–72. For evidence of a decline in mobility, see Table A-1, Annual Geographical Mobility Rates, by Type of Movement: 1947–2003, Current Population Survey, His-

torical Geographical Mobility Reports, U.S. Census Bureau, http://www.census
.gov/population/www/socdemo/migrate/past-migrate.html, accessed June 22,
2004; Jason Schacter, Rachel S. Franklin, and Marc J. Perry, *Migration and Geographic Mobility in Metropolitan and Nonmetropolitan America: 1995–2000, Census
2000 Special Reports* (Washington, D.C., 2003), 1–2.

4. Marion M. Jones, "The Roaming Empire," *Psychology Today* 30 (May/June
1997): 24; Katharine Griffin and Michael Mason, "New Home, Heavy Heart,"
Health 11 (April 1997): 17; Shirley Fisher, "The Psychological Effects of Leaving
Home: Homesickness, Health, and Obsessional Thoughts," in *On The Move: The
Psychology of Change and Transition,* ed. Shirley Fisher and Cary Cooper (Chich-
ester, UK, 1990), 153–70; Marc Fried, "Grieving for a Lost Home," in *The Urban
Condition: People and Policy in the Metropolis,* ed. Leonard J. Duhl (New York,
1963), 151–71.

5. Witold Rybczynski, *Home: A Short History of an Idea* (New York, 1986), 9–10.
The idea of the invented tradition comes from *The Invention of Tradition,* ed. Eric
Hobsbawm and Terrence Ranger (Cambridge, UK, 1983, 1988).

6. Rybczynski, *Home,* 15–77; John Lukacs, "The Bourgeois Interior," *American
Scholar* 39:4 (Autumn 1970): 616–30; Phillipe Aries, *Centuries of Childhood: A Social History of Family Life,* trans. Robert Baldick (New York, 1962), 399.

7. Alexis de Tocqueville, *Democracy in America,* ed. J. P. Mayer, trans. George
Lawrence (New York, 1966, 1988), 536.

8. Jack Larkin, *The Reshaping of Everyday Life, 1790–1840* (New York, 1989), 206;
Stephen Thernstrom, *Poverty and Progress: Social Mobility in a Nineteenth-Century
City* (Cambridge, MA, 1964), 85.

9. Richard C. Wade, *The Urban Frontier: The Rise of Western Cities, 1790–1830*
(Cambridge, MA, 1959), 50, 54.

10. *The Delaware Register and Farmers' Magazine* 1 (Feb.–July 1838): 195, 196,
quoted in Richard Bushman, *The Refinement of America: Persons, Houses, Cities*
(New York, 1992), 209.

11. N. Parker Willis, *The Rag-Bag: A Collection of Ephemera* (New York, 1855),
101, 36, emphases in the original.

12. Rybczynski, *Home,* 9.

13. John Howard Payne and Henry Rowley Bishop, "Home Sweet Home,"
reprinted in *Popular Songs of Nineteenth-Century America: Complete Original
Sheet Music for 64 Songs,* ed. Richard Jackson (New York, 1976), 80–82.

14. Andrew Jackson Downing, "Rural Architecture," in *Rural Essays by Andrew
Jackson Downing,* ed. George William Curtis (New York, 1853), 209–13. See also
Gwendolyn Wright, *Building the Dream: A Social History of Housing in America*
(New York, 1981), esp. chaps. 5 and 6.

15. Harriet Beecher Stowe, *Uncle Tom's Cabin or Life Among the Lowly* (New
York, 1966), 172.

16. Bushman, *The Refinement of America,* 249, 263.

17. See, for instance, Sara M. Evans, *Born for Liberty: A History of Women in America* (New York, 1989), 67–70.

18. Jean Starobinski, "The Idea of Nostalgia," *Diogenes* 54 (Summer 1966): 81–103; "Homesickness," *The Oxford English Dictionary,* 2nd ed., vol. 7 (Oxford, 1989), 330; Damien Reid, "Nostalgia," *British Medical Journal* 323 (September 1, 2001): 496; Krystene Irene Batcho, "Personal Nostalgia, World View, Memory, and Emotionality," *Perceptual and Motor Skills* 87 (1997): 411.

19. Leslie Page Moch, *Moving Europeans: Migration in Western Europe since 1650,* 2nd ed. (Bloomington, IN, 1992, 2003), 1–59.

20. Millet Thompson, *Thirteenth Regiment of New Hampshire Volunteer Infantry in the War of the Rebellion, 1861–1865* (Boston, 1888), 104; E. Lawrence Abel, *Singing the New Nation: How Music Shaped the Confederacy, 1861–1865* (Mechanicsburg, PA, 2000), 218.

21. DeWitt C. Peters, "Remarks on the Evils of Youthful Enlistments and Nostalgia," *American Medical Times, being a weekly series of the New York Journal of Medicine* 6 (1863): 75–76.

22. Stacey Menzel Baker and Patricia F. Kennedy, "Death by Nostalgia: A Diagnosis of Context-Specific Cases," *Advances in Consumer Research* 21 (1994): 169–74; Charles A. A. Zwingmann "'Heimweh' or 'Nostalgic Reaction': A Conceptual Analysis and Interpretation of a Medico-Psychological Phenomenon," Ph.D. diss., Stanford University, 1959, 163.

23. See, for instance, "Homesickness Is Normal but Doesn't Last Long," *Parents' Magazine* 20 (October 1945): 178; "Wish You Were There: Dealing with Homesickness," *Seventeen Magazine* 37 (September 1978): 57.

24. See Peter N. Stearns, *American Cool: Constructing a Twentieth-Century Emotional Style* (New York, 1994), 102–6.

25. See, for instance, Peter Stearns, *Battleground of Desire: The Struggle for Self-Control in Modern America* (New York, 1999), 110; Susan J. Matt, *Keeping Up with the Joneses: Envy in American Consumer Society, 1890–1930* (Philadelphia, 2003), 57–95.

26. Marc Fried, "Grieving for a Lost Home," 151–71. British studies have shown that while only 20 percent of surveyed populations will spontaneously identify themselves as homesick, when offered that label from a list 50–70 percent will choose the word to identify their own psychological condition. A similar silence on the subject is visible in American society. See Fisher, "The Psychological Effects of Leaving Home," 154; Jones, *The Roaming Empire,* 24.

27. Katherine Lanpher, "A Manhattan Admonition," *New York Times,* August 31, 2004, A21.

28. See Morton Beiser and Ilene Hyman, "Refugees' Time Perspective and Mental Health," *American Journal of Psychiatry* 154:7 (July 1997): 996–1001.

29. Mindy Thompson Fullilove, "Psychiatric Implications of Displacement:

Contributions from the Psychology of Place," *American Journal of Psychiatry* 153:12 (December 1996): 1516–23.

30. Heather Chaplin, "Past? Perfect," *American Demographics* 21 (May 1999): 68–69. For a discussion of why possessions might help to assuage the pain of homesickness, see Russell Belk, "Possessions and the Sense of the Past," in *Highways and Byways: Naturalistic Research from the Consumer Behavior Odyssey*, ed. Russell Belk (Provo, UT, 1991), 114–30; Russell Belk, "Possessions and the Extended Self," *Journal of Consumer Research* 15 (September 1988): 139–68.

31. J. Walker Smith and Ann Clurman, *Rocking the Ages: The Yankelovich Report on Generational Marketing* (New York, 1997, 1998), 46.

32. Douglas Frantz and Catherine Collins, *Celebration, USA: Living in Disney's Brave New Town* (New York, 1999), 24.

33. Stephanie Coontz, *The Way We Never Were: American Families and the Nostalgia Trap* (New York, 1992), esp. chap. 2.

34. Steven Mintz and Susan Kellogg, *Domestic Revolutions: A Social History of the American Family* (New York, 1988), 293n.

35. Kenneth T. Jackson, *The Crabgrass Frontier: The Suburbanization of the United States* (New York, 1985), 283–84.

36. Jackson, *The Crabgrass Frontier,* 239–40.

37. Mintz and Kellogg, *Domestic Revolutions,* 185.

38. Ibid., 203; Margaret Andersen, *Thinking about Women: Sociological Perspectives on Sex and Gender* (Boston, 1983, 1997), 145; *News: United States Department of Labor, Employment Characteristics of Families in 2001* (Washington, D.C., 2002), 2.

39. Barbara Le Bay, "American Families Are Drifting Apart," *USA Today Magazine* 130 (September 1, 2001): 20–22.

40. Quoted in Chaplin, "Past? Perfect," 69.

41. Geoffrey Colvin, "What the Baby-Boomers Will Buy Next," *Fortune Magazine* 110 (October 15, 1984): 30.

42. Chaplin, "Past? Perfect," 68–69.

43. J. Walker Smith and Ann Clurman, *Rocking the Ages,* 270.

44. Debra Goldman, Home Improvements, *Brandweek* 35:43 (November 7, 1994): 20, 21.

45. Chaplin, "Past? Perfect," 68–69.

46. Patricia Leigh Brown, "A Hardware Store with a Big Ego," *New York Times,* February 20, 1997, C1, C4.

47. Stephen Drucker, "Living Traditions," *Martha Stewart Living Magazine* (September 1998): 29.

48. Promotional flier for *Martha Stewart Living Magazine,* Summer 2004, 7.

49. Letters to the Editor, *Martha Stewart Living Magazine* (September 1996): 24.

50. "What is your decorating style?" Posted by Anakens, March 19, 2004, Message #6230891, http://www.bhg.com/bhg/dgroups/viewForum.jhtml?forum=33, accessed March 28, 2004.

51. "Why do you like the styles you do?" Posted by breezie, March 27, 2004, Message #6276564, "Why do you like the styles you do?" Posted by deedlerock, March 25, 2004, Message # 6265898, all on http://www.bhg.com/bhg/dgroups/viewThread.jhtml?forum=33&thread=7254036&start=0&thRange=15,   accessed March 28, 2004.

52. Claire Cooper Marcus, *House as a Mirror of Self: Exploring the Deeper Meanings of Home* (Berkeley, LA, 1995), 36.

53. Kevin Blair, *Nostalgia Home Plans Collection*, vol. 2, *A New Approach to Time Honored Design from the Home Plan Design Service* (Omaha, NE, 1999), 4.

54. Philip Langdon, "Suburbanites Pick Favorite Home Styles," *New York Times*, April 22, 1982, C12.

55. Nick Harder, "Front Porch Makes Comeback in Home Architecture," *Chicago Tribune*, June 5, 2004, sec. 4, 21.

56. Sarah Boxer, "A Remedy for the Rootlessness of Modern Suburban Life?" *New York Times*, August 1, 1998, B7, B9.

57. Robert Steuteville, "The New Urbanism: An Alternative to Modern, Automobile-Oriented Planning and Development," *New Urban News*, June 28, 2000, http://www.newurbannews.com/, accessed June 24, 2004; Andrew Ross, *The Celebration Chronicles: Life, Liberty, and the Pursuit of Property Values in Disney's New Town* (New York, 1999), 331.

58. Carl Hiaasen, *Team Rodent: How Disney Devours the World* (New York, 1998), 50–52; Russ Rymer, "Back to the Future: Disney Reinvents the Company Town," *Harper's Magazine* 293, 1757 (October 1996): 68.

59. Frantz and Collins, *Celebration, USA*, 24.

60. Ross, *The Celebration Chronicles*, 74.

61. "Why do you like the styles you do?" Posted by Newspace, March 26, 2004, Message #6270494, all on http://www.bhg.com/bhg/dgroups/viewThread.jhtml?forum=33&thread=7254036, accessed April 1, 2004.

62. Marjorie Garber, *Sex and Real Estate: Why We Love Houses* (New York, 2000), 69.

63. "Why do you like the styles you do?" Posted by Jen7DOL, March 26, 2004, Message #6271946, http://www.bhg.com/bhg/dgroups/viewThread.jhtml?forum=33&thread=7254036, accessed April 1, 2004.

64. Martha Stewart, "Remembering: Warm Thoughts of Home," *Martha Stewart Living* (October 1996): 170; Martha Stewart, "Remembering: Dreaming of Linen," *Martha Stewart Living* (May 1997): 188. For a fuller discussion of how Stewart's current style represents a reaction to the deprivations of her youth, see Christopher M. Byron, *MARTHA INC.* (New York, 2002).

65. Joan Kron, *HOME-PSYCH: The Social Psychology of Home and Decoration* (New York, 1983), 176.

66. Many historians have commented on this. See, for instance, Nancy Woloch, *Women and the American Experience*, 2nd ed. (New York, 1994), 108–13.

67. Marjorie Garber, *Sex and Real Estate*, 57.

68. See Grant McCracken, "Homey-ness: A Cultural Account of One Constellation of Consumer Goods and Meanings," *Interpretive Consumer Research*, ed. Elizabeth Hirschman (Provo, UT, 1989), 168–83.

69. David Brooks, "Acquired Taste," *New Yorker* 74 (January 25, 1999): 41.

70. Dominique Browning, quoted in Elayne Rappling, "Burrowing Within," *The Progressive* 60 (December 1996): 39.

6

Horseless Horses
Car Dealing and the Survival of Retail Bargaining

Steven M. Gelber

News reports suggest that in the near future, electronic chips on every item in a store will allow consumers to be charged for purchases automatically by simply walking out through the door.[1] No checkout clerks will ask the shoppers if they found everything they were looking for; no checkout robots will ask if the customers would prefer to hear their oddly inflected voices speak in English or Spanish; nothing tangible will mark the exchange of value. This invisible transaction will be the latest evolutionary step away from the complex face-to-face negotiation between buyer and seller that once marked almost every retail transaction, one that uniquely survives in the purchase of an automobile.

Would-be buyers who walk into automobile dealerships in the 21st century enter a time warp. They are transported back to the early 19th century, to an era before goods were sold to all shoppers at the same posted price and before dissatisfied customers could return their purchases. They are confronted by sales personnel who are masters of the ancient arts of flattery, high pressure, misdirection, misrepresentation, and patience. They are willing to sit for hours haggling over the cost of everything from the basic car itself, to the moonroof, the floor mats, the interest rate on the car loan, and the trade-in value of the owner's current vehicle—to name just a few of the price points open to negotiation.

It makes no difference if the customer is interested in a new or a used car; the process is roughly the same. In the worst (and fairly common) case, the shopper is met at the curb by a "greeter" who tries to determine if he or she is a "looker" or a serious buyer. Buyers are then turned over to a more experienced salesman who finds a car the buyer wants and opens a period of painful and protracted price negotiation, retreating often to an office in the back to check offers and counteroffers with his manager. Eventually the sales manager himself will appear to continue the dickering over price, and, if the customer is unyielding, the sales manager is sometimes replaced by his manager. In the meantime, the buyer has had to work with the dealer's used-car appraiser to determine the trade-in value of his or her current car. Once the price of the new and used cars are agreed to, the customer is turned over one more time to the business manager who not only negotiates finance and insurance charges, but also tries to sell dealer-installed add-ons such as fabric protection and rust proofing.[2]

As bad as this system may seem, historically things were even worse. Prior to 1958, the buyer often had no idea what the dealer's standard asking price was, because there was no established way to represent the price of cars on the lot. The requirement that all new cars carry a sticker listing the "manufacturer's suggested retail price" (MSRP) created a common starting point for price negotiations, but no more than that. The advent of the Internet has armed some buyers with more accurate information about dealer costs, but that has only made the negotiations fiercer, forcing dealers to give better prices to informed buyers and then trying to make up the loss of profit by keeping up the costs to others. With the isolated exception of General Motors Saturn division, dealers adjust the prices of their vehicles to the local market, charging additional markup on highly sought after cars and cutting the price of slow-selling ones. And even on a Saturn lot, where sticker prices are stuck to, negotiation can take place on ancillary products and services, and will always occur on the trade-in allowance for the customer's current car.

The process of haggling over the cost of an automobile evokes buyer consternation about prices and dealer grumbling that their legitimate profit margins are being shaved. Nevertheless, retail price negotiation has persisted during virtually the entire historical lifetime of the automobile. For one hundred years, even as marketplace bargaining gave way to set prices in nearly every other consumer transaction, the tradition of "horse trading" for cars has resisted all attempts to bring it into line with the retail norm. The anomalous persistence of what dealers themselves have often disparagingly referred to as an "oriental bazaar" confirms how dramatically American attitudes toward the marketplace changed over the course of the 20th century. It also shows how the unique cultural meaning of automobiles shielded them from the normal one-price marketplace.

Car buying is an area of contemporary life where behavioral economics meets behavioral history. Behavioral economics seeks to understand the psychological reasons why people make economically irrational choices, and behavioral history tries to explain how historical patterns construct current behavior. The psychological meaning of automobiles is a cliché of popular literature, and there are few more overused double entendres than "auto-eroticism."[3] What is less obvious, but just as true, is the psychological meaning of the historical pattern of bargaining for a car. The meaning of the car and the meaning of the way that car is obtained are linked by their continuity with the meaning and method of getting horses. Horse trading established the pattern for car dealing. Even though both buyers and sellers complain about the way the car business is conducted, and even though there is an obvious alternative model, behavioral history is one of the prime reasons we continue to subject ourselves to the ordeal of negotiating the price of both new and used cars.

Automobiles began to be marketed as a mass-produced consumer product at the turn of the 20th century. This was the same period when the posted-price retail model pioneered by department stores became the standard for selling manufactured goods. Consumer-oriented contract law had evolved to extend unprecedented warranty protection to the purchasers of factory-made products. These implied warranties, together with open and nonnegotiable prices, created an opportunity for cars to be merchandised in the same manner as other new mechanical conveniences. Automobile retailers tried to emulate the one-price policy, but economic and technical issues combined with social/psychological forces to make the car market an anomaly in the contemporary retail world. Rather than following the lead of other expensive mechanical appliances such as refrigerators and washing machines, car dealing retained the essential elements of the preindustrial marketplace. There were multiple reasons for cars' anomalous status, but most of them were related in one way or another to the fact that, socially and psychologically, cars were not so much horseless carriages as they were horseless horses, emblems of manhood to be acquired in a peculiarly "manly" way.

One Price to All

The retail transformation from individually negotiated prices to charging the same advertised price to everybody occurred in the late 19th and early

20th centuries and was the result of a shift in the psychological and social contexts of consumer behavior. Prior to the 20th century, consumption was almost always a personal transaction between a vendor (who was often also the producer) and a buyer, both of whom were likely to know each other as individuals in a unique interpersonal relationship. That broader knowledge of the other complexified the commercial relationship because it triggered feelings that transcended the simple exchange of value. Knowing that the other person was, for example, wealthy or strapped for cash, had a large family or was living alone, was a member of one or another socioethnic subculture, and so forth all altered the power relationship in the deal, and virtually every purchase was indeed a deal. Because the price for any item was established at the time of its sale through negotiation, that price often reflected not only the strict exchange value of the item to each party, but possibly also the constraints of in-group sympathy, the opportunism of out-group antipathy, or particular knowledge of the other person's strengths or vulnerabilities.

To the extent that participants in the preindustrial marketplace took extraneous factors into account when negotiating prices, they were deviating from a narrowly neoclassical model of economic behavior. Their freedom to buy low or sell high was constrained (or "bounded") by what others, whose opinions they valued, would think of them and/or by how they would feel about themselves if they took advantage of, or failed to have sympathy for, the other person in a transaction. These are the kinds of subjective psychological considerations that distinguish the work of contemporary behavioral economists from that of their more objectively analytic colleagues. Feelings, which may have deep biological origins and of which people may hardly be aware, can influence the "rationality" of economic decisions. Certain of those feelings are given much freer rein when people have to negotiate with each other to determine the purchase price of an item. In terms of the standard neoclassical model of economic behavior, face-to-face negotiation is a rational way to strike a bargain so long as it is an agreement between self-interested individuals, each of whom has the same information about the commodity for sale. However, this standard model is thwarted when a bargainer makes a decision on emotional (that is, economically irrational) grounds. Opportunities for emotional responses are increased considerably by having to haggle over price.

The complexity of making retail decisions was simplified considerably with the advent of a marketplace in which sellers sold their products to buyers at a publicly stated price. In effect, posted prices depersonalized the marketplace by making every customer a stranger and, by the same token, ensuring every stranger (customer) that he or she was not being cheated. This depersonalization (or, what advocates at the time liked to call "democratization") of point-of-sale interactions was the direct result of urbanization, which made people more anonymous, and industrialization, which did the same for products. Just as city dwellers became nameless metaphorical cogs in the machinery of urban life, the real cogs of the real machines generated identical products whose sale was removed far from their production. Both sellers and buyers alike came to value the less socially and emotionally inflected system of a one-price-to-all. Posted prices removed the necessity of "knowing somebody in the trade" to get a good deal and, as department store magnate John Wanamaker put it in 1874, "assuring equal rights to all" and "ruling out the possibility of unfairness."[4] When each unit of a product was the same, with sameness assured by product branding, the nature of marketplace competitiveness shifted. The competition among manufacturers and retailers heated up with multiple producers vying for sales of functionally similar products at both the wholesale and retail level, and multiple retailers competing with one another to sell identical brand-name items.[5] At the same time, competition between the retailer and the customer cooled down; in fact, it went away completely. Within a given store, every customer received the same treatment and paid the same price.

In a traditional transaction, for example, an individual buying cornmeal from a storekeeper supplied by a local miller would typically ask the retailer how much the cornmeal was per pound and then ask for certain number of pounds. The storekeeper could shade the price higher or lower depending on his relationship with the buyer. And, depending on local practice, there might be a certain amount of dickering on the per pound price and the amount to be purchased, especially if the quality of the meal were open to question.

However, after 1906, when factories began to transform cornmeal into identical boxes of corn flakes, a new set of assumptions came into play. The consumer now had to trust the manufacturer, not the retailer. Even if they wanted to, there was no way for malevolent store owners to adulterate the product or rig the scales used to weigh it out, nor could benevolent retailers take special care that the product was fresh and weevil free. Quality was now the responsibility of a distant business. Those companies began to take pains to make the consumer believe that their brand of corn flakes was superior to similar products from other cereal companies and that the purchaser could count on a uniform product, which, now that it was packaged, could not be examined until after it was bought. Consequently, price competition developed among these similar products on two levels. Manufacturers sought to keep prices to the retailers low enough to allow the stores to sell at an acceptable profit, and retailers had to compete with one another in price since a box of brand-name corn flakes was the same no matter where it was bought.

There was, of course, no reason why shopkeepers could not bargain with consumers over the price of individual boxes of breakfast cereal. During the long transition from negotiated to set prices, a period from roughly 1860 to 1920, many stores did precisely that. The retail convention was to put a code on each manufactured item that told the shopkeeper or clerk how much it had cost the store and then for the clerk to tell customers what their price would be. Because this system allowed the store to charge some people more than others for the same item, haggling continued to be part of the retail transaction, although the extent to which it was used apparently varied widely.[6]

At first, consumers were worried that paying the posted price meant they were paying too much, but once it became clear that one-price stores really did charge everybody the same amount, the practice spread, particularly in urban areas. The first advocate of one-price merchandising appears to have been Quaker founder George Fox. Fox noted in 1653 that he wanted his followers to be so honest "that if a child were sent to their shops for anything, he was as well used as his parents would have been."[7] Even though single price policies helped Quaker businesses prosper, and there were more Quakers in America than in any other country, the practice did not spread widely in the United States until after the Civil War. Two merchants, R. H. Macy (a Quaker convert in New York) and John Wanamaker (in the Quaker center of Philadelphia) are most commonly credited with popularizing the concept of one-price at their respective department stores.[8] During the same period, the mail-order houses of Montgomery Ward and Sears Roebuck extended the fixed price concept to rural residents by taking advantage of the decreasing costs of printing and postage and, in effect, creating department stores in a catalog.

Nonnegotiating Women

Historians invariably link the rise of Macy's, Wanamakers, and their many imitators to the new role of women as consumers.[9] What was new for women, however, was the location and the scale and the method of consumption, not the act itself of buying goods. In the preindustrial economy, American women seem to have purchased those items that they used in their household work, such as flour, cloth, and personal items for themselves and their children. Things used by men, such as farm equipment (including horses), were bought by them. Expensive household items such as china and furniture appear to have been most often bought jointly in the sense that spouses negotiated an agreement with each other on what items to buy before one or both of them did any negotiating with a merchant.

If women as well as men had a history of marketplace bargaining, then studies indicating that modern women are less likely to dispute the first offer made to them are probably identifying a postindustrial cultural phenomenon.[10] It may well be that American women participated in a culture of negotiation until the 19th century, when a confluence of historical forces removed them from the role of price bargaining. In this way the change in how women shopped can be seen as a contributing factor to the broader Victorian idea that women had no place in activities that involved competition and confrontation. Just as the middle-class cult of true womanhood and domesticity compensated women for their separation from the business world, the one-price model of the department store provided a way to get out into the world without having to engage in unfeminine bargaining contests with shopkeepers.

Victorian and early 20th century department stores, like homes of the same era, were women's worlds where men were welcome but where female sensibilities prevailed. The stores catered to women's needs and tastes in a variety of ways. They were decorated sumptuously, providing tea rooms and lounges; they would deliver purchases to the women's homes so they did not have carry their acquisitions through the streets; they began to employ female clerks to sell the more intimate items to women customers; they accepted returns; and they openly posted the price of every item and sold it at that price to every customer.

In a city where everyone was a stranger, the ad hoc pricing system that had prevailed in rural areas made less sense. The neighborly social codes that protected small-town buyers from exploitation did not exist. The fixed-price system provided protection to the customer while it relieved clerks of the time and effort needed to negotiate a price each time an item was sold. Once the retail distinction between neighbors and strangers had been eliminated, all other distinctions disappeared as well—including the distinction between men and women. One price for all meant that in the consuming world of the department store, men became women, although in the working world of men, conflict, competition, and negotiation remained the norm.

The division of living space from working space imposed by industrialism meant that many women became unfamiliar with the sphere of production and thus had little knowledge of the costs (both human and monetary) of earning a living. Whether or not they controlled the day-to-day finances in a particular household, women were dissociated from the negotiating that went on regularly at every level in every business. Men tried to get more money for less work, or vice versa; or they tried to get more product for less money, or vice versa. Men tried to get promoted ahead of their coworkers, acquire customers ahead of their competitors, and otherwise win in the competitive game that was the daily world of work. Women were not expected to exercise these combative skills. There was, to be sure, rivalry for status and recognition among women, and vying for position in a social hierarchy created its own culture of competition, in which a keen sense of the cost of material possessions was essential for one's own status and an accurate assessment of other women's economic standing. Brand names and published prices only made this form of invidious comparison easier.

From the store's point of view, having set prices significantly lowered some of the costs of doing business. Most notably, a single price, along with the invention of a cash register that printed dual receipts, meant that salesclerks did not have to be given much latitude in the handling of money, so they could be trained more quickly for positions that paid less for less responsibility. Furthermore, clerks in the new department stores were usually paid straight wages rather than being compensated by commissions like outside sales representatives. While this may have lowered their incentive to sell, it also eliminated their incentive to cut prices to gain a sale on the theory that a small commission was better than none. Of course, the same was also true for the store as a whole. That is the rationale behind mass merchandising, but in the case of stores, the lower price could be advertised since it would be available to everybody who walked in the door.

The department store one-price policy quickly became the model for all retailing. By the end of World War I, shopping had become, for the most part, a much more transparent process than it had been a century before. Items were uniformly manufactured and labeled, and the retail consumer could systematically plan what to buy and where to buy it based on brand names and advertised prices. Business-to-business transactions, which continued to be dominated by men, were much slower to come around to a one-price policy. In fact, business-to-business sales prices are still subject to a very high level of variation based on negotiation. While inside retail sales became one of the few occupations open to women before the last half of the 20th century, outside sales remained a cutthroat male domain, a source of dramatic material from Arthur Miller's Willy Loman in *Death of a Salesman* to David Mamet's Shelly Levine in *Glengarry Glen Ross*. These are people who, like car salesmen, are paid by the sale, not by the hour.

Cars as Consumer Commodities

Because the shift to single-price retailing was taking place during the infancy of the automobile industry, it might be expected that cars would be sold under the new one-price system. Cars were different from the horses they were replacing in enough ways that the moment was ripe for the breaking of old horse-oriented patterns. First, there was the possibility that cars would be less identified with men than were horses. As mechanical conveyances they would not require as much physical strength to control as a twelve-hundred-pound beast with a mind of its own. As a general rule, women rarely rode horses and while some drove horse-drawn carriages or wagons, men often assumed that women lacked the requisite wrist, arm, and grip strength to control a pulling horse. In 1906 a writer in *Outing* magazine warned that "the husband, father, or other male relative who turns [a woman] loose upon the highways and byways, unattended by groom or other thoroughly competent [and obviously male] companion . . . does a wicked and reprehensible thing." As far as the writer was concerned, the frequent avowal that a horse for sale was "safe for a woman to drive" was an oxymoron.[11] Early automobile manufacturers took advantage of these doubts about horse-driving skills of females and the ease of car driving to advertise their electric cars as quiet, clean, and easy to maneuver, and therefore especially suited for women.

A second reason that cars might have been sold differently from horses was their distinct legal status as fabricated goods. "Purchasing a horse is a very different thing from buying a manufactured article," explained a 19th-century legal guide. The seller of a manufactured item knew exactly how it was made and could therefore confidently warrant its performance, but nobody could know what was going on inside a horse. It was foolish, therefore, advised the writer, to give or expect a warranty on a horse.[12] By the same logic, manufacturers could offer and buyers could expect a warranty on manufactured goods such as automobiles. The courts, and then the legislatures, concluded that consumers could not be expected to accurately judge the quality of something made by a machine the same way they had been traditionally expected to judge the quality of a natural product, so courts extended unprecedented protection to the purchasers of manufactured goods.

Horse buyers traditionally operated under the principle of caveat emptor ("let the buyer beware") and were not protected against problems with their purchases unless they had managed to get an explicit written warranty. Car buyers, however, could operate under the assumption of an "implied warranty."[13] This meant that with new (but not used) cars, it was in the manufacturer's and dealer's interest to make sure their product worked as advertised for at least the first couple of months, because if it did not, they would have to fix or replace it. Automobile advertising boasted about guarantees as early as 1908.[14] This new set of assumptions about the nature of retail transactions expressed itself most dramatically in the late 19th century practice of department stores accepting returns of unsatisfactory items. There was no legal obligation for this new accommodation, but it was a logical extension of the idea that any manufactured product should perform in a particular way, and it was one more way that stores could compete with one another for customer loyalty without haggling over purchases.

Finally, one might expect that a new form of retailing for automobiles might have emerged at the beginning of the 20th century because the initial demand for cars far exceeded the supply. The *New York Times* reported in 1903 that dealers were demanding and getting 250 dollars over list price on 2500-dollar cars.[15] Despite their high price and the barriers posed by muddy unpaved roads, and their limited operability in winter, the new machines were wanted by more people than there was capacity to build them. Since this was the first generation of car owners, there were few used cars for either the buyers or sellers to worry about. Some new car buyers wanted to trade in horses as partial payment for their new cars, but dealers did not have to accommodate them since there was no shortage of other customers willing to close a "straight" (i.e., no trade) deal. In other words, it appeared as though a motor car could be sold exactly the same way as a box of manufactured breakfast cereal; one price to all buyers from the same retailer, but with price competition among retailers and among manufacturers based on brand identification.

As newly invented, ungendered machines, protected by a warranty and sold without a trade, there seemed to be little reason why automobiles could not be distributed through female-friendly department stores, rather than by outlets more akin to the old male bastion of the livery stable. This certainly was the reasoning of department store merchant (and early auto buff) John Wanamaker who was selling automobiles in his New York store as early as 1900.[16] In 1903 Wanamaker, added the new 800-dollar Ford to his other brands. As a leader in the field of single-price mass merchandising, Wanamaker saw the retail logic of carrying a car that claimed to be 40 percent cheaper than any other automobile in its class.[17]

Wanamaker was not alone in his belief that automobiles, as standardized products, could be sold like other manufactured consumer goods. In 1909, a year after Henry Ford began producing his Model T, Sears Roebuck offered its house-brand "Motor Buggy Model P" to the public through its catalog. At half the price of a Model T, which itself was about half the price of most other cars, and presumably protected by the same money-back guarantee of satisfaction that covered the other items in the Sears "Wish Book," the Sears Model P was a prime example of the new retail paradigm. Unfortunately for Sears, not many potential drivers were attracted to the bare bones buggy with its large carriage wheels, even with the company's assurance that "you do not require mechanical training in order to operate the Sears Automobile; our Book of Instruction tell you how in thirty minutes." The car was discontinued after three years, unable to compete with the much more popular Ford.[18]

Neither department stores nor catalogs were ever able to establish a firm place in the automobile retail market. Although the terms "department store" and "supermarket" would continue to pop up periodically as ways to describe a variety of approaches to retailing automobiles, the core department store concept of selling competing brand names at a posted price was difficult to implement for a number of reasons. First, the sheer cost of the car set it apart from other manufactured goods. From its beginning, the automobile was the most expensive mass-produced item most people ever bought. In constant dollars, that 800-dollar 1903 Ford cost about the same as a low-end car one hundred years later, and the average unskilled worker in 1903 would have had to work five times as long as his 2003 counterpart to afford it.[19] In addition, there were practical problems selling cars in department stores: they were large and heavy and they needed to be prepared for sale and repaired under warranty by skilled mechanics. In this sense, cars were much like horses—they not only cost a lot, but also required extensive storage space and specialized care for their upkeep.

Size and mechanical complexity made it more practical to sell cars from specialized automobile dealerships, but that in itself did not rule out the possibility of a one-price sales policy. Automobiles were a standardized commodity that lent themselves to uniform advertising, which often included price. Even in the very early days of the automobile era, advertisements for new cars were much more likely to state a specific price than ads for horses. Because the prices of new cars were often published in national advertisements, and included in local newspapers and in dealer brochures, buyers of a particular model used car had a much better idea of what a reasonable price for it might be than did the buyer of a horse.[20] This decreased the opportunities for dealers to take advantage of buyers.

A one-price policy for cars was actually furthered by the emergence of specialty retail dealers because they led to exclusive franchise agreements with manufacturers as early as 1910. An exclusive franchise meant that there would be only one dealer for a particular brand in a defined geographic area. That dealer would get his cars at a standard discount and would be prohibited from reselling them to secondary dealers who might create additional brand-name competition. If dealers could be assured that they would be the only store in the community that was selling a particular brand, that removed the store-to-store level of competition that characterized the regular retail industry. This meant that car dealers could (and sometimes were contractually obligated to) charge the full factory-set retail price.[21]

Nascent manufacturers benefited from this arrangement because they were frequently undercapitalized. They financed production by imposing minimum sales quotas on their dealers and requiring advance cash deposits and full payment on delivery. As long as demand outstripped supply, the manufacturers could create a long list of franchise conditions that required the dealers to maintain attractive premises, stock only factory replacement parts, employ competent mechanics, and not sell cars made by competing companies. Any violation of the rules meant the dealer lost his franchise and his livelihood. Most of these retail principles were firmly established before 1917 and remained substantially unchanged until 1949 when key anticompetitive elements were struck down by the courts.[22]

Its exclusive geographic franchise system distinguished automobile retailing from the sale of most other consumer items because it guaranteed that there would be little or no competition among sellers of the same brand. High consumer demand for cars and lack of competition among dealers meant there was less pressure to cut prices, but high prices meant it was more difficult for people to afford a new car. To make matters worse, car buyers could not get credit. Older neighborhood storekeepers would carry customers on their books because they knew them as individuals. Most newer urban department stores continued the custom for their best customers.[23] Even though middle-class customers had developed a habit of charging purchases, car dealers and banks were reluctant to extend credit to buyers. It was not until 1914 that either auto retailers or finance institutions began to make loans for new car sales.[24] And it would be years before dealers and manufacturers realized they could make as much money from selling credit as they did from selling cars. In the meantime, cars were ostensibly sold for the advertised price and for cash.

Scattered evidence indicates that despite the one-price policy demanded by manufacturers and given lip service by dealers, some car merchants did give discounts off the retail price, although the magnitude of that practice is not clear. To the extent that it did occur, some price cutting on cars might have been expected because dickering over prices did not disappear entirely with the advent of the department-store model. Even after the beginning of the posted-price era, a certain amount of bargaining continued when so-called big ticket items were being bought and sold.[25] Canny shoppers who knew that there were usually wide profit margins on high-priced goods might ask for and get a discount off the ticket price of large appliances or expensive jewelry. There was, however, no expectation by either buyer or seller that a price concession would automatically be asked for or given. Still, negotiating for the price of a car became the standard very early on despite the forces that might have discouraged it.

Making the Car Male

Had women, who were so closely associated with department stores and the one-price policy, become drivers sooner, cars might have been sold in a more straightforward fashion. However, unlike their response to sewing machines and typewriters, few women became active operators of automobiles. Historian Virginia Scharff attributes much of the female exclusion to the way in which the culture of male mechanics dominated the world of early automobiles.[26] There were a few adventuresome women who drove cars, some for long distances under quite adverse conditions, but they were notable exceptions.[27] The idea that there could be a car for women drivers disappeared with the last of the electric autos.

Women were often included in the marketing strategies for automobiles, but it was mostly men who drove them prior to World War I. Day-to-day driving was a man's game for some very practical reasons. Until 1912 cars had to be hand-cranked to start, a process that was both difficult and dangerous. Most cars were open to the weather, prone to mechanical breakdowns and flat tires, and regularly got stuck in the mud of unpaved roads. By the time electric self-starters and enclosed body styles became readily available, the die had been cast. Increasing numbers of women would drive in the 1920s, but the masculinity of the car business would remain essentially unchanged for the ensuing century.

The high cost of most pre-Ford cars limited their market to upper-income men who lived in or near the city where roads were more likely to be paved. These wealthy first-generation auto owners were used to having their horses and carriages attended by grooms and coachmen, and this pattern was initially embraced for the new horseless carriages as well. Grooms and coachmen became chauffeurs, men who not only drove the cars but also attended to their mechanical well-being, just as they had looked after the day-to-day needs of horses. Since grooms and carriage drivers were historically male professions, the tradition of professional male control of personal transportation shifted easily with the new vehicles.

At first, nobody was quite sure who should sell and service the new machines. The job fell to bicycle mechanics who were familiar with one form of mechanical transportation, to blacksmiths who could fashion or repair broken parts, and to stable owners who had the room and equipment to maintain carriages and cars. These latter two professions were made up of men who lived and breathed horses and were steeped in horse-trading culture. It is not surprising then that the male ethos of the horse trader would transfer to the new car dealers. Although they were curiosities, even at the time, stories of car dealers taking horses in trade reinforced the sense that there was some sort of equivalence to these purchases. Moreover, just as gentlemen or businessmen had depended on their grooms to buy and sell their horses, early automobile owners often delegated the purchase of cars to their chauffeurs. Grooms had a reputation for accepting (or demanding) bribes from traders to choose their horses. Chauffeurs did the same, undermining attempts to maintain a transparent one-price policy and planting the seeds of unethical marketplace negotiation.

Speed kills. It also sells—perhaps because it kills—and pre–World War I automobile advertising was rife with boasts about how fast a particular car was, which races it had won, and which endurance trials it had run. Manufacturers sought publicity and attempted to prove the reliability of their machines by demonstrating their speed and durability. Both with company sponsorship and on the their own, car owners took part in street races, track races, cross-country races, and hill climbs that were all demonstrations of the quality of early cars—and their drivers. By doing so, these early drivers were creating mechanized versions of the quintessentially male pastime of horse racing.

Delight in speed had been part of the culture of young men for generations. Rural youth raced their horses on the roads and at fairs, and urban "scorchers" drove first their carriages and then their bicycles around city streets at breakneck speed, showing off to spectators and one another. A fast horse, noted the economist Thorstein Veblen in 1899, was a way for a man to appropriate "the animate forces of the environment" and "so express his own dominating individuality through them."[28] Horses were, as cars would be, the public statement of a man's sociobiological success. Both were the bright plumage with which he could intimidate rival males and attract desirable females.

To use Veblen's term, men used horses to express their "dominating individuality." As much as, and probably more than, anything else a man would ever own, a horse was an expression of male identity and the desire to dominate other males. Owning a fast and fancy horse or carriage meant to the pre-20th century man exactly what owning a fast and fancy car means to a modern man: new was better than old; shiny was better than dull; fast was better than slow; tricked out was better than pared down; expensive spoke volumes about one's success. A man's means of personal transportation was a representation not only of his wealth, but also of his virility: "Being still under middle age," observed a horse buyer in 1836, "I am of course far from indifferent whether I am well mounted."[29]

The psychological meaning of horses is an obvious historical example of behavioral, and perhaps even "cognitive," economics in action. That is to say, the process of acquiring and owning a horse involved deep feelings that shaped economic decisions and could cause people (in this case, men) to act in a way contrary to their best economic interests. While cost, size, and mechanical complexity were practical reasons why cars would be bought and sold in a particular way, the many irrational (emotional) factors had roots in the historical relationship between horses and the male psyche.

The Precedents in Horse Trading

Horses have a long history as trophies. Like gold and women, they were traditional war booty because one could transport and display them. Horses continued to serve this symbolic function in America in two ways. As economic trophies they represented victory in the more generalized competition of the marketplace. Good horses were expensive, and owning one advertised business success. They were a particularly conspicuous form of conspicuous consumption. They were also, however, trophies of a much more immediate competition: the purchase and sale of the specific animal. As though the transaction for this trophy were a distilled example of the larger system, two men tested their business mettle to see who could emerge with the better deal, and because horse sales often involved trades, both parties ended up with material representations of the success or failure of their bargaining (combat) skills.

When observers spoke and wrote about horse trading, what fascinated them were the one-on-one negotiations for a particular animal, not corporate purchases of hundreds of horses or mules for drayage companies or mines. Every individual horse could be bargained for, and if a trade were involved, the bargaining concerned two horses. On the surface, there was nothing irrational about bargaining for a horse. As a natural commodity, every horse was different; nobody could know for sure what was going on inside a horse's body or brain, so buying one was always something of a gamble. Custom, and the law, assumed that buyers were competent judges of horseflesh, and therefore horses were sold "as is" except if there was a specific warranty that the animal was free of a given fault. There was frequently, however, an irrational subtext to a horse trade; just enough dissimulation was tolerated by the male community of traders to make the transaction a game and, by definition, a game, has a winner and loser.

According to the unstated rules of the horse-trading game, direct lies were unacceptable, as were clearly fraudulent devices that altered the appearance or behavior of a horse. The rules were flexible and varied from place to place and over time, but they were widely enough understood that an entire genre of folklore evolved celebrating the victories and relishing the defeats of men who traded horses. As late as 1979, Deane C. Davis, the ex-governor of Vermont, enjoyed telling the undated story of a trial in which the buyer claimed that the seller had assured him the horse did not have a particular breathing disorder called "heaves." However, it turns out that the seller, who was a severe asthmatic, had in fact assured the buyer, "If this horse has got the heaves, I got the heaves." The jury concluded that the seller had, at least within the norms of the horse-trading game, told the truth and no fraud had been committed.[30] In this incident the seller won and the buyer lost, and each in turn presumably experienced the pleasure of winning and the humiliation of losing. A humiliation, it might be supposed, that the buyer experienced anew every time his broken-winded steed stopped to catch its breath.

The disingenuous tradition of horse selling depended on two factors. Horses could come with a wide variety of hidden faults, and a buyer often had a horse to unload. The professional horse dealer could, therefore, make a profit in a number of ways. He could act as an honest broker, distributing horses with particular traits to people looking for that kind of a horse, and, in essence, charging a fee for that service by buying a bit low and selling a bit high. He could also charge the buyer "boot," or an extra fee in addition to the animal he took in trade. This was often done when private parties were trading unequal animals. The boot was usually cash, but it also might be tack, a second animal, or anything else one of the parties was willing to give or take to make the deal. Finally, and most notoriously, the dealer could make money by disguising a horse's faults and selling it for much more than it was worth. Legendary horse traders had animals with easily hidden, but quickly discovered, faults, which they would buy back from the duped purchaser at a steep discount, in order to sell again to the next sucker. Such animals were actually worth more to traders than healthy or vice-free horses since they could be sold over and over again.

The competitive game aspect of horse trading created an emotional (one could almost say, hormonal) context that made the process of acquiring a horse part of the meaning of owning one. As manufactured goods, automobiles lacked the individual variations of horses and therefore lacked the essential quality of the unknown that enabled the horse-trading game. This was the characteristic that made dealers think they could sell cars at a set price. History, however, conspired to trap new car dealers into a gendered negotiating role that they have both reveled in and regretted ever since.

Even if they could hold the line on the retail price of new cars, the homogeneity that made it possible to have a one-price policy for new manufactured items disappeared with secondhand automobiles. The used-goods marketplace retained a preindustrial haggling character because the unique history of every item offered for sale meant its price had to be determined on an ad hoc basis. For new cars to be sold like other manufactured goods, that transaction had to be isolated from any connection to the sale of used cars. Thus, it was not the fact of bargaining that distinguished the used-car market from the buying and selling of other used goods, but where that bargaining took place: at a retail store that sold new cars.

By purchasing the new car buyer's old car, automobile dealers re-created a sales situation very similar to the time-honored, if somewhat dishonorable, custom of horse trading. Car dealers were ambivalent about inheriting the mantle of the much-maligned horse trader. The old-time stableman had the reputation of taking advantage of his superior knowledge to trick his customers by hiding the faults of his stock. So in the pre–World War I era, many car dealers tried to establish themselves as modern urban retailers, more like department stores than livery stables, but the culture of trading infiltrated the new industry, sometimes in remarkably direct ways. For example, an early Iowa Ford dealer who regularly accepted horses in trade for cars had a hostler who, he boasted, could "take any old nag, feed him oil meal for a couple of weeks, brush him up, put on a nice harness and hitch him in a nice rig" and end up with a horse that not even its old owner would recognize.[31] It did not take much of an imagination to see how analogous techniques could also be applied to cars taken in trade.

As secondhand commodities there was no implied warranty in used-car sales, and few dealers were willing to give any explicit guarantees on previously owned vehicles. Instead, the car dealers embraced the ancient art of doctoring the product so that it looked better than it was. For almost every trick that horse traders had used to hide the organic shortcomings of their stock, car dealers invented an analogous mechanical ruse. Where traders had dyed horses' gray hair, dealers painted over rust spots. Filing a horse's teeth to make it look younger gave way to turning back the odometer. Special diets to hide gastric problems in horses turned into extra heavy oil to dampen excessive engine noise. An unscrupulous hostler could rub red pepper or ginger on the anus of a placid horse to make it act frisky, or feed the lethargic animal a stimulant. Similarly, secondhand car dealers would add ether to the gasoline to temporarily improve performance. On the used car lot as in the horse trader's stable, things were seldom what they seemed, and skim milk did in fact masquerade as cream.

The historical stage was set for used-car dealers to follow in the lead of horse traders, but it was not inevitable that the used car would be bought (and then sold again) by the same person who retailed the new car. The public did not expect that any other merchant of manufactured goods would take the buyer's current article as a trade-in, with one very telling exception—the bicycle. For many younger men, the switch in personal transportation from horse to car went through an intermediate detour via bicycle. Bicycle mechanics were prominent among early automobile manufacturers, and men who sold bicycles joined men who sold horses as early automobile dealers and mechanics. There is some indication that during the first years of the bicycle craze in the 1880s, as riders sought newer and better models, they asked dealers to buy back their older bikes, but as long as demand exceeded supply, dealers resisted the used-bicycle business. However, once the peak of the fad passed, cycle sellers began to emulate horse dealers by taking in trades.[32] At one hundred dollars, a safety bicycle of the mid-1890s would be worth something over two thousand dollars in today's money. That bike was cheaper than most horses, but still expensive enough to make a cyclist think twice about buying a new one without having a buyer for his old model.

Their very cost was one of the reasons that horses and cars bestowed prestige on their owners, and cars were ten or twenty times as expensive as bicycles. If men wanted to maintain or improve their social standing by buying newer or better automobiles, there had to be a way to make them more affordable. The goal of affordability was achieved in car dealing as it had in horse trading and bicycle sales by sellers taking the owners' current transportation as partial payment for a new one. As early as 1903 new-car dealers were advertising good deals on used cars. While the demand for new automobiles was still high, these used cars may have been offered on consignment as a favor for new-car buyers.[33] However, in just a couple of years, when the supply caught up with demand, new-car dealers were buying used cars directly from their customers. Just as they had come to expect that horse dealers would accept trades, car owners wanted auto dealers to extend the same service.

In the retail sense, the car had already become a horseless horse, and, in turn, the automobile *dealer* had become a car *trader*. Reselling used cars opened up another market in which dealers could provide cars for men who could not afford a new vehicle, but it also opened up the opportunity for price negotiation and marketplace dishonesty. While it might have been easier to estimate the trade-in value of a used car than a horse, new-car buyers still could not know exactly what their old car was worth. The value of a used automobile was based on too many variables. The age, mileage, and condition of the car all affected its resale price, but so did market circumstances that had nothing to do with the condition of the car itself. For example, shifting consumer brand preferences and the rapid rise and fall of automobile companies could make a perfectly good car much less desirable. Value was also affected by the time of year because cars sold best in spring and summer. Since the dealer had to sell any used car he bought, he had not only a strong incentive to pay bottom and charge top dollar, but also to doctor the car so that it appeared to be better than it actually was.

Early dealers developed a full repertoire of techniques to improve the resale value of trade-ins. New paint and tires were almost standard, as were other cosmetic improvements. These kinds of changes might make an automobile look better cared for than it actually had been, but they were no more dishonest than getting a haircut, shoeshine, and new suit for a job interview. Many of the other techniques, however, were meant to deliberately disguise serious faults. It did not take long for used-car buyers to learn to distrust used-car dealers. In 1904, even before the first wave of demand had been satisfied, the Broadway Automobile Exchange, a used-car lot in New York City, headlined its display ads, "No Junks, No Misrepresentations."[34] Clearly, the company was trying to disavow a dubious reputation that used-car dealers had already inherited from horse traders. Used-car dealers who operated independently of new-car dealers were heirs to the notorious "gypsy" horse traders who never expected a customer to return for a second purchase. But because new-car dealers appear to have bought more used cars than independent used car lot operators, both the shady techniques and the shady reputation that grew up around used cars infected the new-car environment as well.

Dealer competition for the new-car buyer turned out to be stronger than dealer desire to be a modern merchant who dealt only in new items. Thus, the old tradition of men swapping transportation (and lies) in the marketplace was reborn. At the same time, the idea of a one-price policy became impossible, because now the real price of a new car was the difference between what the buyer gave the dealer for the new car and what he got back from the dealer for his trade-in, usually called the "allowance." It made no difference if the price of the new car were fixed and public, because the price of the used car always had to be negotiated. The dealer may have been contractually obliged to sell the new car at a specific advertised price, but nobody could tell him what to pay for a trade-in. It did not take customers long to figure out that when a dealer would pay him more than a used car was worth (an "over-allowance") he was getting a de facto discount on a new car. And reciprocally, the dealers began to figure out ways to jack up the price of new cars to cover the additional cost of over-allowances. This was often done by adding spurious transportation charges, or requiring that the buyers purchase overpriced accessories known in the trade as the "pack."

Conclusion

If department stores turned male customers into women by offering them a single price in a feminine environment, then car dealers turned women into men by not posting one true price for their new cars and always negotiating what they would pay for a trade-in. Even as cars became easier to drive in the 1920s and larger numbers of women drove, men continued to sell them, mostly to other men. Car salesmen recognized that women played a role in the purchase of new cars, and training literature frequently reminded salesmen to include wives in their presentations, but it also acknowledged that husbands did the actual buying of a new car and even more so, the selling of the old. Occasional campaigns to sell cars directly to women were invariably short-lived, and experiments with female car "salesmen" were similarly brief. In effect, the car sales lot became a battleground or playing field, a place where men locked horns in an attempt to dominate one another. It was hardly more welcoming to women than a pool hall or barbershop.

By focusing on the survival of horse-trading traditions in car dealing, behavioral history allows us to understand why we continue to engage in the unpleasant anachronism of bargaining for the price of a car. New cars could be sold like new electronic equipment, and used cars, like used houses, might be sold in a transaction completely divorced from the purchase of a new car. But the male traditions of horse trading created an expectation that the dealer would buy the customer's existing car. As high-priced representations of their owners, automobiles had meaning beyond mere transportation, and the process of acquiring them came to be infused with the same emotional significance that had marked horse trades. For the next hundred years, neither buyers nor sellers were able to extricate themselves from a system both claimed to hate. Market realities combined with psychological forces to keep them both in an arena where the masculine clank of arms drowned out the reasoned feminine position of one price to all, with returns cheerfully accepted.

NOTES

1. Judy Muller (abcnews.com), "Bar Codes Could Be Replaced by Electronics," *ABC News*, December 13, 2003.

2. Michael Royce, *Beat the Car Salesman* (Boca Raton, FL, 2002).

3. Eric Dregni and Miller Karl Hagstrom, *Ads That Put America on Wheels* (Osceola, WI, 1996), 78.

4. *Golden Book of the Wanamaker Stores* (Philadelphia, 1911).

5. Mira Wilkins, "When and Why Brand Names in Food and Drink?" in *Adding Value: Brands and Marketing in Food and Drink*, ed. Geoffrey Jones and Nicholas J. Morgan (London, 1994), 15–40.

6. Susan Strasser, *Satisfaction Guaranteed: The Making of the Mass Market* (New York, 1989); James D. Norris, "One Price Policy among Antebellum Country Stores," *Business History Review* 36, no. 4 (1962): 454–58.

7. George Fox, *Autobiography of George Fox*, chapter 8: "A Visit to Oliver Cromwell" (Grand Rapids, MI, n.d.), http://www.ccel.org/f/fox_g/autobio/cache/autobio.html3.

8. *Golden Book*, 109; Ralph M. Hower, *History of Macy's of New York, 1858–1919* (Cambridge, MA, 1946), 26–29.

9. William Leach, *Land of Desire: Merchants, Power, and the Rise of a New American Culture* (New York, 1993); Robert Hendrickson, *The Grand Emporiums: The Illustrated History of America's Great Department Stores* (New York, 1979), 35–37.

10. Barbara Babcock and Sara Laschever, *Women Don't Ask: Negotiation and the Gender Divide* (Princeton, NJ, 2003).

11. F. M. Ware, "How to Know the Horse You Buy," *Outing*, 1906, 505–508.

12. George Henry Hewit Oliphant, *The Law Concerning Horses, Racing, Wagers, and Gaming* (Philadelphia, 1847), xxvii.

13. Kevin M. Teeven, *A History of the Anglo-American Common Law of Contract* (New York, 1990), 140.

14. "Bargains in New Automobiles" (Display Advertisement), *New York Times*, 22 November 1908, 82.

15. "Automobile Topics of Interest," *New York Times*, 17 May 1903, 14.

16. "The Untold News" (Wanamaker Display Advertisement), *New York Times*, 7 December 1900, 4.

17. "The Ford Dealer Story," *Ford Dealer Magazine*, May–June 1953, 10–12.

18. Boris Emmet and John E. Jeuck, *Catalogues and Counters: A History of Sears, Roebuck and Company* (Chicago, 1950), 220–21.

19. "What Is Its Relative Value in U.S. Dollars?" in Economic History Services, economic history.net, http://www.eh.net/hmit/compare/, 2004.

20. David Q. Bowers, *Early American Car Advertisements* (New York, 1966).

21. James M. Rubenstein, *Making and Selling Cars: Innovation and Change in the U.S. Automobile Industry* (Baltimore, 2001); Congress, House, Subcommittee of the Committee on Interstate and Foreign Commerce, *Automobile Marketing Legislation*, 84th Cong. (6 July 1955, 11–18 April and 2 May 1956), 94–95.

22. Thomas A. Dicke, *Franchising in America: The Development of a Business Method, 1840–1980* (Chapel Hill, NC, 1992), 61–65.

23. William Leach, *Land of Desire: Merchants, Power, and the Rise of a New American Culture* (New York, 1993), 126–30.

24. Theodore H. Smith, *The Marketing of Used Automobiles* (Columbus, OH, 1941); Art Spinella et al., *America's Auto Dealer: The Master Merchandisers* (Van Nuys, CA, 1978), 31.

25. Walter J. Primeaux Jr., "The Effect of Consumer Knowledge and Bargaining Strength on Final Selling Price: A Case Study," *Journal of Business* 43 (1970): 419–26; Stanley C. Hollander, "Discount Retailing: An Examination of Some Divergences from the One-Price System in American Retailing," Ph.D. diss., Economics, University of Pennsylvania, 1954, 22–25.

26. Virginia Scharff, *Taking the Wheel: Women and the Coming of the Motor Age* (New York, 1991), 1–14.

27. Curt McConnell, *A Reliable Car and a Woman Who Knows It: The First Coast to Coast Auto Trips by Women, 1899–1916* (Jefferson, NC, 2000).

28. Thorstein Veblen, "Pecuniary Canons of Taste," in *The Theory of the Leisure Class*, chap. 6 (American Studies at the University of Virginia, 1899; http://xroads .virginia.edu/~HYPER/VEBLEN/chap06.html.

29. George Stephen, *The Adventures of a Gentleman in Search of a Horse* (Philadelphia, 1836), 14.

30. Deane C. Davis, "Nothing but the Truth," *Blair and Ketchum's Country Journal* (March 1979): 35.

31. John H. Eagal, "The Reminiscences of Mr. John H. Eagal, Sr.," Henry Ford Museum and Greenfield Village Research Center, Record Group 65, Box 17, July 1953, 4–5.

32. Smith, *Marketing of Used Automobiles*, 2.

33. "Automobiles: For Sale" (Display Advertisement), *New York Times*, 30 August 1903, 14.

34. "Automobiles. Challenge Sale!" (Display Advertisement), *New York Times*, 5 April 1904, 7.

Part III

Death and Mourning

7

American Death

Peter N. Stearns

Three points are clear about the reception of death in contemporary American society, in even a crude historical context. First, death is always a complex preoccupation for humankind, which means that many problems visible today are not necessarily new. But second, massive changes in death and death practices have occurred over the past century or century and a half (some debate here), and current society is unquestionably, if sometimes unwittingly, still adjusting. So, third: there are some problems and blind spots in contemporary approaches to death that are both untraditional and troubling. Behavioral history, exploring the second point but with an eye to the third, can explicitly help us understand where we are concerning death reception, why we are where we are, and whether there are important adjustments to consider.[1]

Points 2 and 3 used to add up to a ringing indictment of contemporary society for distancing itself from some of the traditional solaces concerning death, for turning into a destructively death-denying culture with real costs to the dying and to those around them.[2] Some of this indictment still holds, but we know a bit more now about some successful adaptations that followed the 20th-century watersheds concerning death. Some aspects of death are handled better than others in contemporary life, so that a blanket condemnation of contemporary death-as-taboo misses the mark. Previous historical work, from the 1960s, actually played some role in leading to partial reconsiderations, though not reversals, of the dominant contemporary approach. Behavioral history can and should now work in these complexities.

Contemporary death practices and experiences have been criticized from various angles, some of them contradictory (particularly, in this regard, a long campaign against excessive expense on funerals versus a belief that contemporaries have inadequate rituals and grief outlets). Almost always, there is at least passing juxtaposition to superior values and practices in the past—a judgment that accurately captures huge changes but sometimes overdoes the resulting contrast in the quality of encounters with death.

As against the blanket condemnation approach, two facets stand out for particular concern. Most dramatic, confirmed by a 2003 study, is the fear and isolation in which large numbers of Americans face their own death. Though understudied, especially since the classic formulations of Elisabeth Kübler-Ross of forty years ago, this is undoubtedly the most troubling feature of contemporary death, one that does contrast with premodern experience. The Institute of Medicine report, while calling for more research, notes explicitly that "a significant number of people experience needless suffering and distress at the end of life." Simple facts confirm: a vast majority of people wish to die at home but a vast majority do not do so. Forty percent of all dying individuals are isolated in intensive care for more than ten days. Despite modest improvements, discussed below, end-of-life care is "still a roulette wheel, with only slightly better odds now."[3]

But the receptivity for grief at the death of others, particularly grief that is unusually expressive or prolonged, comes next on this list. This can be closely associated with great tensions experienced on the deaths of children. This is a tragic encounter that more often than not splits a marriage because of the diffuse blame and unresolved grief, in contrast to the frequent tightening of family ties around a shared grief experience just a century or so ago. Victorian practices of a century and a half past also made extreme grief more manageable or easier to conceal, or both, than is true in the contemporary United States.[4]

Other aspects of contemporary death reactions, though different from those of either Victorian or more traditional society, seem, however, to work fairly well for most people. We're dealing with a differentiated experience, in which some adjustments to change, though considerable, have proved functional while other categories are badly served.

One final preliminary approach, analytically interesting though not central to a behavioral history, focuses on explanation of current patterns: historians of death, though not a huge breed, have generated one important debate over when the "contemporary" begins. Some note that nineteenth-century culture began to lose confidence in traditional death formulas, which themselves were not unchanging. Death began to become more unacceptable. Certainly, Victorians painfully accepted guilt whenever children died, even though the mortality rate at this point remained high. More elaborate grief and huge funeral monuments and fancy cemeteries denoted the new uncertainty. The relocation of cemeteries, away from residential areas, showed new fears (as well as new knowledge of disease transmission). So did the idea of a garden atmosphere and, above all, the growing practice of embalming, to make the dead look undead—a practice that continues today. Even the new idea of families reuniting in heaven can be seen as an essentially contemporary effort to sugarcoat death. But even if this first erosion of traditional beliefs and practices began to set the contemporary stage, the more strictly post-Victorian changes, discussed below, beginning with a dramatic shift in the incidence and causes of death itself, really shaped the scenery and the ensuing drama.

With this initial contemporary sketch, we can jump back to the massive transformation of death between about 1880 and the 1930s. Several facets relate, though with some independent causation and impact as well.[5]

First, young children stopped dying in large numbers, for the first time in human history. Between 1880 and 1920, in the United States and western Europe, infant mortality dropped from about 30 percent to under 10 percent, and the drop continued. Also for the first time ever historically, the average family no longer had to expect any child to die. Maternal mortality, which traditionally at some points claimed about 10 percent of all women who bore children, virtually disappeared as well. Following this, from the 1930s onward, new inoculations and medicines beat back most deaths from communicable diseases. Attention shifted to less tractable degenerative diseases, and by the same token the common experience of death began to be reserved for the elderly and those who cared for them. All this added up to a death "revolution."

At the same time, the locus of death shifted from home to hospital, and the professionals most associated with death became doctors and other medical personnel, not clergymen, who were now relegated to an ancillary role, at least until death finally occurred. Most people no longer saw death or handled dead bodies, which unquestionably made the whole process more removed, both literally and figuratively.

The shift to doctors, dedicated to fighting death, and the turn to increasingly impersonal (though more therapeutic) hospitals, changed the experience of dying and the prospect of death, and also altered the outlets for those attached to the dying. Older ideals of a good death in later age, ideally of a respiratory ailment that took a bit of time but did not impose incapacitating pain, allowed for farewells and for the settling of older disputes. But these ideals now faded from expectation, or at least from a normal prospect of realization. A gulf opened between the death most people wanted for themselves—sudden and unexpected—and the death that loved ones could prepare for.

Following on the heels of the new incidence of death, the new location, and the new management, traditional rituals and even emotions began to decline as well, or to come under new attack.[6] By the 1920s the visual symbols of mourning—dark clothing, crepe-decked windows, and prolonged periods of seclusion—receded steadily. Demands of work made it harder to take much time off for mourning, even for the well-to-do (compounded later when married women began to work outside the home), while the consumer ethic, finding relatively few market opportunities in grief, urged quick recovery in order to pursue life's material joys. Other changes, such as the increasing rate of cremation after World War II (though lower in the United States than in crowded Europe), pointed in the same direction, toward less ritual and open emotionality. Finally, grief itself was attacked, as part of the outdated self-indulgence of Victorianism. From the 1910s onward, popular articles and advice manuals in the United States blasted grief as a nuisance, an imposition on others, and, in any duration, a sign of mental illness that demanded psychological intervention. Psychiatric "grief work," correspondingly, was devoted to shortening the grief period and treating sufferers as patients. Etiquette manuals, which in the late 19th and early 20th centuries had focused on elaborate protocols for paying respects to grieving families, by the 1950s turned the tables: it was the grievers who now needed to be schooled in manners, for they risked bothering others.[7] The traditional emotional apparatus applied to death had, at least according to prescriptive guidelines, effectively been stood on its head.

A crucial subset of these changes—particularly the rise of hospitals but also the insistence on emotional restraint—involved the effort to remove children from much knowledge of death or participation in funerals. Euphemisms began to conceal the facts of death from children—a few schools even renounced the term "dyeing" for Easter eggs, lest children be disturbed—and possibly from many adults as well. People, like football quarterbacks, now passed, they did not die.

All these changes affected those around death (or now shielded from it) more obviously than they affected the dying, which may be one reason that subsequent adaptations focused more on the former. Death was still death, just less openly discussed, but the experience of deaths of others now seemed particularly problematic. Anticipation of the death of a loved one clearly changed when the act of dying moved out of the home, and the strictures on grief added to constraint. Indeed, the new emotional standards constituted the most striking reversal of 19th-century norms, which had emphasized the importance, even sanctity of grief—another reason that remedial attention focused on this area more than on dying itself. Reactions by others were further complicated by the fact that death became an occasional thing, not part of normal existence, even routine. But in fact, dying changed, too, especially given its new location among strangers and in a professional setting vowed to combat rather than to ease death. The likelihood of loneliness and confusion increased, all the more in that death was now most likely the result of degenerative disease that brought incapacities of its own. Many reports showed how medical personnel turned away from those who were irrevocably dying because they represented failure. Rigid hospital visiting hours (though relaxed a bit after the 1970s) affected imminent mourners, but even more those about to be mourned, who waited largely alone. But the new antideath culture affected more than the final days or months. The growing lack of familiarity with death, given its altered incidence and location and the discouragement from discussing the subject, made personal preparation more difficult. Many people seriously considered the process of dying only when it became unavoidable. The psychological challenge of death increased.[8]

These big changes, however, are not the whole story, or we really would be dealing with a systematic contemporary collapse rather than a selective one.

The funeral home, developing from the late 19th century onward, was the most important innovation in response to the revolution in death.[9] Here was recognition that death no longer occurred domestically, and that neither modern families nor modern legal requirements allowed bodies to be handled domestically, either. Here was acknowledgment, also, that people should be spared the sight of decay, as embalming served as the centerpiece of the undertaker's skill. But here, also, was a real outlet for rituals—albeit new ones—and grief. People visiting the body at the funeral home quickly established community. They could be assured that death was being handled properly, in a religious-like environment without, however, narrow denominational commitments. Funeral homes, indeed, carefully combined a sense of religious reverence with a domestic atmosphere. As

Gary Laderman notes in his masterful recent study, Americans become uncomfortable with the death of others primarily when there are no bodies for a funeral home farewell. Hence the strenuous contemporary efforts to bring bodies home from war; hence the dismay at the pulverizing effects of the 9/11 attacks. But for normal death, by contrast, funeral directors became expert in helping family members and friends discuss their grief, making the modern American funeral a genuine psychological solace.

From the standpoint of people affected by a death, a new version of the good death emerged. Acceptable death continued to assume occurrence at a reasonably advanced age. It also assumed initial death-fighting efforts, often including extensive, and expensive, hospitalization, urged on by loving relatives eager to delay grief and avoid the guilt that might come with anything less than an all-out commitment to sustaining life. Once this stage ended, a ceremony in which people could say farewell and comfort one another, but also a sanitized presentation that avoided a starker confrontation with the physical realities of death, seized center stage. Small wonder that critiques of the expense of contemporary funerals missed the mark, with little real impact on popular practice, save perhaps in the modest rise of cremations.[10] Indeed, for many family members a certain amount of expense became part of the expiation funeral homes could provide. And, as against the rise in cremation, American coffins have become not only more elaborate and costly, but also impervious to dirt, which can be interpreted as a further effort to deny death while indulging, one last time, in the national battle against filth and decay.[11]

But the contemporary good death, in its mixture of novel forms with many traditional emotions, was mainly beneficial for survivors. It did little to cushion the act or prospect of dying. To be sure, knowledge of funeral home comforts might help an individual pleasantly envisage reactions to his or her own death. The rise of death awareness by the 1970s added to this prospect, as an increasing number of individuals not only ordered funeral plots in advance, but also planned their own ceremonies, which allowed more individual expression and a greater personal connection to the good death scenario. But this recourse was limited, because most people sidestepped this level of advance acknowledgment and because, before dying outright, primary attention continued to rivet on medical efforts to combat death, not to attempts to ease the prospect of death for individuals directly involved. Indeed, one of the reasons for funeral home rituals, including embalming, derived from the limited contact family members were normally allowed with hospital patients, especially if in intensive care, and the distorted views of bodies that were being administered to before death.

Funeral homes were not, of course, the only innovation that responded to the new context of death. Even before experts began to urge greater openness toward death, Americans who faced unusual grief or the premature loss of a loved one tried to comfort one another. Building on the self-help support groups pioneered by Alcoholics Anonymous in the 1930s, Thanatos societies and other organizations sprang up during the 1950s. These were associations of strangers whose only bond was their shared emotion plus the recognition that society in general, often including members of one's own family, was not likely to prove very supportive. Parents whose children died, spouses who could not end their grief easily, populated these groups, though with varying benefits and while—deliberately—leaving the larger social climate untouched.

During the cultural experimentation of the 1960s, a variety of writers, including Kübler-Ross and Ivan Illich, encouraged a review of the initial, rather extreme, responses to contemporary death.[12] As a result, doctors became somewhat more open to thinking about the act of dying and its implications for medical practice. Many became more willing to be candid with terminally ill patients, exchanging their own sense of alienation and failure for a patient's improved capacity to prepare. Ordinary people, according to opinion polls, increased the frequency of their own thinking about death, or at least their willingness to admit such thoughts. New concern also applied to grief, offering some alternatives to the recourse to therapeutic grief work without, however, entirely dislodging this approach and its ongoing hostility to emotional intensity.[13]

The 1970s saw a revival of a kind of guidance that had been available in the 19th century and before: the advice book on mourning. Bookstores by the 1980s and 1990s usually had ten to fifteen titles in hand, by authors such as Harold Kushner and Stephen Levine.[14] Speaking against contemporary antideath culture, but with obvious sincerity and self-interest, these books urged that grief at death required a great deal of effort and a prolonged period of time. But the remedy was not tradition. The books also insisted that each individual must chart his or her own grief course, for community norms could not be revived and there was no one-size-fits-all.

Most impressive, because most directly addressing the limitations of the postrevolutionary death experience for the dying themselves, as well as for loved ones close by, was the hospice movement. Imported from Britain beginning in the 1970s, here was the most ambitious effort to provide a de-liberate alternative to maximum death-fighting through conventional doctors and hospitals. Hospices offered advice and facilities to allow indi-viduals to adjust to their fate, often with assistance in easing pain toward the greatest possible dignity in death. The same approach encouraged family members to attend the ailing individual, so that they too could re-capture the benefits of the traditional good death. Often, indeed, with hos-pice backing, death could occur in the home, precisely what most hospice patients professed to desire.

All of these adjustments were important, and the hospice movement was particularly significant—though the very need for so many innova-tions reflected the magnitude of the death revolution during the 20th cen-tury as a whole. Contemporary American death was not immobile. But, not surprisingly given the larger shifts, many of the remedies fell short for many people, particularly for the dying themselves.

We have noted one deficiency that followed quite directly from 20th-century experience and culture, and that was hard to remedy. When, for whatever reason, grief is unusually great, or when the combination of guilt and grief accrues in the death of a child or young adults—now unusual, statistically, but by the same token extremely hard to handle—the absence of ritual and predictable community support still take a toll. Despite some increased awareness of the problem of grief suppression and lack of symbolic outlets, the fact remains that contemporary grief that spills well beyond the funeral home and a brief adjustment period is very hard to accommodate. Most people manage, creating their own, fairly private markers of remembrance and recovery in a process now intriguingly indi-vidualized.[15] But some fall short, and the company of sharing strangers or therapists remains the best that contemporary America has to offer.

More troubling, if only because more common, are the loneliness and alienation of most dying people themselves, save those cut off swiftly. American culture, for all its adjustments, remains closed to much talk of death. Children, though less rigorously excluded from funerals than fifty years ago, know little of death. (Adults still worry far more about children and death than they need to, as unnecessary anxieties about the impact of 9/11 on largely oblivious children remote from the event revealed.) With little death experience until mid- to late adulthood, and few opportunities to explore the topic, it is small wonder that people enter later age with scant apparatus either to plan or to cope, despite some success since the 1970s in acknowledging one's thinking about death. Then, when they start to die, they are cut off from relevant social contacts—the dominant nursing home experience—or they encounter extended medical care from doctors still reluctant to shift from curative to palliative efforts lest they seem to surrender.

While hospital authorities have become more aware of the need to help handle the dying process, the steady improvement of medical technologies, and the growing concern about lawsuits for malpractice, have pushed in the opposite direction. The dying lack control, in other words, of their own death process, which takes place often against their own repeatedly, if futilely, expressed wishes to prefer dignity over prolongation. The hospice movement, designed to redress this problem, has accomplished much, but its impact has been limited. Only 19 to 25 percent of dying Americans have any contact with a hospice, and even this minority figure is misleading for contacts often occur too late to do much good, delayed until the final few days by the insistence of well-meaning relatives and doctors that death-fighting should continue well beyond any probability of success. Contact for minority groups is particularly limited. Concern about possible Medicare fraud has further impeded access to the hospice alternative. And the story does not end here: 75 percent of all Americans are unaware that hospices allow home care. Eighty percent say they know that predeath stipulations, about the kind of care desired, are vital, but almost no one follows through (and those who do often find their instructions ignored).[16]

It is impossible to avoid the conclusion that we know how to improve the experience of dying but remain inhibited by contemporary culture from putting our knowledge to more than limited effect. Loving relatives and medical professionals contribute, no doubt, but what is particularly striking is the gap between admitted knowledge and actual preparation on the part of the ultimate victims themselves. Specific communication gaps also contribute, but the lack of opportunity to explore death in advance lies at the core of the dilemma.[17]

Small wonder, then, that the dying most frequently despair over the context that adds to whatever anxieties naturally attend death. Their most common goals—"relationships and belonging," "having control," and "being human"—simply do not normally meet much fulfillment as contemporary death actually occurs.

The continuities from the contemporary transformation of death, whether they reflect the standard location of death, the personnel involved in overseeing it, or the emotional experience that prepares for the final act, are compounded by two characteristics of those who most commonly die. They are old, and they are usually severely ill—both qualities that reduce voice and bargaining power and leave the way open to well-intentioned loved ones, eager to express their caring but also to delay grief and guilt, and to the death-fighting apparatus of the professionals still most involved with death. A significant, if seldom broadcast problem remains, and behavioral history shows how it has been determined by recent changes in experience and culture that are not fully matched by subsequent adjustments. Extreme claims that death is taboo in contemporary society are off the mark—for some accommodations have proved extremely constructive—but it remains true that, for many in contemporary society, death is harder than it once was. Individual exceptions aside, many contemporary Americans no longer know how to die well, or help others die well; or, at the least, they face severe barriers in putting their knowledge into practice.

Applying the behavioral history approach to issues in contemporary American death and grief furthers the identification of some deficiencies noted, admittedly, in purely presentist research. Indeed, the focus on the loneliness and confusion of many deathbed situations begins with current findings and then works backward to the historical context. The historical perspective, nevertheless, contributes in several ways. First, it allows a fuller delineation of the causes of the problems with contemporary death. It highlights as well the deep roots of these problems in the death revolution of a century past; it will be no easy task to effect improvements because the contemporary approach responded to an interlocking set of fundamental shifts in the death experience. Realizing that a number of successful adjustments accompanied these shifts, or added in later as certain drawbacks became apparent, provides more than a glimmer of hope; there is no barrier between contemporary hesitancy and useful innovation. But the same adjustments remind us that it is the grief stricken, rather than the dying, who have seized center stage in undoing the worst excesses of the death revolution. Elements of a good death have been revived, but save for a minority in the hospice, the dying have been pushed to the sidelines.

Behavioral historical analysis suggests, then, a clear set of problems that merits attention. It provides richer context in which individuals can consider their own approaches to death—particularly, their own death—in a situation that has become unprecedentedly individualized. No clear prescriptions result, for on this as other topics behavioral history improves understanding without offering exclusive remedial formulas. If loneliness and confusion are likely deathbed companions, fueled by the contemporary relocation and redefinitions of death, it is possible to prepare. Available legal provisions about the kind of death one seeks provide one kind of recourse that might be more widely recommended and discussed—for example, in disallowing heroic life maintenance at the cost of rationality and dignity alike. Law aside, some candid discussion with family members about desired scenarios could directly address some of the changes that otherwise deteriorate the experience of dying. Greater knowledge of death's recent history is an essential starting point for individuals themselves and for renewed discussions about best practices in key institutions such as hospitals.

Without greater understanding, things may get worse, if I may add a bit of forecasting to behavioral history. In about a decade, in societies with age structures like that of the United States, more death will begin to occur, indeed a lot more, as the baby boomers begin to meet their actuarial grim reaper. A return to more death by disease, widely though less definitively forecast as well, would also challenge contemporary death expectations. It will be interesting to see if the inevitable escalation of death generates additional adjustments to the contemporary death context, or simply more suffering amid the rawest disjunctures that remain from a century of change in virtually all aspects of the final human experience.

NOTES

1. Generalizations about death and reactions to death must always be qualified, whether for the present or past. Individuals vary, and subcultures vary, as the next essay by Suzanne Smith makes clear. With a decline in overall community norms and rituals, variations and therefore degrees of adjustment or suffering have probably increased. But Robert Wells's study of the 19th century shows variations in acceptance of earlier norms (in this case, high grief norms) as well. See Robert Wells, *Facing the "King of Terrors": Death and Society in an American Community, 1750–1990* (Cambridge, MA, 1999).

2. Phillippe Ariès, *Western Attitudes toward Death* (Baltimore, 1974); David Stannard, *Puritan Way of Death* (New York, 1991).

3. Elisabeth Kübler-Ross et al., *Death: The Final Stage of Growth* (New York, 1986); David Stannard, *Death in America* (New York, 2003).

4. Paul Rosenblatt, *Bitter, Bitter Tears* (Minneapolis, 1983); Peter N. Stearns, *American Cool: Constructing a Contemporary Emotional Style* (New York, 1994).

5. Some attacks on contemporary superficiality toward death point more to wider changes in the 20th century, notably more regimented work routines for the

middle class, including women, and especially the feel-good aspects of consumerism. These claims can be overly general, as we will see, because most people manage some aspects of death fairly well; but in some ways, as we will also see, they complement the results of the shifts in death itself.

6. Stearns, *American Cool.*

7. Amy Vanderbilt, *The New Complete Book of Etiquette* (New York, 1954).

8. Contemporary apprehension about death has impacts that go beyond personal experience but that merit additional attention and exploration. American performance in contemporary wars has been strongly shaped by revulsions against deaths of Americans and a reluctance to experience resultant grief. The extent of shock at 9/11 was also intensified by dismay at death and resentment at the need to shoulder so much grief—as a number of foreign observers, more accustomed to mass death, have pointed out.

9. Jessica Mitford, *The American Way of Death* (New York, 1963).

10. Gary Laderman, *Rest in Peace: Cultural History of Death and the Funeral Home in Twentieth-Century America* (New York, 2003). On ethnic adoption of funeral homes (while preserving some other customs), see Richard Meyer, ed., *Ethnicity and the American Cemetery* (Bowling Green, Ohio, 1993).

11. Christie Davies, "Dirt, Death, Decay and Dissolution: American Denial and British Avoidance," in Glennys Howarths and Peter Jupp, eds., *Contemporary Issues in the Sociology of Death, Dying and Disposal* (New York, 1996)

12. Kübler-Ross, *Death;* Ivan Illich, *Medical Nemesis: The Expropriation of Health* (New York, 1999). Darwin Sawyer, "Public Attitudes toward Life and Death," *Public Opinion Quarterly* 46 (1982): 521–33.

13. Donna Dickenson and Malcolm Johnson, eds., *Death, Dying and Bereavement* (London, 1993); see also an excellent review of post-1960s developments, John W. Riley Jr., "Dying and the Meanings of Death," *Annual Review of Sociology* 9 (1983): 191–216; Margaret Stroebe et al., "Broken Hearts in Broken Bonds," *American Psychologist* 47 (1992): 1205–12; Cas Wouters, "Changing Regimes of Power and Emotion at the End of Life," *Netherlands Journal of Sociology* 26 (1990): 151–55.

14. Harold Kushner, *When Bad Things Happen to Good People* (New York, 1981, 2002); Stephen and Andrea Levine, *Who Dies?* (New York, 1982).

15. Katherine Ashenburg, *The Mourner's Dance: What We Do When People Die* (New York, 2002); this book also offers a larger discussion of contrasts between traditional and modern death rituals, without excessive editorial lamentation.

16. "Natural Hospice and Palliative Care Upgrading," *NHPCO Facts and Figures* (Alexandria, VA, 2003).

17. Stroebe et al., "Broken Hearts."

8

Laid Out in "Big Mama's Kitchen"
African Americans and the Personalized Theme Funeral

Suzanne E. Smith

The personalized theme funeral, a new trend in the funeral industry, has gained popularity and considerable press coverage in the past few years. The concept is relatively simple: instead of the casket being laid out rather austerely in a funeral home visitation room, it is displayed against a staged backdrop that has a specific theme that evokes the personality or hobbies of the deceased. For example, if the deceased person had been an avid fisherman, the casket would be set next to a faux fishing pond with a tackle box, fishing reels, and a "Gone Fishing" sign added as props nearby. Another option is the sports motif, in which a basketball hoop, football, or a favorite golf bag and putting green surround the casket. Some themes include special effects such as the barbecue motif in which a grill is packed with dry ice to simulate barbeque smoke and microwaved food is set out to add the aroma of a grilled feast. A movie buff might also be memorialized in a movie theater set with fresh popcorn handed out to mourners. One of the most popular theme funerals, created by Perpetua, Inc., a leading company in the personalized funeral market, is "Big Mama's Kitchen." In "Big Mama's Kitchen," the casket is laid out in a kitchen set, which includes familiar appliances, food props such as fried chicken, a loaf of Wonder bread, and fresh-baked goods served to the mourners.[1]

The popularity of "Big Mama's Kitchen" attests to the appeal of personalized funerals specifically with African American consumers. The product's name, "Big Mama's Kitchen," evokes a common nickname and stereotype of the African American matriarch in a family, "Big Mama," who appears regularly in African American folk life and contemporary

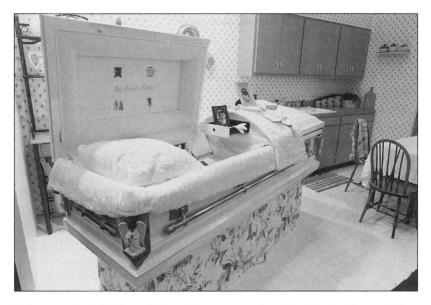

"Big Mama's Kitchen" set, designed by Perpetua, Inc. (Reprinted with permission
of The Press of Atlantic City)

popular culture.[2] Slivy Edmonds Cotton, the founder of Perpetua, Inc.,
and herself an African American, has been interviewed about her objec-
tives for marketing personalized theme funerals and has commented that
her own paternal grandmother "seemed always to be over a stove or at a
cutting board . . . and 'Big Mama,' as everyone called her, was never unhappy about that and died a happy woman."[3] Cotton has also remarked
that theme funerals assist the "tongue-tied" mourner: "When they come
into these sets they immediately have something to say to the family. They
say 'Oh my goodness, this is just like him.'"[4] In general, Cotton has argued
that the personalized theme funeral buys "into the idea that funerals
should be a meaningful experience reflective of the person's life . . . [and
help mourners] feel the person is really there."[5]

The emergence of the personalized theme funeral offers a rich opportunity for analysis for the cultural and behavioral historian. What does this
phenomenon of a Hollywood-style "staging" of a funeral reveal about current behavioral responses to grief and mourning? In some of the press
coverage about these funerals, journalists have noted that it is just another
manifestation of the baby boom generation's need to distance itself from

difficult emotions vis-à-vis conspicuous consumption.[6] For some, the personalized theme funeral can be dismissed as just another example of the
capitalistic excesses of the funeral industry. In other words, "Big Mama's
Kitchen" and the other themed funeral sets are just new fodder to support
Jessica Mitford's argument in her landmark study, *The American Way of
Death,* first published in 1963 and then revised and updated posthumously
in 1998. In Mitford's muckraking book, she contended that the funeral industry exists to profit quite ruthlessly from grief-stricken mourners,
whom it convinces to purchase needless, kitschy products as a means to
cope with loss. Certainly, the personalized theme funeral can be critiqued
quite easily on these grounds.[7]

Yet, recently, Mitford's arguments have been challenged as too reduc-
tive. In his book, *Rest in Peace: A Cultural History of Death and the Funeral
Home in Twentieth-Century America,* historian Gary Laderman questions
Mitford's central claims about the funeral industry as *only* capitalistic exploitation at its worst. Laderman writes, "Contrary to the accusations lev-
eled by Mitford and others, there is more to the business of death than
simply economics—the emotional, psychological, religious, and cultural
dimensions of disposal must also be taken into historical account when
investigating American ways of death."[8] Given Laderman's argument for a
more multifaceted approach to studying American death rituals, the personalized theme funeral demands a more nuanced historical analysis.

Behavioral history provides a meaningful way to understand the new
cultural phenomenon of the personalized theme funeral. The contemporary trend of transforming funeral visitations into staged theater-style
productions—and attempting to redefine the grief process as a result—
needs to be contextualized in relation to its historical antecedents. Tracing
the history of American funeral rituals offers insight into the current popularity of the personalized theme funeral. For the purposes of this chapter,
I focus my analysis on the appeal of the personalized theme funeral within
African American communities. Funeral rituals unique to African American life, whose history can be connected to African and early African
American slave culture, help explain the particular appeal of staged funerals specifically with African American consumers. I argue, therefore, that
exploring the historical roots of the personalized theme funeral illustrates
the continuity, rather than discontinuity, of African American grief rituals
over time. Moreover, the impulse to celebrate, rather than mourn, a person's life during a funeral is a common characteristic of many American
funerals but is especially popular among African Americans.

In the first half of this chapter, I examine the history of early African American funeral traditions. These premodern rituals act as a baseline from which later, more commercial, funeral and burial rituals will develop in the late 19th century. Most notably, premodern funerals were conducted in the private sphere of the home, and burial usually took place on family-owned property. The rise of the funeral industry in the 19th century dramatically changed the death experience in America and ultimately defines what can be called the modern funeral. In the second half of the chapter I will show how the modern funeral, which becomes most pervasive in the 20th century, moved death and mourning out of the private sphere of the home and into the public sphere of the commercial marketplace. In some respects, therefore, the invention of the personalized theme funeral in the 21st century might aptly be described as the postmodern funeral, as it reinvents some of the traditions of the modern funeral yet also reconnects in some direct ways with original premodern funeral rituals. To conclude, I discuss why sets such as "Big Mama's Kitchen" have such appeal in African American communities in terms of how they reflect specific communal needs as well as celebrate the individual personalities of the deceased.

Early African American Death Rituals: The Premodern Funeral

Early African American funeral customs reflected the influences of both West African funeral rituals that were retained in the New World and of life under enslavement. In West African cosmology, the relationship of the deceased to the living was a dynamic one in which the spirit of the departed had the ability to interact with the living long after burial had occurred. Research on the ancient Kongo civilization has revealed that the Bakongo peoples saw the world as divided into two regions: the known realm of the living and the realm of the dead, which exists underneath the world of the living—almost as a mirror image or as a world upside down from the living realm. As historian Elizabeth Fenn writes, "The two worlds are connected by water, and the Bakongo believe that gleaming ancestral spirits can be seen in the flash of the sun's rays off of oceans, lakes, and streams."[9]

The belief that the spirits of the deceased could actively engage with the living—for good or evil—profoundly influenced Kongo and early African American funeral practices. As Albert J. Raboteau has noted,

Improper or incomplete funeral rites can interfere with or delay the entrance of the deceased into the spiritual world and may cause his soul to linger about, as a restless or malevolent ghost. Funeral ceremonies are long, complex, and expensive, but it would be a great disgrace for a family not to observe proper rites, even if they must go into debt to do so.[10]

The rituals of Kongo and early African American funerals illustrate how mourners allayed these fears of improper burial through symbolic acts that sought to free the deceased spirit from the earthly realm. Most notably, mourners decorated gravesites with the last objects the deceased touched or with objects the deceased particularly cherished. In the Kongo, mourners placed plates, cups, or drinking glasses on the burial site, as it was believed that the spirit of the dead person was still present in these objects.[11]

This ritual continued in North America as enslaved African Americans maintained the belief that the last-used objects of the dead were embodied with the spirit of the deceased and, moreover, that the objects might be useful to the deceased in the spirit world. During the colonial period, African Americans who had recently been enslaved and had survived the Middle Passage were especially preoccupied with a proper burial, as it was believed that if these African rituals were honored, the deceased's spirit would return to Africa. Evidence of the endurance and meaning of these rituals was discovered into the 20th century. In 1939, as a part of the Georgia Writer's Project, African Americans in Brownsville, Georgia, were interviewed about the practice of leaving possessions on a loved one's grave. Although the interviewers transcribed dialect in a racist style, its essence reveals that this ritual was commonplace. One woman commented, "Dis wuz a common ting wen I wuz young. Dey use tuh put duh tings a pusson use las on duh grabe. Dis wuz suppose tuh satisfy duh spirit an keep it frum followin yuh back tuh duh house."[12] It was also common both in West African and early African American funeral traditions to leave food or wine at the grave for the deceased to enjoy.

The position and condition of the items left on the gravesite were also significant. Grave decorations were often inverted, which was a symbolic gesture in the Kongo tradition that signified how the spirit world was upside down or a mirror of the lived world.[13] As Robert Farris Thompson has described, "Indeed, the verb 'to be upside down' in Ki-Kongo also means 'to die.' Moreover, inversion signifies perdurance, a visual pun on the superior strength of the ancestors, for the root of *bikinda*, 'to be upside down, to be in the realm of the ancestors, to die' is *kinda,* 'to be strong,' 'because those who are upside down are strongest.'"[14] Another important burial ritual involved breaking or damaging the objects left on the grave. In an 1891 article titled, "Fetishism in the Congo," E. J. Glave observed that the "crockery, empty bottles, and old cooking pots," left on Kongo graves were "rendered useless by being cracked or perforated with holes."[15] Unaware of the spiritual significance of the damaged objects, Glave speculated that mourners damaged these items to prevent them from being stolen.

Glave's research on these Kongo rituals quickly caught the attention of American folklorists, who had observed similar practices in the American South. H. Carrington Bolton wrote to *The Journal of American Folklore* in response to Glave's article. Bolton commented on how Glave's observations illuminated his visit to a cemetery for "poorer negroes" in Columbia, South Carolina, that same year where he witnessed "graves decorated with a variety of objects, sometimes arranged with careful symmetry" and included "crockery of every description, glass bottles, and nondescript bric-a-brac of a cheap sort—all more or less broken and useless."[16] A subsequent issue of the same journal included yet another confirmation of this practice when Ernest Ingersoll wrote in, explaining that he had also visited these South Carolina burial sites ten years earlier in 1881 and observed similar objects. Ingersoll's description of the gravesites was the most vivid:

> When a negro dies, some article or utensil, or more than one, is thrown upon his grave; moreover it is broken. . . . Nearly every grave has bordering or thrown upon it a few bleached sea shells. . . . [m]ingled with these is a most curious collection of broken crockery and glassware. On the large graves are laid broken pitchers, soap-dishes, lamp chimneys, tureens, coffee-cups, sirup jars, all sorts of ornamental vases, cigar boxes, gun-locks, tomato cans, teapots, flower-pots, bits of stucco, plaster images, pieces of carved stone-work from one of the public buildings destroyed during the war, glass lamps and tumblers in great number, and forty other kitchen articles. Chief of these, however, are large water pitchers; very few graves lack them.[17]

Ingersoll's level of detail confirms the astonishing array of items left on African American gravesites by the mid- to late 19th century. Subsequent research on these objects has revealed that—contrary to Glave's early

Etching of a Congo gravesite. (From *Century Magazine* 41, no. 6 (April 1891): 827)

claim that the objects were broken to prevent theft—the damage was believed to free the deceased's spirit from the earthly objects and facilitate a transition to the spiritual realm.[18]

Enslavement also shaped African American funeral rituals quite dramatically from the colonial to the antebellum period. As previously noted, African slaves in the New World believed that death would return their souls to Africa. Later, as more enslaved African Americans converted to Christianity—especially after the First Great Awakening—death and the afterlife symbolized freedom from bondage and spiritual release. In terms of specific funeral rituals, enslaved African Americans were quite restricted in their ability to properly honor the dead. In most cases, the initial burial took place at night—often in what was known as the hush harbors, which was an area near the slave quarters that was usually surrounded by trees and offered slaves private sanctuary at night to gather and mourn. The more official funeral service or sermon often happened much later, sometimes weeks or months after the burial. The delay of the second service occurred if clergy or additional family members were not available at the time of the burial. Until the funeral sermon was preached, the family did not have peace of mind that the deceased's spirit was free. By the mid-19th century and especially after Nat Turner's rebellion in 1831, slave masters increasingly monitored slave funerals out of fear that these late night ceremonies might offer a means to plan slave insurrections.[19]

The traditions of the antebellum slave funeral reflected both the unique style of the African American funeral and similarities to general trends in death rituals in 19th-century America. Funeral practices changed fairly dramatically over the course of the 19th century. At the beginning of the century, the death experience in the United States was still primarily a rural and private phenomenon. By the end of the century, the death experience was dominantly an urban and a public life passage. In the rural funeral of the early 19th century, death would often take place in the home, and the funeral proceedings reflected the premodern model. Family, friends, and perhaps the local physician or a member of the clergy gathered around the bedside of the dying person. When death finally occurred, close relatives of the deceased prepared the body for burial, which facilitated the grief process and reaffirmed family relations during a time of loss.

The preparation of the dead body, therefore, required tasks that both upheld the dignity of the deceased while also aiding the mourning process of those left behind. The first step in the treatment of the corpse was to "lay out" the body. Survivors, usually the women of the household, ritually washed and dressed the corpse in a shroud or "winding sheet" and then placed it in a coffin. To preserve the corpse in warmer weather, survivors often put a large block of ice in a tub underneath the coffin. The body of the deceased might be in the home for one to three days and was rarely, if ever, left alone. Family members kept the deceased in the front room or parlor, which was often draped in black crepe, with furniture removed and mirrors covered.[20]

When it was time for the corpse to be moved to the place of burial, mourners congregated in the home of the deceased and said prayers over the body before the funeral procession commenced. Depending on the economic status of the family, mourners then moved to a meetinghouse or church for a more formal funeral service. After the service, the family transported the body to the place of burial, which—in the early 19th century—was often the grounds of the family farm. In rural 19th-century America, burial was a very intimate ritual in which survivors of the deceased interacted closely with the dead.

The Rise of the Modern Funeral

By the mid- to late 19th century, industrialization and urbanization transformed the death and funeral experience from a private, rural phenomenon into a more commercial and public event. Several key aspects of the death experience changed dramatically by the mid-19th century, which led to the formation of the funeral industry and a complete transformation of the ways in which Americans treated their dead. As many scholars who study American death practices have noted, the use of embalming to preserve the corpse legitimized the funeral industry as it created a specialized skill that funeral directors could market. Moreover, the medical profession began to have more authority over the death experience by the turn of century as most deaths occurred in hospitals rather than in one's own home. Finally, the development of the funeral chapel or home, by the 1920s, solidified what would become the modern funeral of the 20th century. Examining the history of embalming, the medicalization of death, and the invention of the funeral home can help explain the current appeal of the postmodern personalized theme funeral.[21]

Embalming, a practice that can be traced back to ancient Egypt, first became prevalent in the United States during the Civil War. The Civil War marks perhaps the most dramatic turning point in Americans' relationship to the death experience. The sheer volume of deaths that occurred during the Civil War—over 600,000—completely altered Americans' perceptions of death and burial and resulted in the development of the funeral industry. Wartime conditions challenged deeply held beliefs about what constituted a dignified and spiritually meaningful burial. In general, soldiers who died in battle were buried quickly, often in makeshift graves near the site of combat. As the war progressed and the death tolls rose, more families—especially of Union soldiers—wanted the bodies of their dead returned home for proper burial. Transporting a dead soldier back home was logistically challenging, especially in the summer months when decomposition occurred more quickly.[22]

As a result of these difficulties, embalming became popular as a means to preserve the corpse until it could be shipped home for proper burial. The war not only introduced the public to the usefulness of embalming, but it also helped to determine which professionals would be associated with it in the future. Until the outbreak of the Civil War, embalming was used only for the preservation of cadavers for dissection in medical schools. As the war dragged on, some enterprising undertakers began to offer their services to families who wanted to transport a corpse across the country. Embalming was an expensive procedure that quickly became a lucrative business and near the end of the war, the federal government sanctioned embalming as the most acceptable form of preservation. The

Civil War conflict completely legitimized embalming and was critical to the formation of the funeral industry.[23]

During the war, Washington, D.C., became a popular training ground for embalmers. By 1863, at least four "embalmers of the dead" listed their services in the Washington directory. Some embalmers moved even closer to the front lines and distributed advertisements that promoted their efforts to preserve the "honored dead." At this time, the first African American embalmer also appears in historical documents. W. R. Cornelius, a successful white embalmer, kept a journal of his experiences and described with admiration his assistant, a man he refers to as Prince Greer. Cornelius wrote, "I undertook embalming myself with a colored assistant named Prince Greer, who appeared to enjoy embalming so much that he became himself an expert, kept on at work embalming through the balance of the war, and was very successful." Cornelius continued that Greer could "raise an artery as quickly as anyone, and was always careful," and needed Cornelius's guidance only when there was "a critical case," indicating that he viewed Greer not simply as a servant but as a valued and well-trained colleague.[24]

While embalming became more common throughout the war, it became institutionalized after the assassination and funeral of Abraham Lincoln. The new wonders of embalming allowed Lincoln's corpse to be transported across the country quite soon after his death. Starting in Washington, D.C., Lincoln's funeral journey lasted a full twenty days, with its final destination in Springfield, Illinois. Throughout this extended funeral cortege, American citizens—both black and white—viewed Lincoln's corpse in a way that was exceptional in terms of proximity. By the time the body finally arrived in Springfield, the embalmer who had been escorting the corpse across the country was having a difficult time maintaining its integrity. Nevertheless, this famous journey solidified in the public's mind the importance of embalming as a means to facilitate the grieving process.[25]

Consequently, from 1865 on, the American funeral industry grew significantly, and a new era began in which death became another commodity in a growing industrial society. As the death experience was increasingly influenced by the demands of a more consumer-oriented market, the funeral industry diversified to offer a wider range of goods and services to the American public. The coffin—now "casket"—industry began to produce a large selection of increasingly elaborate designs. Undertakers offered more funeral products for grieving families to purchase, including

burial robes and "mourning cards" that were given as a memento to grieving friends and relatives. These types of ancillary funeral merchandise illustrate how, by the late 19th century, the death experience was becoming
an increasingly commercial and public enterprise.[26]

The post–Civil War period also witnessed the growth of burial societies
within African American communities, which served individuals and families who could not afford all of the accouterments of the modern funeral.
Members of these societies contributed money into a central fund that
would then help pay for the costs of embalming and other funeral services
when a member passed away. Eventually, many African American funeral
directors founded burial societies of their own as a means to generate
business. Over time, burial societies were questioned as a business practice. Opponents believed that they simply capitalized on people's fears of
dying without a proper funeral, while proponents felt that they created a
sense of communal responsibility to bury the dead respectably. On either
side of this debate, the existence of burial societies proved how successful
the funeral industry had become at selling the idea of a dignified burial to
African Americans with all of the requisite products and services.[27]

The cultural shift to a more commercial, market-driven, funeral coincided historically with a larger trend to an increasingly medical, rather
than familial, death experience. By the turn of the century, hospitals increasingly became the place in which most people died, as opposed to
dying at home in one's own bed. This trend was directly connected to the
rising professionalization of doctors, who were beginning to see patients
most frequently in a clinical setting rather than via house calls. Moreover,
this trend corresponded to the proliferation of hospitals. Historian
Thomas Schlereth has documented remarkable statistics about the growth
of hospitals between the 1870s and 1920s. He writes that during this time
period, "the American hospital changed in size and clientele. An 1873 survey counted 178 hospitals, about 50 of which were institutions for the
mentally ill. A 1923 tabulation listed 6,830, or an increase of about 3,800
percent."[28] As a result of this remarkable growth, doctors and hospitals
began to control the death experience and to fundamentally alter societal
attitudes about death itself. As Gary Laderman describes,

> A new perspective on death began to take hold in the United States: Life
> must be sustained at all costs, with death viewed as a devastating defeat. . . .
> The cultural implications of this environmental shift from death in the
> home to death in the hospital were profound, and contributed to the literal

displacement of the dead from the everyday social worlds of the living. Dying in the isolated space of the hospital room institutionalized the experience as a passage requiring scientific, and increasingly technological intervention, rather than prayers and the presence of community.[29]

This new clinical approach depersonalized the death experience and limited family members' ability to tend to the dying person or to perceive death as a natural process.

The rise in hospitals paralleled an equally important trend in the funeral industry: the creation of the funeral home or chapel. Until the 1920s, most funeral directors worked out of a small office and went to the home of the deceased to embalm the body. Most families at the turn of the century continued to prefer to have their loved one laid out in the family's own parlor for visitation before the funeral ceremony and burial. By the 1910s and 1920s, the funeral home began to take over as the location for all phases of the funeral arrangements. The embalming, viewing of the casket, and often the funeral ceremony itself were performed at the funeral director's business establishment. The development of the funeral home was related to the historical evolution of the undertaker, who originally was a cabinet maker who simply sold coffins and organized funeral processions, into a funeral director, who embalmed corpses, offered grief counseling to mourners, and coordinated every aspect of the funeral experience. As Robert Habenstein and William Lamers describe in *The History of American Funeral Directing*, the rise of the modern funeral home involved "the consolidation of . . . three functional areas, the clinic [for embalming], the home [for visitation], and the chapel [for religious services], into a single operational unit."[30]

The growing popularity of the modern funeral home reflected much larger changes in Americans' relationship to death and mourning practices. For the funeral directors, consolidating all phases of the funeral into one building was more efficient in terms of productivity and, therefore, more profitable from a business perspective. For grieving relatives, the funeral parlor allowed family members to remove the often-ominous presence of the deceased from the home, which alleviated some of the intensity of the mourning process. In Victorian America, the parlor was the site of formal ceremony in the home where guests were welcomed and weddings and funerals usually took place. As historian James J. Farrell explains, "In the privatization of the home that the proliferation of rooms and functions implied, the parlor represented the last public space in a private home." By the 1920s, however, the formal parlor in the home was becoming more obsolete—especially as a site for life passage events.[31]

Part of this shift to the funeral parlor reflected an impulse to segregate death from the home, which would place more clear parameters around the grieving process. In the architectural world, a clear movement arose to completely remove any associations with death from the home. As Farrell has noted, "Edward Bok, the editor of *Ladies' Home Journal,* stipulated that home designs for the journal never show a 'parlor.' Instead, he preferred that the room be called the 'living room.'"[32] Along with this tendency to emphasize "living" rather than death in home design, the funeral itself was getting a facelift as a movement arose to replace the dreary black drapes and other symbols of mourning with bright flower arrangements that were more uplifting. In 1917, *The Literary Digest* published an article titled "The Unseemliness of Funerals," which included comments from a mourner, who described this cultural shift to a less somber funeral quite vividly:

> There should be no memories of my mother but bright ones. The evening that my mother died her body was taken to the chapel. There was no crape [*sic*] on the door. There was no weeping; there were no black dresses; and except for an occasional catch in the voice now and then, my sister and my aunts and uncles went right on with life in such a way that a stranger could never have guessed. . . . [After the funeral] I returned home to the house and looked around it, and it was still as bright with my mother's spirit as it was before. Then we all went out to work again.[33]

Several distinct characteristics, therefore, define the modern funeral, including: the occurrence of death usually in a hospital rather than a home setting; a preference for embalming as a means to preserve the corpse for viewing; and a shift from holding any funeral rituals such as the viewing or the ceremony from the home to the funeral parlor. These changes reflect a societal desire to limit grief to a more constricted time and a place that is clearly distinct from the home and family. Understanding the contours of the modern funeral sets the stage now to turn to the phenomenon of the personalized theme funeral and to explore the appeal of its postmodern style.

Personalized Theme Funerals:
The Appeal of the Postmodern Funeral

At first glance, the idea of surrounding the deceased's casket with a theater-style set that evokes his or her personality or hobbies appears to be a
rather garish way to honor the memory of a loved one. It is a phenomenon that can be too easily disparaged as a showy and overly packaged way
to divert mourners from the realities of death and grief. Yet, to quickly
discount this funeral ritual as kitsch that is counterproductive to the
mourning process inhibits one's ability to see the personalized theme funeral as the product of larger historical trends in American, and specifically African American, death practices. In important respects, the personalized theme funeral can be seen as postmodern as it both revises features of the modern funeral and reconnects with certain premodern
rituals.

In terms of its relationship to premodern rituals, it is important to return to the West African and early African American burial rite of leaving
the cherished objects of the deceased on the gravesite. In her article "Honoring the Ancestors: Kongo-American Graves in the American South," historian Elizabeth A. Fenn recounts both the West African roots of this tradition and its contemporary manifestations in the American South. Most
notably, she describes how these premodern burial rituals continued to
influence the style of African American burials into the late 20th century.
In her research in the mid-1980s, Fenn located African American graves
that were still covered with items such as ceramics, glassware, guitars, and
other personal belongings, some of which were as large as bed frames. She
also observed objects that appeared to honor the trade or profession of the
deceased. Mourners decorated one grave of a Fort Bragg mechanic with a
shiny car wheel with two wrenches welded to it. Another contemporary
African American grave in New Orleans was covered with a kettle, metal
grillwork, and a basketball hoop.[34]

These objects indicate the endurance of the idea, within certain African
American communities, that decorating the grave with these artifacts both
honors the memory of the deceased and facilitates the grieving process for
those left behind. It managed to survive despite the larger changes in funeral practices and may well have been essential to making these changes
acceptable. The personalized theme funeral, therefore, stands in direct relation to these abiding burial rituals. Whether it is the sports motif that in-

Wheel and wrenches on a mechanic's grave in Cumberland County, North Carolina. (Photo courtesy of Elizabeth Fenn)

cludes props such as basketball hoops, footballs, or golf equipment or the barbeque theme that might feature a faux grill and picnic table, the personalized theme funeral reproduces the same symbolic gestures of early premodern African American funerals. At the heart of these rituals lies the belief that properly acknowledging the loss of a loved one involves fetishizing material objects from the deceased's life. The personalized theme funeral involves, of course, an obvious irony in that the featured objects are not personal, but purchased (or rented), and therefore are generic rather than unique to a particular individual. In the early Kongo and African American burial rituals, mourners believed that the material objects on the gravesite literally contained the spirit of the deceased because they were either cherished personal belongings or the last object touched by the deceased. The personalized theme funeral sells the idea that the deceased's spirit can be honored vis-à-vis the various theater-style sets, but, in some ways, it is less personal than a funeral that might feature a simple photo collage or a display of the actual personal possessions of the deceased.

In spite of the ironies embedded in the personalized theme funeral, the popularity of the staged visitations raises other questions about the state of the modern funeral in a postmodern age. In several significant ways, the personalized theme funeral indicates the endurance of certain types of mourning rituals over time. Nevertheless, personalizing death and grief with these staged sets is a unique 21st-century behavior that needs to be explained in relation not only to past history, but also to contemporary circumstances. Why, in other words, has this impulse to customize death in such an individualized manner emerged at this particular moment in time? In part, the invention and popularity of the personalized theme funeral can be seen as a facet of larger 21st-century trends in which the boundaries between the private and the public have become increasingly blurred. Reality television in which "real" individuals, rather than paid actors, go on shows to supposedly find a spouse and get married or get a job are only one example of this phenomenon. Similarly, the Internet has dramatically altered how Americans create their sense of self-identity. Any individual, for instance, can create a "home page" about him or herself, which then can be loaded onto the Internet for public consumption.

Not surprisingly, the Internet and other developing technologies such as digital recording via DVDs have begun to reshape the funeral industry and how people mourn and remember the deceased. Death has entered cyberspace and become big business. In recent years, companies have begun to sell Internet memorial and obituary pages as well as e-mail services that allow individuals to send farewell e-mails to friends and relatives after they die. Personalized DVDs, which capture the life of the deceased with film, photographs, and music, are also a new product that funeral directors are offering to mourners. Although it is not high-tech, another recent trend in mourning is affixing memorial decals onto one's car windows as a means to honor a loved's ones passing. These individualized acts of remembrance became especially popular and powerful in the wake of the 9/11 tragedy as flyers of the dead or missing were strewn all over lower Manhattan. All of these behaviors bespeak a desire to personalize death and customize grief in a public way that is a clear departure from more traditional and formal mourning rituals. The personalized theme funeral clearly operates on this level and reflects the particular ways in which death and grief are being reimagined in the 21st century.[35]

Of all these contemporary mourning trends, personalized funeral sets such as "Big Mama's Kitchen" best illustrate the fascinating tensions surrounding the ever-evolving place of grief and mourning in American life. As the history of the American funeral reveals, death and funerals originally occurred entirely in the private sphere. The dying person remained at home; family members tended to the corpse and made all funeral arrangements; and burial usually took place on privately owned family property. It was not until the emergence of the funeral industry after the Civil War that death and burial moved into the public sphere and became another product to be purchased in an increasingly commercial society. The invention of the funeral parlor signified the final stages of this shift. The deceased, who now usually passed away in a hospital, was quickly transferred directly to the funeral director for embalming, and mourners eventually viewed the corpse at the funeral "home" rather than in the intimate surroundings of their own parlor.

Funeral sets such as "Big Mama's Kitchen" disclose, however, a real longing on some level to reinsert death and mourning back into the private sphere, but in a public way. Since it is no longer acceptable to keep the deceased at home for visitation, sets such as "Big Mama's Kitchen" allow mourners to bring at least the essence of their mother's or grandmother's kitchen into the funeral home setting.[36] The appeal of the "Big Mama's Kitchen" theme funeral with some African American consumers indicates a strong desire to process grief amid the backdrop of "home"—no matter how prefabricated the kitchen set might be. The most extreme example of this trend is one of the other standard sets that Perpetua, Inc., offers to its customers: a backdrop known simply as "Traditional." In the "Traditional" set, the casket is laid out in a replica of a turn-of-the-century family parlor, including antique-style furniture and props that simulate how funeral visitations were held before the emergence of the funeral chapel. Interestingly enough, Perpetua's CEO, Slivy Edmonds Cotton, acknowledged in an interview that "Big Mama's Kitchen" was far more popular than the "Traditional" set. According to Cotton, "'Big Mama's Kitchen' has been so popular that they [mourners] will change the date of the funeral so that they can use the 'Big Mama's Kitchen' set. That's pretty powerful stuff."[37] Perhaps the antique, late-19-century design of the "Traditional" set comes across as too old-fashioned for 21st-century consumers. In other words, the feeling of "home" sought by personalized theme funeral customers is a present-day rather than a Victorian one.

The appeal of the personalized theme funeral also attests to the persistence of the belief that the death of an individual be celebrated rather than mourned. The idea that grief should be tempered with optimism has a powerful pull in American, and particularly African American, culture. As noted earlier, the desire to remove the gloom from funerals was expressed as early as 1917 in essays such as "The Unseemliness of Funerals" published in *The Literary Digest*. The anonymous author of this piece quotes another writer who expressed the wish that every funeral service might become "a ceremony of holy joy rather than the pitiful acknowledgment of defeated hopes . . . a man shall die as he lives, in the same spirit of confidence and joy.'"[38] These longings for a "joyous" funeral were clearly rooted in the Christian tradition, which envisions the afterlife in heaven as the ultimate reward for a life lived righteously.

Ever since African Americans began converting to Christianity, these narratives about the spiritual freedom found in the afterlife have had an understandably powerful allure. In African American life, a funeral is most commonly referred to as a "homegoing," distinct from "homecoming," which refers to a literal return home, usually to reconnect with family. "Homegoing" refers "to the transition one makes in going from this earthly life to a spiritual one in heaven with God and deceased loved ones. It is the ultimate destination of the traveler seeking spiritual rest and joy."[39] Much of the press coverage and publicity about the personalized theme funeral trend highlights how the staged sets create a more upbeat tone for the funeral that emphasizes this sense of death as a welcome homegoing rather than a somber and frightening end. As Aaron Grimes, manager of the Wade Funeral Home, commented about the personalized funeral sets, "It's not like you're at a funeral home; it's like you're at home. It makes it just a happy place to be."[40]

African Americans were, of course, among the earliest groups to transform funerals into festive celebrations of the deceased's life. The New Orleans jazz funeral, which includes a parade of upbeat Dixieland jazz, offers the best example of this tradition.[41] The pageantry of the jazz funeral and theater-style sets of themed funerals are similar in that they illustrate the continued importance in African American life for a proper, jubilant, and sometimes extravagant funeral. As Edith Churchman, an African American funeral director, remarked in a news article on minority-owned funeral homes, "We still believe in that sweet by-and-by. . . . You may have been a domestic all your life, worked in somebody's house . . . but when it comes time, you can have a wonderful funeral. This is something that you can plan for, set aside money for. You might not be living equally on earth, but you can certainly lie equally in heaven."[42] This is not to imply, however, that personalized theme funerals do not appeal to other racial groups, but that African Americans are a viable market for the product given their long-standing funeral traditions.

The history of these African American funeral traditions offers significant insight into the current appeal of personalized theme funerals such as "Big Mama's Kitchen" to African American consumers. From the early Kongo rituals of leaving cherished possessions of the deceased on the grave to later "homegoing" customs of the 20th century, African Americans have exhibited strong cultural tendencies to celebrate the spiritual life of the deceased through the material objects that a loved one left behind. This impulse translates quite readily into the recent trend of personalizing a funeral through theater-style backdrops—even though these sets often involve more ersatz props than genuine personal items from someone's life. For some African Americans, however, specific sets such as "Big Mama's Kitchen" are problematic in that the product sells a stereotype of black womanhood that is outdated and reductionist. The myth of "big mama" cooking up a fried chicken dinner may, in other words, stir warm nostalgia of family togetherness, but it also erases other important and more complex narratives about black women's lives and their accomplishments outside of the kitchen.[43] Whether personalized theme funerals will continue to be popular over time remains to be seen. They ultimately may prove to be much more of a temporary fad than a permanent change in American and African American styles of mourning.

To conclude, the phenomenon of the personalized theme funeral, which can—at first glance—appear easy to dismiss as another excess of our overly commercial, late-capitalist age, looks quite different when viewed in its proper historical context. By using the methodology of behavioral history, themed funerals such as "Big Mama's Kitchen" can be understood as a postmodern gesture to recapture some of the qualities of premodern burial practices by staging funeral visitations that re-create a familiar sense of home that was lost with the emergence of the modern funeral at the beginning of the 20th century. Moreover, in terms of specific African American traditions, personalized theme funerals resonate with burial rituals that can be traced back to West Africa. The behaviors that emerge around grief and mourning in any culture deserve careful analysis as they reveal how death is negotiated—whether it is embraced as a natural end of life, resisted through medical intervention, or envisioned as a spiritual "homegoing" journey into an eternal afterlife. Using history to understand contemporary mourning trends such as personalized theme funerals deepens our appreciation of the ways in which death and mourning rituals—even commercialized ones—evolve and reflect real cultural needs to come to terms with the end of life.

NOTES

1. For general press coverage about personalized theme funerals, see Joseph Swavy, "Truly Grand Finales: You'll Be Dying to Star in Personalized Adieu," *The Press of Atlantic City,* August 6, 2002, A2; Tiffany Kjos, "Theme Funerals: A Trend outside the Box," *Arizona Daily Star,* September 16, 2002, A9; NPR Segment, "Funeral Sets," August 8, 2002, audio archive can be found at http://discover.npr.org/features/feature.jhtml?wfId=1148022. For images of the various sets offered by Perpetua, Inc., see the company's website at http://www.perpetuainc.com/html/photo_gallery.html.

2. For an example of the figure of "big mama" in African American popular culture, see the film *Soul Food* (Director, George Tillman Jr., Twentieth-Century Fox Films, 1997), in which the matriarch of a middle-class, African American family is depicted as holding her family together by hosting her Sunday dinner and cooking for everyone in "Big Mama's Kitchen."

3. Robert Strauss, "Slivy Edmonds Cotton, WG'79, Celebrating Life in Death," *Wharton Alumni Magazine,* Spring 2003, retrieved from the World Wide Web at http://www.wharton.upenn.edu/alum_mag/issues/spring2003/wharton_now_8.html.

4. Kjos, "Theme Funerals."

5. Swavy, "Truly Grand Finales."

6. For commentary on baby boomers and death, see David Brooks, "The Valley of Death, Another Boomer Test," *New York Times,* June 25, 2000, 9; Joe Queenan, *Balsamic Dreams: A Short but Self-Important History of the Baby Boomer* (New York, 2001), 96–107.

7. Jessica Mitford, *The American Way of Death* (New York, 1963); and *The American Way of Death Revisited* (New York, 1998).

8. Gary Laderman, *Rest in Peace: A Cultural History of Death and the Funeral Home in Twentieth-Century America* (New York, 2003), xlii.

9. Elizabeth A. Fenn, "Honoring the Ancestors: Kongo-American Graves in the American South," *Southern Exposure* 13, no. 5 (September/October 1985): 43; and Robert Farris Thompson, *The Flash of the Spirit: African and Afro-American Art and Philosophy* (New York, 1984), 103–16.

10. Albert J. Raboteau, *Slave Religion: The "Invisible Institution" in the Antebellum South* (New York, 1978), 13.

11. Thompson, *Flash of the Spirit,* 132–34.

12. Georgia Writers Project, *Drums and Shadows: Survival Studies among Georgia Coastal Negroes* (Athens, GA, 1940), 54.

13. Fenn, "Honoring the Ancestors," 43.

14. Thompson, *Flash of the Spirit,* 142.

15. E. J. Glave, "Fetishism in Congo Land," *Century Magazine* 41 (1891): 835.

16. H. Carrington Bolton, "Decoration of Graves of Negroes in South Carolina," *Journal of American Folklore* 4, issue 14 (July–September 1891): 214.

17. Ernest Ingersoll, "Decoration of Negro Graves," *Journal of American Folklore* 5, issue 16 (January–March 1892), 68–69.

18. Raboteau, *Slave Religion,* 83–85; Fenn, "Honoring the Ancestors," 43–44; and Dorothy Jean Michael, "Grave Decoration," *Publications of the Texas Folklore Society* 18 (1943): 131.

19. Raboteau, *Slave Religion,* 230–31; and Eugene D. Genovese, *Roll, Jordan, Roll: The World the Slaves Made* (New York, 1976), 194–202.

20. For more detailed discussion, see James J. Farrell, *Inventing the American Way of Death, 1830–1920* (Philadelphia, 1980), 147–48; and Gary Laderman, *The Sacred Remains: American Attitudes towards Death, 1799–1883* (New Haven, 1996), 30–38.

21. For more background on these trends, see Farrell, *Inventing the American Way of Death,* 146–83; Laderman, *Rest in Peace,* 1–44; and Robert W. Haberstein and William M. Lamers, *The History of American Funeral Directing,* 5th ed. (Brookfield, WI, 2001), 257–90.

22. For more details, see Laderman, *Sacred Remains,* 104–5.

23. Haberstein and Lamers, *History of American Funeral Directing,* 5th ed., 205–18.

24. Haberstein and Lamers, *History of American Funeral Directing*, 5th ed., 211.

25. For a more detailed description and analysis of Lincoln's funeral, see Laderman, *Sacred Remains*, 157–63.

26. Haberstein and Lamers, *History of American Funeral Directing*, 5th ed., 257–90.

27. For additional information about the history of burial leagues, see Roberta Wright Hughes and Wilbur B. Hughes III, *Lay Down Body: Living History in African American Cemeteries* (Detroit, 1996), 267–90; Karla F. C. Holloway, *Passed On: African American Mourning Stories* (Durham, NC, 2002), 33–36; and Langston Hughes and Arna Bontemps, *The Book of Negro Folklore* (New York, 1958), 105.

28. Thomas J. Schlereth, *Victorian America: Transformations in Everyday Life, 1876–1914* (New York, 1991), 286.

29. Laderman, *Rest in Peace*, 3–4.

30. Robert W. Haberstein and William M. Lamers, *The History of American Funeral Directing*, 1st ed. (Milwaukee, WI, 1962), 439.

31. Farrell, *Inventing the American Way of Death*, 175; and, Clifford E. Clark Jr., "Domestic Architecture as an Index to Social History: The Romantic Revival and the Cult of Domesticity in America, 1840–1870," *Journal of Interdisciplinary History* 7, no. 1 (Summer 1976): 49–52.

32. Farrell, *Inventing the American Way of Death*, 176.

33. "The Unseemliness of Funerals," *Literary Digest* 54 (April 21, 1917): 1170.

34. Fenn, "Honoring the Ancestors," 44–45.

35. For more information on these trends, see Dan Eggen, "Death Finds Life on the Web: Sites Offer Caskets, Tributes, Posthumous E-Mail," *Washington Post,* May 17, 2000, A1, 12–13; Alex Wong, "DVDs: The Time of Your Life," *Newsweek,* August 23, 2004, 16; Susan Kinzie, "A Window into Memories: Auto Decals Gain Popularity as a Way to Honor a Loved One," *Washington Post,* August 28, 2004, A1–2; A. S. Berman, "Gone to the Big Domain in the Sky: Site Creators Die, but Home Pages Live On in Afterlife," *USA Today,* April 6, 2000, 3D; William Lee Adams, "E-Mail: Voice from the Grave," *Newsweek,* September 6, 2004, 15.

36. In some of the press coverage on personalized theme funerals, I have seen passing references to funeral directors who would be willing to stage a visitation in your own home, but this would be after the corpse had been properly embalmed and does not appear to be a common or popular practice.

37. Kjos, "Theme Funerals."

38. "The Unseemliness of Funerals."

39. Elaine Nichols, "Introduction," in *The Last Miles of the Way: African-American Homegoing Traditions, 1890–Present*, ed. Elaine Nichols (Columbia, SC, 1989), 10.

40. "Theme Funerals Set the Stage to Head for the Hereafter," *OffBeat News,* CNN.com, November 2, 2002; available at http://www.cnn.com/2002/US/11/01/offbeat.theme.funeral/.

41. For more background on the history and cultural meaning of jazz funerals, see Leo Touchet, *Rejoice When You Die: The New Orleans Jazz Funerals* (Baton Rouge, 1998); and Helen A. Regis, "Blackness and the Politics of Memory in the New Orleans Second Line," *American Ethnologist* 28, no. 4 (November 2001): 752–77.

42. Hugh R. Morley, "Minority-Owned Funeral Home in New Jersey Buffeted against Industry Changes," *Knight-Ridder Tribune Business News,* February 3, 2002, 1.

43. Interviews with Edith Churchman and Claudia Nash Thomas, National Funeral Directors and Morticians Association Convention, Baltimore, MD, August 9, 2004.

Part IV

Perception of the Senses

9

Making Scents Make Sense
White Noses, Black Smells, and Desegregation

Mark M. Smith

He sat in my office, giving me candid answers to awkward questions. A white South Carolinian, born in the 1940s, he'd grown up with African Americans and maintains close contacts with some to this day. I'll call him "Norm." Norm didn't see "black folk" as necessarily inferior, but he did think them different. I was talking with Norm for research on my book, *How Race Is Made: Slavery, Segregation, and the Senses,* an exploration of how white southerners believed that they could "sense" race and racial identity using not just vision but their sense of smell, hearing, taste, and touch.

Refreshingly, wonderfully forthcoming, Norm told me that it was a widely held belief among whites when he was growing up that black people had a distinctive odor—a musky fragrance. Certainly, he said, that odor was more difficult to detect today—it'd been "covered up" by a combination of perfume and air conditioning. But Norm's nose was accustomed to the smell and even today he reckoned he could smell blackness. On this point, I pushed him. "So, let me get this right," I said. "If I were to blindfold you and bring two men into this room, two perspiring men, one visually 'black,' the other visually 'white,' sit them side by side, you think you could tell which was which by smelling them?" Norm paused just long enough to make his answer entirely credible: "I have no doubt that I could."

Now, let me be clear: Norm is an intelligent, thoughtful, decent man, has black friends, and has shown many kindnesses to African Americans over the years. I later interviewed black people from Norm's hometown who confirmed this. Nor did Norm consider "black" odor necessarily bad.

But he did think race was detectable by odor. In this regard, Norm bore the weight of over two centuries of southern—indeed, American—history that made "blackness" detectable by white noses.[1]

This essay ponders the link between olfaction—real and invented—and behavior. Its main focus is on segregationists' anticipation of, and response to, the 1954 *Brown v. Board of Education* Supreme Court decision which, in effect, demanded integrated public schools. Olfaction played an important role in white protests over integration because of smell's associative meaning. Historically, many whites believed black people had a different odor and they associated that wholly constructed smell with disease, dirt, inferiority, and, interestingly enough, sex (the imagined scent acting as both repulse and allure). All were matters of enormous concern to those determined to preserve segregation in the mid-1950s. I end on a deliberately and necessarily speculative note where I attempt to sort out the links, if any, between smell, race, and behavior today. For a while this facet of the history of the senses bears more on mid-20th century patterns than those today. Norm's reaction suggests an ongoing link that can only be understood through behavioral history.

Why Smell?

Why examine race through the nose and not, say, through the eye? I might begin by noting that most historical writing is largely, if often unwittingly, already visual in its drive for focus, perspective, in its happy embrace of Enlightenment epistemology. Here, I attempt to restore some balance by appealing to a nonvisual sense. Moreover, it sometimes seems as though we only "see" race, which is to say that we construct "race" by relying on a constructed visual trope. But when we've ventured beyond the eye, we have done so profitably. Most obviously, there has been a lot of helpful work on whether or not "the commercially inspired fusion of black and white music that lay at the heart of rock and roll has made a significant contribution to interracial understanding." Expanding our historical sensorium to include smell might prove equally fruitful and could teach us about the different ways in which whites have understood and constructed blackness. As Trudier Harris remarks, "The nonblack American public will tolerate 'blackness' more *in the ear* than *in the eye* (think of white suburban kids, in the 'safety' of their homes, listening to black rap artists who spout lyrics directed specifically against them). So the public doesn't have to see James Earl Jones or Ruby Dee, and it can tap its foot or work its muscles to the spa music without giving too much thought to the musicians." This essay suggests that blackness was tolerated even less in the white nose.[2]

We also need to study olfaction and race because it has an unusually long and deep history. For white Americans generally and southerners in particular, claims that race could be smelled were critical not only for helping establish the inferiority of blacks but also for valorizing whiteness. Historically, most claims were made about the smell of blackness; by implication the scent of whiteness was normative, even odorless. Statements regarding the smell of black people pepper the national past, and few whites were immune to the stereotype. Antebellum abolitionists weren't shy about expressing their conviction about putative black stench, not least because pseudoscientific treatments of the late 18th century made a clumsy but powerful case for a distinctive and largely unalterable "Negro" or "African" smell. In the Old South, similar claims helped justify black enslavement and several proslavery ideologues, ethnologists most prominently but also a divine or two, elaborated colonial arguments to explain why just black people should be enslaved. Old associations died hard, and the same olfactory arguments were used to justify segregation after the Civil War. Southern segregationists found the olfactory argument immensely helpful, even essential, principally because the claim that black skin had an innate fragrance enabled them to claim that in the case of visually ambiguous, light-skinned blacks, a white nose could always detect who was and who wasn't really black.

Psychologically and socially, such an argument was very important for white southerners trying to fix and stabilize racial identity. Segregation, after all, was premised on the argument that immutable and identifiable differences separated the races. As blackness became increasingly defined by the presence of one drop of "African" blood—in other words, as blackness became ever less visible to the eye—segregationists had to rely increasingly on their cherished belief that the other senses—the nose included—could detect race. Without white claims concerning the detective and policing power of the nose, segregation would have been even more unstable than it already was.[3]

Smell, then, helps explain historical behaviors. Because of its associative function, smell gave racial prejudice an emotional, irrational edge. Sensory stereotypes generally, olfactory ones in particular, maintained Harvard psychologist Gordon Allport in 1954, are potent and, once acquired, "bring a shudder and lead us to move away or otherwise protect ourselves from the stimulus." Allport reminds us that once we begin to understand that people sensed their worlds—had to smell smells they didn't want to smell (unlike lids for eyes, there are no covers for nostrils)—we begin to understand better the visceral, irrational, emotional aspect to racial construction and racism. The segregationist belief in the smell of racial identity not only enabled them to maintain the fiction of distinctive races (and the system that the fiction supported), but it also enabled them not to have to think about race, their nose and gut feeling instead of their brain thinking. And, as Allport suggested, it was very difficult indeed to dispel emotionally driven prejudice with appeals to hard, empirical evidence.[4]

I need to make one other point now rather than later. Simply: there is no scientific, empirical basis to the argument that race can be smelled not least because race is a social construction, not a biological fact. In 1950, psychologist George K. Morlan conducted one of only two experiments about which I know on race and smell. Morlan's experiment was the most thorough: "Fifty-nine subjects" smelling "two whites and two Negroes," once with the boys just having showered, the second after heavy, sweaty exercise. Conclusion? "The overwhelming majority of the subjects"—northern or southern—"were unable to tell any difference in body odor or they made incorrect judgments." There was no olfactory dimension to race, except in the mind of the segregationist. Those supporting segregation undoubtedly believed that they could detect race by smell. But the demands of an ideology, the insistent requests of a way of life, take their toll, contorting beliefs to suit larger social ends.

Objectively, poor whites throughout southern history, for example, likely smelled as rank as laboring blacks: both were usually engaged in manual labor, both had similar diets, neither had ready and steady access to soap and water. Chances are, the nose could detect class more reliably than it could race. But in a society based on race, poor whites and blacks couldn't smell the same to white noses lest whiteness lose its social and cohesive value. White need for black inferiority, white demands for black difference, backed up by dubious but influential "science," ensured that many white people of all classes believed that black people smelled. The smell of blackness, then, was a cultural construct rather than a real or recoverable phenomenon, a point that both sensory historians and those interested in behavioral history would do well to keep in mind. How a smell is manipulated and consumed depends more on the nose doing the smelling than on the body producing, chemically, the scent.

Neither was the smell/race argument always logical. It didn't have to be. Racial prejudice often has its own dynamic that makes sense only to those who invent and apply it and then come to accept it unthinkingly. For example, whites who complained about the offensiveness of black stench were often the same people who had blacks cook their food, iron their clothes, wash their bodies, clean their houses, and attend to other bodily needs and desires. Segregationists squared numerous circles here, arguing that their maids smelled less than most or that putting up with their nurse's odor reflected their own largesse. Naturally, none of this undermined the truth of the general proposition that blacks smelled and should be kept apart from whites. Ideological constructions can and do effect behavior in powerful ways even if their logic is contorted.[5]

All of which brings us to the sensory, olfactory importance of the May 17, 1954, *Brown v. Board of Education* decision and the federal mandate to integrate public schools. With this ruling, two hundred years of American history came rushing into the present. Segregationists understood *Brown* as a sensory concertina in which whites believed they now had to see, hear, touch, and smell blackness in contexts defined by African Americans. In letters written to southern governors between 1953 and 1957, segregationists—from the North and West as well as from the South—expressed their opinions in alarmingly visceral and olfactory terms. Smell imparted a gutlike quality to white reaction over *Brown* that far outweighed the intellectual component of massive resistance. In short, smell gave the segregationist argument a visceral, highly emotional quality that tended to relax already loose prohibitions against extreme, often violent, certainly insulting, behavior.[6]

Smelling Black, Smelling Brown

In 1906, Lloyd Eady, aged fifteen, became a miner in Walker County, Alabama; by 1950, he'd moved to Chicago to find work; in 1956, he wrote Alabama governor "Big Jim" Folsom telling him what an integrated Alabama would smell like to white nostrils: "My Children Attends the Same School and Classes with Some Negro Children and Complain of the *Smell*."[7]

Those who'd stayed in the South already knew this. While integrationists tended to appeal to a theology that was both reasoned and emotional, segregationists invoked a visceral, primitive form of religious agitation, one largely devoid of careful theological reasoning, to justify the preservation of the existing order. The senses held center-stage in their arguments. "I have Gods proof we are different," wrote one supporter of segregation in 1955: "My eyes and ears tell me we are different." True faith, after all, came through hearing, seeing, and, apparently, smelling. Ben Howard of Athens, Alabama, argued in 1957 that God had impregnated stink into black skin: "No one wants there [sic] Child to go to School with Stinking [Negroes] they stink they all do God Put that Sent [sic] on them." The future smelled bleak, too: "Why if the Negroes force Integration our next President will be a Stinking Negro."[8]

Because of its old associations with sex, disease, and invasiveness, smell preoccupied segregationists during the debate over *Brown*. Integration meant black invasion of white space, affecting not just the visual world of whites but also their olfactory one. According to Mrs. B. B. Tart, "In working with Negroes here on the farm in open air is all right but get in a tight place like gradding [sic] tobacco . . . you have to get out in the air for their oder is like Cloriform, now think of closing up a warm school room, & you will see, & hear of more & more disease." "My association with the colored people," Mrs. John F. Watlington of Reidsville, North Carolina, wrote to Governor William B. Umstead in June 1954, "has been very pleasant." "The reason for this," she explained, "is it has always been in airy places—plenty of fresh air." This was olfactory "crowding" of white space. Mrs. Lella M. Galvani of Nashville wrote a letter to Alabama governor Gordon Persons and Virginia governor Thomas B. Stanley in 1954 with sixteen objections to desegregation. Her second: "If race segregation laws were broken down, it would mean white people would be pushed out, imposed upon or be made to bear the *very offensive odor* of negro people *under crowded conditions at work, study, rest, recreation or play.* Our country is large enough that we do not have to be crowded up with thousands of Negroes." Making blacks wash wouldn't alleviate the problem because, as Mississippi segregationists believed, the "characteristic odor of the Negro's skin . . . is inherent and not caused by uncleanliness."[9]

Stereotypes concerning race, smell, sex, and hygiene were resurrected eagerly and loudly. *The White Sentinel* of Fort Lauderdale, Florida, argued, "The Negro carries stench glands as does the dog and in his natural state these may serve as a means of identification in place of a name. . . . This stench (from extra sweat glands) is partly under control and is put out when the Negro is excited." Mrs. John E. Schmidt Jr., of Valdosta, Georgia,

believed, "Most of our 'darkies' take too infrequent baths and consequently have a decided unpleasant odor about them." She and others of
her ilk tried to help, of course, but their hands were tied by their respect
for black personal freedom: "Aside from insisting upon cleanliness while
in our homes and trying to teach them the value of cleanliness we can do
nothing—it is not for us to make laws saying how often one is to take a
bath." Anyway, bath or no bath, black people smelled and they would remain that way as long as segregationists said so. "I was learned & reared in
Ala. have been around Negroes all my life," offered one man in 1955, "and
am sure I have Never smelled a Negro I wanted to Call Bro."[10]

Southern whites had their arguments confirmed by nonsoutherners.
Although some of these people were part of national organizations opposed to integration, such as the Citizens' Councils that had a presence in
"at least 30 states" by 1956, many of them were not part of any formal organization. Judging by their letters to southern governors, for every non-
southerner happy to challenge segregation, one endorsed it. As a New
Yorker told South Carolina's governor in 1955, "The subway trains are
crowded with Negroes with a revolting body stench which almost suffo-
cates the white passengers." Another New York resident offered Jim Folsom "an argument favoring the maintenance of segregation in the South"
and warned of the effects of integration and how it would now be difficult
"to avoid contact with this undesirable, obnoxious boisterous element."
Nostrils would indicate when things had gone too far: "The overpowering,
nauseating stench of blacks is intolerable to white residents. The Supreme
Court Judges who rendered the decision for integration should be obliged
to live in the same neighborhood and associate with foul smelling
Africans."[11]

Then there was the advice of "The Comforter," Father William E. Riker
of "Holy City, California." Riker published a pamphlet tracing the process
and effects of interracialism that he sent to several officials including Alabama governor James Folsom. Integration threatened "the Great Christian White race" and was the work of "the Devil Himself" who "actually
stole in to ill smellingly pollute our people and country." Trust your eyes
and nostrils, counseled The Comforter: "The White race man . . . will
naturally create a beautiful blue eyed, golden-haired baby; and not one
of those kinky-haired non-creative black baby with a foul smell attached
to it."[12]

The smell of blackness was, it seems, national.

"Hadn't you better look into that luggage?" (From the Georgia Archives)

Lingering Scents

A 1963 psychiatric study of six- and seven-year-olds in New Orleans and sixteen- and seventeen-year-olds in Atlanta found that "the [white] child has been taught to associate extreme danger and hurt or harm with dark skin." But the researchers also found that familiarity bred tolerance: "What one sees after some months is the slow development of discretion and selection in the white child, the breakdown of quick and total vision and the beginning of particular vision based on daily experience." There was, then, hope: "In weekly meetings one can hear even the most segregationist-minded child describe the different personalities or mannerisms of the several Negro children."[13]

The *Brown* decision also forced some adults to think hard about the society in which they lived, and a handful tried to untangle race and smell by pointing to class. Pauline Easterm, a nurse from Houston, Texas, made the point with devastating precision in 1960: "The ratty, bum, reaking of the smell of liquor, drunk, dirty and degenerate may sit down at any Lunch Counter and eat beside us—if, when the filth, sweat and slime were removed we saw his skin is WHITE. Yet, the refined, intelligent, educated, clean, Citizen can't if his skin is dark? Just how stupid can we get?" Mrs. Easterm threw up her hands at the nonsense of it all: "Negro[es] all over the South prepare and cook our foods in Restaurants, Cafes, Lunch Counters. Yet they aren't allowed to sit with us at a counter to eat it. Now really does that sound sensible to you?" She concluded, "Am I white? Yes Sir—Born in Meridian, Mississippi."[14]

But the likes of Pauline Easterm were few, and so continuity, not change, marked most white attitudes regarding smell and race during the late 1950s and into the 1960s. Olfactory racial stereotypes were remarkably tenacious, not least because the *Brown* decision tended to galvanize white resistance, which in turn permitted the outpouring of raw emotion. As a 1975 report on "Psychiatric Aspects of School Desegregation" explained, desegregation "is not merely a legal problem; it is also a social problem, an economic one," and "a psychological one," north and south. The report correctly tagged ardent segregationists as suffering from an "emotional disorder" and argued that even in instances where integration had yet to occur, the reactions could be visceral precisely because they were anticipatory.[15]

Black smell, then, lingered in white noses. Three years after the first *Brown* decision, the nine black teenagers who integrated Central High

School in Little Rock, Arkansas, nervously walked down "white" halls. Newspaper headlines proclaiming "Situation at School Is Getting Smelly" were tepid compared to white voices shouting "Niggers stink. The room smells now" and "They got in. I smell something." The usual "evidence" was trotted out just as it had been for years, although now with a tone of resigned affirmation, white predictions having come true. The Augusta *Courier* of March 1959 splashed a report of the impact of integration on northern railroads on its front page. Titled "Hell on Earth," the article told of the experience of a Florida man on Philadelphia train cars. He reported how blacks "shoved the white people," how their very presence led to "Filth and Foul Odors" in the cars. The "smell was awful."[16]

Black activism only upped the emotional ante. In 1963, one segregationist drew up a bruisingly sarcastic list of "Rules for Conduct in Sit-In Demonstrations," subtitled "As directed by the NAACP, on suggestions by Brother Shuttlesworth and on the advice of Attorney-General Robert Kennedy, and Sanctioned by the Communist Party." Of the ten rules, the matter of smell and hygiene came in at number one: "1. TAKE A BATH— don't be afraid. Five New York doctors have proved that a bath will not hurt you and it will be an experience for you." This construction of black olfactory otherness and difference was ahead of how blacks looked. Rule 4: "DRESS NEATLY, CONVENTIONALLY—Wear yellow or green sharp pointed shoes, pegged pants, purple or black hat with large white or black and white coat." Black people couldn't win for trying. Efforts to smell "nice" were ridiculed: "Girls should use extra amounts of perfume and at least two pounds of Royal Crown Hair Dressing."[17]

As the civil rights movement gained momentum, the number of groups that stank grew. In 1961 *The Citizens' Council* newspaper out of Jackson, Mississippi, ran a front-page cartoon that left no doubt of what they thought of various civil rights organizations and the dubious, sinister groups behind the movement for desegregation. Support civil rights, shouted the cartoon, and you'll reek too. More than that, official noses could smell disloyalty, un-American behavior, and downright subversion as sure as a segregationist could smell blackness (see fig. 9.1). White venting against "stinking" blacks was more than metaphorical abstraction. When one Spartanburg, South Carolina man wrote to Governor George B. Timmerman in 1957 railing against the Supreme Court's decision "to admit nine stinking Negroes into an all white school" and "Adam Clayton Powell and His stinking NAACP field Agents," he likely believed in their literal stench.[18]

Norms, Old and New

So, where are we now? Does the imagined smell of blackness still have currency in contemporary American culture or has integration exposed the myth, forced people to question—and think about, not just feel—the black/smell association? It is, of course, very difficult indeed to say with any assuredness. Generational, ethnic, class, gender, and other factors undoubtedly influence the way people use their noses and the nature and potency of their olfactory stereotypes. It is also reasonable to assume that the demise of segregation, a system that relied on the conviction among whites that it was possible to authenticate race reliably and predictably, has lessened the importance of the association between scent and blackness. The structural and cultural imperatives of a system that mandated regular, daily, social verification of race in part through the nose plainly no longer apply. In short, there is less reason for whites to identify race on a daily basis. But the end of segregation doesn't necessarily mean the wholesale abandonment of olfactory stereotypes in white U.S. society.

Trouble is, there simply isn't much contemporary evidence on, or discussion about, the topic. Perhaps this dearth itself suggests a shift in attitudes: might people feel less comfortable talking about race and smell now than they did prior to *Brown?* As two recent commentators put it, "What may be even more surprising, given this age of political correctness, is that anyone would mention a racial difference [in smell] at all." But silencing a belief doesn't necessarily erase it. Indeed, the contained, unarticulated conviction might fester, gain strength, and bubble to the surface in moments of heightened emotion. We should be careful not to overstate contemporary squeamishness about the topic, just as we should not too readily assume insensitivity on the matter before *Brown.* Not only can evidence be found today, but researchers looking into peoples' perceptions about smell and race before the mid-1950s didn't always have an easy time. As George Morlan found in 1950: "To ask Negroes or whites to undergo the humiliation of being smelled by a variety of people cannot be done lightly. To ask others to sniff at whites or Negroes stretches the limits of what can be expected from volunteers."[19]

History weighs heaviest on people who lived through the civil rights movement. Predictably, when the contemporary racist of that generation wants to express utter contempt, the claim that black people smell is still a weapon of choice. One of my white colleagues who wrote a hugely popular and evenhanded history of a southern state—one that rightly made African Americans as important as whites to the story—discovered the following message on his answering machine one day: "And I read your book . . . and I think it stinks 'cause it was reeking with being politically correct. And why don't you get some cork and fire and put it all over your face and you can get to be a black face and then you could get to be a smelly fucking nigger." Not much separates this from the kind of gut reaction common in 1954.

But Americans have also learned how to dissociate race and smell, developed new tools to manage the association, or kept the association intact but reconfigured it more positively. The matter of racialized smell has, for example, become something of a joke, a comedic, if still slightly edgy, touch point between the races. Thus, Phillip J. Milano can title his book, *Why Do White People Smell Like Wet Dogs When They Come Out of the Rain? And Other Questions Worth a Smack on the Head from Mom* with impunity and, in fact, earns praise for raising difficult questions in a light-hearted manner. And some things wholly unimaginable just a generation ago are now happily embraced. As Peter Coclanis points out in his astute reading of the impact of Booker T. Washington's crusade for cleanliness among African Americans: "Few white males of any class, I submit, wished to smell like Jack Johnson, for example, or, for that matter, like Jackie Robison, or even like Muhammad Ali. But by the mid-90s, everyone wanted to be like Mike and smell like Mike—as both Gatorade and Bijan realized." Indeed. Between October 1996 and Christmas of that year, Bijan sold 1.5 million units of Michael Jordan's cologne at $23 for a 1.7 ounce bottle; in 1950 it was inconceivable that white men would have bought a fragrance advertised by a black man.[20]

Things are, I suspect, a little more complicated than that, not least because two-hundred-year-old stereotypes tend not to evaporate with the stroke of a legislative pen, no matter how potent the ink. There is, after all, little indication that Bijan sells Michael Jordan's scent principally on the basis of his race. Rather, Jordan's cologne is marketed by his iconic status as a stunningly successful sportsman, his blackness probably only marginally relevant to how the cologne is packaged, sold, and consumed.

But there are constituencies who actively want to consume blackness with an eagerness that, ironically, comes awfully close to reaffirming the notion of an identifiable black scent. Ostensibly, white youths—"wiggers"—who have adopted "black" cultural norms and forms of expression seem to suggest the fungibility of racial identity and the idiocy of strictly demarcated lines of "race." For David R. Roediger, though, wiggers send mixed messages. Clearly, they suggest "the extent to which white Americans already are culturally African American" and also offer "a telling sign of the dissatisfaction of white youth with whiteness." Yet Roediger worries that some of this cultural appropriation, both in its form and content, should "warn us against romantically mistaking wiggers for the vanguard of antiracism," not least because wiggers can essentialize black culture through their aggressive appropriation of widely accepted and constructed black cultural markers. This is especially true with regard to the enthusiastic and extravagant consumption of black music (especially hip-hop and rap) and efforts to authenticate blackness in language, sound, and dress. And to adopt something perceived as "black" has the effect of stabilizing a racial category that has otherwise become highly fluid. Clearly, the appropriation of a black style by whites has to run the gamut of the senses if it is to be authentic, something seemingly important to wiggers. This raises the question: Is it possible not just to look and sound but also to smell "black" today?[21]

Evidence on this is rare and frustratingly opaque. What little I have found, though, suggests that wiggers do think they have to—and are able to—smell black to be authentic. Support for this point comes, interestingly enough, by way of what appears to be a lament from a former wigger and may be found on the White Aryan Resistance Web site, run by Tom and John Metzger out of Fallbrook, California, the self-proclaimed "most RACIST REVOLUTIONARY newspaper in the world." In early 2001 an erstwhile wigger wrote in confessing how "very ashamed" he was of his past. Lashing out at others yet to see the light, the "28 year old White man" listed what it took to be a wigger: "they all think acting, dressing, and even smelling like a nigger is a good thing." Now, what, exactly, this scent is and how one acquires it—cologne? particular hair-care products? a matter of washing or not washing?—remains annoyingly unclear. But the specifics yield to the general point that modern American culture, even among those dissatisfied with whiteness, endorses something they think smells "black." In other words, even though beliefs about biologically determined racial characteristics appear to carry little weight among young Americans especially, this tempering in and of itself doesn't mean that people have stopped thinking racially. According to George M. Fredrickson, "Deterministic cultural particularism can do the work of biological racism quite effectively." "Race" can be "coded as culture," as John Solomos and Les Back argue, so that "the qualities of social groups are fixed, made natural, confined within a pseudo-biologically defined culturalism." In this way, the association between smell and race is preserved even though the cultural function of the association appears benign, even emancipating.[22]

Wiggers who want to smell black, then, sound very much like segregationists. Both believe in the existence, even desirability, of racialized sensory categories, even if wiggers recognize that culture, not nature, dictates those categories. According to Paul Gilroy's thoughtful work, *Against Race: Imagining Political Culture beyond the Color Line,* there are real dangers here. Working from the premise that "the human sensorium has had to be educated to the appreciation of racial differences," Gilroy argues that the consumption and marketing of blackness tends to rely on, and thereby affirms, sensory stereotypes. To understand the extent, meaning, and significance of that education and how it affects attitudes and behavior, historians need to consider the role of the senses in shaping race, race-thinking, and "raciology's brutal reasonings."[23] If Gilroy is right, and I think he is, there is some irony here: while the segregationists helped produce the association between smell and blackness, wiggers consume it, seemingly oblivious to the way that consumption perpetuates a stereotype whose history is unarguably pernicious.

By helping to explain the historical roots of some aspects of olfactory contemporary attitudes toward race, behavioral history serves a healthy function insofar as it urges us to pause before applauding what we sometimes tout as the generous, enlightened liberalism of our own historical moment. Whiffs, modes of smelling, changes notwithstanding, quietly remind that we still have our own prejudices, biases not only staring us in the eye but, in some respects, lingering right under our noses.

NOTES

1. This conversation took place on August 21, 2001, in Columbia, South Carolina.

2. On the ocular bias of historical inquiry, see my essays, "Making Sense of Social History," *Journal of Social History* 37 (September 2003): 165–86; "Echoes in Print: Method and Causation in Aural History," *Journal of the Historical Society* 2 (Summer/Fall 2002): 317–36. Also, see Martin Jay, *Downcast Eyes: The Denigration of Vision in Twentieth-Century French Thought* (Berkeley, 1993); Alain Corbin, *Time, Desire and Horror: Towards a History of the Senses,* trans. Jean Birrell (Cambridge, MA, 1995); Leigh Eric Schmidt, *Hearing Things: Religion, Illusion, and the American Enlightenment* (Cambridge, MA, 2000); Constance Classen, *Worlds of*

Sense: Exploring the Senses in History and across Cultures (London, 1993); Richard Cullen Rath, *How Early America Sounded* (Ithaca, NY, 2003); Peter Charles Hoffer, *Sensory Worlds in Early America* (Baltimore, 2003); Marshall McLuhan, *The Gutenberg Galaxy: The Making of Typographic Man* (Toronto, 1962); Stephen A. Tyler, "The Vision Quest in the West, or What the Mind's Eye Sees," *Journal of Anthropological Research* 40 (Spring 1984): 23–189. On race relations and music, see James C. Cobb, *The Most Southern Place on Earth: The Mississippi Delta and the Roots of Regional Identity* (New York, 1992), quotation on 305; Brian Ward, *Just My Soul Responding: Rhythm and Blues, Black Consciousness, and Race Relations* (Berkeley, 1998), esp. 89–115. Trudier Harris, *Summer Snow: Reflections from a Black Daughter of the South* (Boston, 2003), 151–52 (her emphasis). On making race, much has been written, but see especially Thomas C. Holt, "Marking: Race, Race-making, and the Writing of History," *American Historical Review* 100 (February 1995): esp. 2, 7.

3. On the evolution of smell and race in southern history and on the African American response to olfactory stereotyping, see my *How Race Is Made: Slavery, Segregation, and the Senses* (Chapel Hill, NC, forthcoming). On the 18th century, see Winthrop Jordan, *White over Black: American Attitudes toward the Negro, 1550–1812* (Chapel Hill, NC, 1968), esp. 256–57, 459, 492, 501, 518.

4. Gordon W. Allport, *The Nature of Prejudice* (Reading, MA, 1954), esp. 109, 132, 136, 137. See also Dan McKenzie, *Aromatics and the Soul* (London, 1923), esp. 48–61; Constance Classen, David Howes, and Anthony Synnott, *Aroma: The Cultural History of Smell* (New York, 1994); Alain Corbin, *The Foul and the Fragrant: Odor and the French Social Imagination,* trans. Miriam L. Kochan (Cambridge, MA, 1986); Stephen Kern, "Olfactory Ontology and Scented Harmonies: On the History of Smell," *Journal of Popular Culture* 7 (Spring 1974): 816–24. Smell has also been used to mark ethnicity. During the world wars, German soldiers claimed they knew the whiff of the English, and the English said likewise. See James Vaughn Kohl and Robert T. Francoeur, *The Scent of Eros: Mysteries of Odor in Human Sexuality* (New York, 1995), 160–61. A good deal of pseudo-scientific nonsense concerning smell and racial identity has made its way into the literature. See ibid., 161–62.

5. George K. Morlan, "An Experiment on the Identification of Body Odor," *Journal of Genetic Psychology* 77 (1950): 264. The other study remains unpublished and is summarized in Otto Klineberg, *Race Differences* (New York, 1935), 130–31. Its findings were the same as Morlan's. On a belief that smell can be re-created, see Hoffer, *Sensory Worlds in Early America* (already noted in full in note 2), 2, 8. My critique of this position is noted in "Making Sense of Social History," 178–79. I necessarily use a broad brush here: slaveholding paternalists were more tolerant of interracial sensory intimacy than southern segregationists. For the full argument, see my *How Race Is Made.*

6. I don't deny the vibrant intellectual life of the South here, but when it came

to race, many white southerners, and Americans generally, suffered intellectual blind spots. See, for example, Paul V. Murphy, *The Rebuke of History: The Southern Agrarians and American Conservative Thought* (Chapel Hill, NC, 2001). On the South's life of the mind, see especially, *The Role of Ideas in the Civil Rights South,* ed. Ted Ownby (Jackson, MS, 2002); Richard H. King, *A Southern Renaissance: The Cultural Awakening of the American South, 1930–1955* (New York, 1980); Daniel J. Singal, *The War Within: From Victorian to Modernist Thought in the South, 1919–1945* (Chapel Hill, NC, 1982). On massive resistance, see Numan V. Bartley, *The Rise of Massive Resistance: Race and Politics in the South during the 1950s* (Baton Rouge, LA, 1969); Neil R. McMillen, *The Citizens' Council: Organized Resistance to the second Reconstruction, 1954–1964* (Urbana, IL, 1971).

7. Lloyd Eady, Chicago, to Governor Folsom, March 10, 1956, Governor James Elisha Folsom Papers, SG 13913, Folder 17, Segregation March 6–March 15, 1956, Alabama Department of Archives and History, Montgomery, Alabama (ADAH). Eady's emphasis.

8. Mrs. T. J.[?] Baker, [Decatur, GA?], to "President Eisenhower," n.d., received July 18, 1955, Record Group 12: Georgia Department of Education, Subgroup 2: Office of the State Superintendent, Series 25: Correspondence of the State Superintendent with the General Public, Box 1: Alphabetical Correspondence Files, 1955, Folder Ba-Br, Georgia Department of Archives and History, Atlanta, GA (GDAH); Ben Howard, Athens, AL, to Folsom, 10-5-57, Folsom Papers, Administrative Files, SG 13908, Requisitions, Allotments—Soil Conservation Committee, Folder 10, Segregation Oct.–Nov. 1957, ADAH. Also see Allison Davis, Burleigh B. Gardner, and Mary R. Gardner, *Deep South: A Social Anthropological Study of Caste and Class* (Chicago, 1941), 16–17. On religion, see the recent treatments by David L. Chappell, *A Stone of Hope: Prophetic Religion and the Death of Jim Crow* (Chapel Hill, NC, 2004), and Jane Dailey, "Sex, Segregation, and the Sacred after *Brown,*" *Journal of American History* 91 (June 2004): 119–44.

9. Mrs. B. B. Tart, Newton Grove, NC, to Umstead, Raleigh, NC, June 21, 1954, Umstead Papers, Segregation Correspondence Files 1954-T, Governor William B. Umstead Papers, Segregation Correspondence Files W (2), Box 58.3, North Carolina State Archives, Raleigh, NC (NCSA); Mrs. John F. Watlington, Reidsville, NC, to Gov. Umstead, Raleigh, NC, June 1, 1954, ibid.; Mrs. L. E. [Lella M.] Galvani, 2116 Pierce Ave., Nashville, TN, to Persons, Mar. 9, 1954, Persons Papers, SG 12761, Administrative Files, Fiscal Year 1954, Segregation Letters—Misc., Folder 15, ADAH (her emphasis); see also Mrs. L. E. Galvani, Nashville, TN, to Stanley, Mar. 9, 1954, Stanley Papers, Accession Number 25184, Box 90—General Correspondence, Racial, Library of Virginia, Richmond, VA (LV). Last quotation in McMillen, *The Citizens' Council*, 162. See also Anonymous, Fort Worth, TX, to Shivers, June 20, 1955, Folder: "Anonymous Letters #2," Governor's Office, Call No. 1977/81-68, Texas State Archives, Austin, TX (TSA).

10. "The Negro, The Ape," *The White Sentinel* (Fort Lauderdale, FL), n.d., J. D.

Rowlett Collection, 1954–1972 and n.d., Acc. No. 71-299, Box 1, Folder 3: White Sentinel, GDAH; "Gentlemen," copy of letter appended to Mrs. John E. Schmidt, Jr., Valdosta, GA, January 22, 1956, to Timmerman, Timmerman Papers, Box 5, Misc. Segregation File, South Carolina Department of Archives and History, Columbia, SC (SCDAH); "A Friend," Bainbridge, GA, to Folsom, n.d., received June 30, 1955, Folsom Papers, Administrative Files, Segregation, SG 13914, Oct. 1 1954–Mar. 31 1956, Folder 1, Segregation, 1954–1955, ADAH. See also Mrs. Taylor, n.p., to Stanley, Richmond, VA, May 24, 1954, Stanley Executive Papers, Box 99—Segregation 1954, LV.

11. On the Citizens' Councils outside the South, see McMillen, *The Citizens' Council*, 138–55 (quotation on 138). Generally, note the remarks in C. Vann Woodward, *The Strange Career of Jim Crow* (New York, 1974; 3rd rev. ed.), esp. 113–15. Similarly, George Wallace got thousands of telegrams from outside the South supporting his 1963 rant. See Dan T. Carter, *From George Wallace to Newt Gingrich: Race in the Conservative Counterrevolution, 1963–1994* (Baton Rouge, LA, 1996), 6. Quotations: Unidentified [New York City?] to Governor George B. Timmerman, Columbia, SC, Apr. 19, 1955, Timmerman Papers, Box 5, Misc. Segregation File, SCDAH; Anon., Brooklyn, NY, to Governor Folsom, n.d., received Mar. 5, 1956, Folsom Papers, Administrative Files, SG 13913, FY 1959 [*sic*], Public Safety—Miscellaneous, Folder 14, Segregation, 1955–1956, ADAH.

12. Pamphlet, "For the First Time in all History Father Wm. E. Riker Lets the Cat out of the Bag," 8, 9, 28, illustrations on 4–5, 12, in Folsom Papers, Administrative Files, SG 13913, FY 1959 [*sic*], Public Safety—Miscellaneous, Folder 15, Segregation, March 5, 1956, ADAH.

13. Robert Coles, *The Desegregation of Southern Schools: A Psychiatric Study* (Atlanta, GA, 1963), 8, 10

14. Mrs. Pauline Easterm, R.N., Houston, TX, to Mr. Philip L. Coupland, Smithfield, TX, in William D. Workman Papers, Box 8, Folder "Books, Case for the South, Reaction, Readers outside the South, 1960, Feb.," South Carolinian Library, University of South Carolina, Columbia, SC (SCL).

15. Group for the Advancement of Psychiatry, *Psychiatric Aspects of School Desegregation* (n.p., 1957), 5, 9, 11, 13, 14.

16. Melba Patillo Beals, *Warriors Don't Cry: A Searing Memoir of the Battle to Integrate Little Rock's Central High* (New York, 1994), 69, 95, 109; "Railroads in North Afraid to Protect Women Because of Federal Government," *Augusta Courier*, March 9, 1959; Integration: The Right Wing Response, 1956–1964, Record Group 48, Series 3, Acc. No. 68-187, Folder "Newspapers—Augusta *Courier*," GDAH, already fully noted in note 8.

17. "Rules for Conduct in Sit-In Demonstrations," [illeg.] McDaniel to "Bob" [Robert T. Ashmore], c. 1963, Robert T. Ashmore Papers, Box 5, Folder 15, SCL.

18. "Hadn't You Better Look into That Luggage?" *Citizens' Council* (Jackson, MS), June 1961; Integration: The Right Wing Response, 1956–1964, Record Group

48, Series 3, Acc. No. 68-187, Folder "Newspapers—Augusta *Courier,*" GDAH; Mr. John G. Littlejohn, Spartanburg, SC, to Governor George Timmerman, Columbia, SC, [October?] 1957, Timmerman Papers, Box 6[?], Misc. Segregation File, SCDAH.

19. Kohl and Francoeur, *Scent of Eros,* 234, n.26; Morlan, "An Experiment on the Identification of Body Odor," 265.

20. On Milano and his book, see the commentary offered by Associated Press writer Ron Word at http://www.yforum.com/wetdogsap.html (accessed September 26, 2001). An edgier, more satirical treatment is at http://www.blackpeopleloveus.com (accessed November 14, 2002), especially the "letters" section. Peter A. Coclanis, "What Made Booker Wash(ington)? The Wizard of Tuskegee in Economic Context," in W. Fitzhugh Brundage, ed., *Booker T. Washington and Black Progress: Up from Slavery 100 Years Later* (Gainesville, FL, 2003), chap. 5; Lisa Chadderdon, "The Sweet Smell of Success," *Fast Company,* issue 14 (April 1998): 144.

21. David R. Roediger, *Colored White: Transcending the Racial Past* (Berkeley, CA, 2002), 213, 227.

22. See Aryan Update, January 7, 2001, 6–7 at http://resist.com/updates/2001updates/1.07.01aryanupdate.htm (accessed September 26, 2001). Quotations by Fredrickson and Solomos and Back in Fredrickson's *Racism: A Short History* (Princeton, NJ, 2002), 8.

23. Paul Gilroy, *Against Race: Imagining Political Culture beyond the Color Line* (Cambridge, MA, 2001), 7, 8, 42.

Part V

Sexuality

10

Tainted Love

The Transformation of Oral-Genital Behavior in the United States, 1970–2000

Kevin White

Growing up in England as a thirteen-year-old, listening to BBC Radio One, my innocence was protected by the Reithian guardians of morality who banned songs in which they saw innuendo such as Chuck Berry's "My Ding-a-Ling" and the Sweet's consummate power pop, "Little Willy," and especially the libertine ditties of Cockney reggae boy Judge Dread: "Big Six," "Big Seven," "Big Eight." Somehow, Lou Reed's paean to Andy Warhol's New York demimonde, "Walk on the Wild Side," escaped any ban. Indeed, for months as the record rose high into the top ten, the hypnotic bass of local jazzman Herbie Flowers could be heard powering the track behind Reed's snarling sociopathic vocal. From Reed I learned about the possibilities of androgyny, "shaved his legs and then he was a she." But it was to be years later that I realized what the line about being "given head" meant.

Little did I appreciate that my teenage encounter with this song on the radio was loaded with meaning. In a globalizing world, by 1973 I could be exposed while quite under age to the latest American fad: oral sex as a cutesy, hip symbol of the new world of sexual liberation where procreative heterosexuality was so last year, where penetrative male heterosexuality was out of favor amid the smorgasbord of erotic options offered by Alex Comfort in his *The Joy of Sex* (which piled up high also in England's largest bookseller, W. H. Smith). But I didn't know what "giving head" meant, so, for now, I survived this early engagement with American sexual imperialism. Probably most of the population of England did too.[1]

These days, girls talk about cunnilingus/fellatio all the time. *Sex in the City* worked in part because it captured how savvy, sassy American women have been shooting the breeze for the last few years. It's all very matter-of-fact; it is no big deal. The term "blow job" appears regularly in the series. In one scene one character visits her doctor and is asked, "Do you have sex?" "Yes." "Do you have oral sex?" "Yes." "Giving and Receiving?" "Yes." In one episode, the boyfriend of one of the characters is told in no uncertain terms that "my clitoris is about two inches from where you think it is." Funny, I don't remember this kind of talk when I lived in the States in the 1980s.

It's all very matter-of-fact. Over the past thirty years technology has brought pornographic films from the dirty movie houses into the home, first with 16 mm film, then with video and now with DVD. This latest format has revitalized the prominence of oral sex, especially in gay pornography. For example, Falcon subsidiary Bel Ami has exploited the willingness of some (once) poor eastern European boys from the Czech Republic, Slovakia, Latvia, and Hungary to have sex with one another for money. Thus, in the classic *Lukas's Story I,* we may observe the famous (in the "gay community") sex scene between Slovak porn superstars Lukas Ridgeton and Johann Paulik in its entirety, or one can click on oral for the oral sex portion or anal for the anal sex bit or one can go right away to the orgasm. This pattern is repeated all over porn, and Bel Ami is a worldwide brand, imitated in all sorts of surprising ways.[2]

Sex advice straddles every area of society from the animated Dr. Ruth Westheimer on the airwaves to sex advice columns that litter every women's and men's magazine. Sex advice books make it on to the bestseller charts, and they affirm the rightness of varied sexual relations. Oral sex can have many functions. Ian Kerner's 2004 best seller, *She Comes First: The Thinking Man's Guide to Pleasuring a Woman,* urges men to become "sexually clitorate" and proclaims "The Cunnilinguist Manifesto," which is a "call to action" (for men) who should "take one small lick for man, one giant lick for womanhood. Cunnilinguists of the world unite. The revolution is upon us. Vive la Vulva!"[3] According to Michele Weiner Davis in *The Sex-Starved Marriage,* varied sex can prevent divorce and its concomitant horrors. So one correspondent reports that "although I didn't like oral sex before, now it actually turns me on and gets me excited. It has become a big part of our lovemaking." Still, "Anal sex doesn't do much for me, but I don't mind it, and because I know he likes it, I want to give that to him." Oral sex remains the clean, uncomplicated alternative sexual practice, and ceasing oral sex can cause marital problems; one correspondent noted, "We used to have oral sex all the time, and I love it." But now she just "does not have any faith that he'll do it."[4]

In the United States today it is hard to avoid such references to intimate acts. Modern technology has assured that older innocence is harder to maintain, and, like virginity, once innocence is lost, it is hard to get back. So, even if one studiously avoids putting risqué terms into Internet search engines, as one must on university computers, a virus will get you. Unless you are a Mennonite, made immune from the forces of history, you soon can become worldly wise.

A consensus is emerging about the new morality in this brave new late modern world of what Anthony Giddens has dubbed "plastic sexuality."[5] Driven by scientific and technological change, this "virtual" sexuality has no respect for traditional morality or historical rootedness. The media is truly the message as technology sets up a momentum of its own. Thus, this late modern "plastic" sexuality is literally artificial as pills and condoms help divorce the sex act from procreation.

The American people, of course, are now jaded, having had to face up to the rift between late modern and traditional forms of sexuality in sharp relief. The publication of the Starr Report on the Internet in 1998 was one of the first events that showed clearly the potential of this medium to override older standards: in explicit detail Starr described the oral sex (fellatio) given to the president of the United States, Bill Clinton, by the former White House intern, Monica Lewinsky. Yet, as dramatically, Clinton, citing ancient precedent that recognized "sex" only as "procreative heterosexuality," insisted that he "did not have sex with that woman." In his autobiography, he expands on this: "I engaged in wrongful conduct that included inappropriate intimate contact with Monica Lewinsky; that the conduct, while morally wrong, did not constitute full 'sexual relations' as I understood the definition of the term."[6] Clinton, of course, famously had to apologize to the American people for misleading them thus, because extraordinarily, Americans saw Clinton as being excessively legalistic and technical in this regard; by 1998, oral sex did constitute sexual relations.

"Oral sex" (fellatio or cunnilingus) is obviously a behavior that is at the core of late modern sexual mores. As a behavior, it both challenges the hegemony of procreative sexuality and penetrative male heterosexuality. And it is clearly a hip and happening practice. Twenty years ago, sociologist John Gagnon, in a famous article, established that the behavior had become part of the "sexual script" of young people.[7] A vast amount of work delineates its prevalence and its safety in the era of AIDS. But neither sociologists nor historians have really addressed the qualitative implications of the acceptance of this behavior as part of the commonsense repertoire of sexuality. This is surprising given the behavior's importance for emotional change. Equally to cite Foucault, "It is through the isolation, intensification and consolidation of peripheral sexualities that the relations of power to sex and pleasure branched out and multiplied, measured the body, and penetrated modes of conduct."[8] Yet sociologists and historians alike have preferred studying sex talk rather than sex behavior despite Foucault's identification of the key role of peripheral sexual behavior in sex history.

This essay will therefore attempt an examination of the historical roots of oral sex in the United States as a behavior. Having started with an examination of the contemporary prevalence of oral sex in public and private discourse, the patterns of change over time will be pinpointed and interrogated.

An overview of contemporary and Western societies historically reveals that the current tolerance and normalization of oral sex in the West is but a mere blip in history. It is unprecedented. There is some evidence that such practices have long been tolerated in marriage, as an aspect of foreplay. But, just as sex outside of marriage has rarely been accepted, fellatio in particular has been associated with deviance, both with prostitution and with homosexuality. Terms of abuse such as "cocksucker" confirm the low value of the practice in the United States. Correspondingly, a powerful taboo has dominated discourse on this subject throughout Western civilization. Much has been made of Gilbert Herdt's 1981 study of the Sambia, a tribe in New Guinea. Like other Polynesian societies, it is striking in its difference from Western norms of morality. This tribe has drawn so much attention because it has made compulsory a kind of homosexual relation. Teenage boys are assigned an older male lover whom they are required to fellate. It is thought impossible for boys to mature into grown adults unless they have swallowed adult semen. But this is a rare society in which fellatio is so normalized.[9]

The great bulk of recorded history reveals a constant, even essentially the same, dominant hegemony of procreative heterosexuality and a counterdiscourse of disapproved sexual behaviors, including oral-genital behavior. The classical Mediterranean does provide an early complication, but one that also ended rather definitively. Most famously in ancient

Greece, certain male on male sexual activities were encouraged. As Plato famously wrote in the Symposium, "Whenever, therefore, it has been established that it is shameful to be involved in homosexual relationships, this is due to evil on the part of the legislators, to despotism on the part of the rulers, and to cowardice on the part of the governed."[10] Of course he meant man/boy homosexual acts. Such love was a key part of what Foucault described as "the care of the self" incorporated into the upper class's civilized aesthetics.[11] Roman sexual morality followed a similar "realistic" view of what acts were natural/unnatural. The Romans differentiated between "fellatio" in which the partner doing the penetrating stays motionless while the partner doing the receiving does the work and "irrumation" in which the active partner thrusts into the larynx. Both activities expand the masculinity of the active partner; as Wayne Dynes comments, "In fellatio the beneficiary of the act luxuriates in making the other service him completely while in irrumation he has the converse satisfaction of being able to give full vent to the impulse to aggressive penile thrusts."[12] Clearly, the role of penetrator used to be more valued.

There is massive evidence of this pattern's prevalence in Graeco-Roman civilization. However, with the rise of Christianity, there arose a discourse that took an idealized notion of the difference between the natural and the unnatural and set up a powerful hegemony for procreative sexuality in Western civilization. The early church and hence the New Testament tended to sidestep this issue by raising up chastity as an ideal. St. Paul did not link sexuality to procreation, but he declared, "Let every man have his own wife," so that sexuality could be utilized as "a way that was not obsessive," in his eschatological and hence limited and temporary worldview. In the meantime, pleasure in sex in marriage was acceptable.[13] Rather, it was St. Augustine of Hippo (d. 435) who was the true macho Christian founding father of procreative heterosexuality as ideology. Augustine's *Confessions* is a paean to how he found the way from sinfulness. Of his influence, Michel Foucault has noted that "the confession was and still remains the general standard governing the production of true discourse on sex in the West." As St. Augustine himself wrote,

> During the space of those nine years, from the nineteenth to the twenty eighth year of my life, I was led astray myself and led others astray in my turn. We were alike deceivers and deceived in all our different aims and ambitions both publicly when we expounded our so called liberal ideas, and in private through our service to what we call religion.[14]

Reading rather like a contemporary Christian Right polemic, St. Augustine's "ideal" view of nature is so extreme that he detests "unnatural" acts, that is, those outside procreative heterosexuality, to the degree that he forbade them to married people and even advised men to visit prostitutes if they wished to engage in such acts. Hence he created a powerful taboo.

St. Augustine's influence on Christian sexual morality has been massive down the ages. He is the patriarch who sets up and names alternative sexuality as sin. In medieval times, Thomas Aquinas clarified, updated, and refined this position. If anything, Aquinas was even stricter than Augustine: "Even married sex, adorned with all the honorableness of marriage, carries with it a certain shame, because the movements of the genitals unlike those of other external members don't obey reason—sexual sin is thought of as more disgraceful than other immoderate activity, partly because of the uncontrolled movements of the genitals, but also because our reason gets submerged." He goes on: "Sex properly ordered for its purpose of human reproduction is no sin. . . . Sexual sin consists rather in a breakdown in proper reasonable order in exercising the sex act, and that can happen in several ways. Sometimes we seek pleasure in a sex act with an objective naturally unsuited to the act's purpose that rules out reproduction by nature." Consenting to an "unnatural" act is indeed a "fatal" sin. Even "kisses and embraces directed toward such pleasure can also be fatal. Indeed those are the kisses we call lustful so we can say that lustful caresses are always fatal."[15] Aquinas's powerful discourse helps explain why there is little reference to oral sex in medieval times.

In Renaissance England, as ideas of individual freedom began to stymie the Church, the late Alan Bray has identified a significant gay subculture where fellatio was commonly practiced, while in "A Rapture" the metaphysical poet, Thomas Carew, celebrated the pleasures of cunnilingus:

> And, where the beauteous region doth divide
>   Into two milky ways, my lips shall slide
>   Down those small alleys, wearing as I go
>   A tract for lovers on the printed snow;
>   Thence climbing o'er the swelling Appenine
>   Retire into thy grove of eglantine,
>   Where I will all those ravished sweets distill
>   Through love's alembic, and with chemic skill
>   From the mixed mass one sovereign balm derive,
>   Then bring that great elixir to thy hive."[16]

Carew and the poems of other metaphysical poets represented the new mood of sexual liberation and libertinism of Restoration England following the repressive Cromwellian interregnum.

Across the Atlantic, the Puritans of the United States are no longer seen by historians as the ascetics portrayed by Max Weber a hundred years ago.[17] As Edmund Leites has indicated, their influence resonates down the decades in American society and culture. By abandoning the stricture that ministers should remain unmarried, marriage ceased to be inferior to life-long virginity, and sex within marriage came to be seen in very positive terms. Thus Richard Baxter urged his fellows to "keep up your conjugal love in a constant heat and vigor." Advising wives, Daniel Rogers proposed that they should "poare upon your own husband, and his parts, let him be the vaile of your eies, and looke no further." To be sure, the Puritans confined sex to marriage, and even here sexual pleasure combined with a strong ethic that demanded continued examination of conscience together with much worth being placed on constancy. As Leites notes,

> Mainstream Puritans did not see marital sexuality as a threat to moral constancy; in fact, they saw it as a remarkable and happy harmony of carnal, moral and spiritual bonds. But, for the unmarried, Puritanism placed severe constraints upon erotic pleasure. This was not because the Puritans thought that sex was in itself bad, but because the erotic life was, at its fullest, highly passionate and agitated.[18]

So the Puritans helped introduce an ethic of sexual pleasure into heterosexual relations that belied Roman Catholic mores.

But while they tolerated sexual pleasure within marriage, they feared deviance with a vengeance outside of it. The Salem witchcraft trials reveal this. Cotton Mather noted that "the Devil in Witchcrafts . . . work(s) upon the Bodies of Men and Women, . . . and that he . . . Extraordinarily afflict(s) them with such distempers as their Bodies were most subject unto" while the "devil . . . makes(s) a deceitful and unfaithful use of the Scriptures to make his Temptations forceable."[19] Equally, the Puritans began the regulation of sodomy. Thus, the Connecticut Law known as "Ludlow's Code" appeared in 1650, forbidding "men lying with men," but like other laws at the time it did not yet refer specifically to oral sex. New England minister Michael Wigglesworth's diaries are full of guilt and fears. He writes of "feeling such filthy lust also flowing from my fond affection to my pupils while in their presence . . . that I confess myself an object of

God's loathing."[20] While regulation of heterosexuality seems to have less-ened at this time, regulation of homosexual acts seem to have increased. Even as an ethic of pleasure entered marriage, ancient taboos still bounded alternative sexual behaviors.

Victorians, too, valued the mystery of sex and sexual pleasure within the confines of marriage or, at the least, within engagement. They devel-oped the powerful ideology of "romantic love." As Karen Lystra has noted, "Sex was treated as BOTH a serious spiritualized sacrament of romantic love and the occasion for a good laugh."[21] One writer noted of friends, "What a terrible warm time Dan and Em had of it for wedding. Probably Em has been obliged to squeal ere long."[22] Sex was less ethereal, but more earthy and intensely passionate. One Lyman Hodge wrote to his fiancée, Mary Granger, a poem:

> To us you belong,
>   Yield us thy love fearless and strong,
>   Kiss us, caress us,
>   Handle us, press us,
>   Toy with us, play with us,
>   Do as you will,
>   Bite us, unlace us,
>   Squeeze us, embrace us,
>   Drink from us, suck from us,
>   Drink up your kiss.[23]

As Karen Lystra put it, "Victorians did not denigrate sex, they guarded it."[24] It seems clear that there was a wide range of acceptable sexual con-duct: kissing and petting were fine, but the line seems to have been drawn at nongenital activity before marriage, and at procreative heterosexuality after.

Yet, despite the expressiveness and emotionality in Victorian women's letters to one another, they still seem to have been unwilling to discuss what it was they got pleasure from. And Victorian marriage manuals fa-mously reveal very little about the mechanics of sex. *Sylvanus Stall*, one of the most famous works, simply does not discuss the subject of behavior. What on earth did Victorians do? However, the best seller by Auguste Debay, *Hygiène et physiologie du mariage* (1848), stated that only the "mis-sionary position" was appropriate in lovemaking.[25] Karen Lystra in her comprehensive survey has only uncovered one possible example of oral sexual behavior. Emily Lovell wrote to her husband Mansfield, "I could not help saying a few words would that I could KISS YOU ALL OVER—and then EAT you UP."[26] But this is obviously inconclusive. We simply do not know what the Victorians did in bed. Yet their veil had a purpose. As Michel Foucault noted, "There is a pleasure on the censor's side in exercising a power that questions, monitors, watches, spies, searches out, palpates, brings to light." Yet the censor finds "a pleasure that kindles at having to evade this power, flee from it, fool it or travesty it."[27]

It was the heightened interest in sexual pleasure in the later Victorian decades that established the first stage of current behaviors regarding oral sex—though in generating equally novel regulatory efforts the same interest did not yet produce the full contemporary reality. Anthony Giddens confirms that Victorian romantic love could be subversive. Its advocates rejected "lust" and an "earthy sexuality." "Romantic love" stressed "transcendence." For Giddens, "Such love projects in two senses; it fastens upon and idealizes another, and it projects a course of future development." Romantic love takes on the guise of the quest "in which self-identity awaits its validation from the discovery of the other."[28] In short, sex as transcendent pleasure had arrived. Therefore, whatever Victorians did in bed, oral sex might well have been on the menu. Men's fascination with oral sex in pornography confirms its presence in male fantasy.

Victorians had set their limits in that sex was to be celebrated in private in the context of marriage and of engagement. The Victorian underworld was where Victorians tolerated nonprocreative sexualities. Just as St. Augustine had recommended, such practices were confined to prostitutes, some of whom performed oral sex, and the emerging gay world. There is much evidence of this from studies by doctors. For example, Dr. G. Frank Lydston gave a lecture to the Chicago College of Physicians and Surgeons. Lydston noted,

> Personally, I fail to see any difference, from a moral standpoint, between the individual who is gratified sexually only by oral masturbation performed (on him or her) by the opposite sex, and those unfortunate mortals whose passions can be gratified only by performing the active role in the same disgusting performance (on a member of the same sex).[29]

Dr. Irving C. Rosse, in a long diatribe on the risks of nonprocreative intercourse, warned of syphilis of the mouth, caused by a "hideous act that marks the last abjection of vice" (oral-genital sex). He had heard of a case in Washington who "with unblushing effrontery did not hesitate to say how it was contracted."[30] Doctors Philip Leidy and Charles K. Mills noted a case of a patient who had a "great propensity to fondle men, both with his hands and mouth."[31] In reaction, the Victorians regulated sexuality and oral sex in particular to an unprecedented extent. It comes as no surprise that they began to add jurisdictions against oral sex to sodomy statutes. California forbade "oral copulation in prison" in 1872. Massachusetts banned "any unnatural and lascivious act with another person" in 1887, building on a 1784 law. Oklahoma and Maryland followed in the progressive era.[32] This sophisticated society had the power to regulate the ancient paradigm of procreative sexuality's hegemony as never before. Yet from 1900 the steadily evolving counterdiscourse supporting alternative sexual behaviors began to gain ground.

Permissiveness advanced further, though haltingly, after 1900. At the turn of the century, using scientific methods, doctors like Kraft-Ebing, Freud, and Havelock Ellis began to categorize alternative sexual behaviors as "perversions." They thus named the taken-for-granted common sense of acceptable behavior of the Victorians. Freud's *Three Essays on the Theory of Sexuality* (1913) was much discussed at the time (as after). In this work, he associated oral-genital sexuality with "infantile sexuality." He described such activity as

> cannibalistic pregenital sexual organization. Here sexual activity has not yet been separated from the ingestion of food; nor are opposite currents within the activity differentiated. . . . A relic of this constricted phase of organization, which is forced upon our notice by pathology, may be seen in thumb-sucking, in which the sexual activity, detached from the nutritive activity, has substituted for the extraneous object one situated in the subject's own body.[33]

Yet while oral-genital activity may have been associated with stunted development, such a sexual trait was shared at some stage by everyone. Indeed, Freud noted that it was "inappropriate to use the word perversion as a term of reproach." Hence Freud especially, through his popularizers, was to help normalize what had been seen as the perverse. As in so much else, Freud here starts to breach the powerful Christian moral systems that had long denigrated nonprocreative behavior like oral sex.

Likewise, Havelock Ellis in volume 6 of his massive tome *Studies in the Psychology of Sex* (1936) detailed oral sexual techniques and practices, material that later became the blueprint for sex and marriage manuals. Even more, if Freud can't be interpreted as approving of oral activities, Ellis is the true precursor of sexual liberalism. He refused to moralize or to judge. He rejected the term "perversion," preferring the term "sexual deviation." Also, while Freud can be used to moralize, Ellis can't. Thus Ellis's role in influencing the sea changes of the future in the English-speaking world cannot be underestimated. In particular, and, significantly, he pioneered the idea that women ought to be satisfied by the sex act. Marriage writers to date had "framed (their work) to suit the supposed physiological needs of the husband, neglecting those of the wife."[34]

The first half of the 20th century entailed a first sexual revolution in sex talk but not in sexual behavior, nor in talk about still tabooed behaviors. To be sure, changes were afoot, but they were evolutionary not revolutionary. In most ways, the period resembles the Victorian era except that the unspoken is spoken more often.

The overwhelming ethos was still that of romantic love, but of an even more intense kind, as a companionate marriage of equals became the vogue. Let's call this system romantic love under stress. It was this amended ethos that, taken on by the new middle class of urbanizing America's culture of consumption, overwhelmed the Victorian culture of production by the 1930s. Marriage manuals from Europe, best sellers in the United States, began to discuss previously tabooed subjects. For example, Marie Stopes discussed premature ejaculation in her *Enduring Passion* (1924) and in *Married Love* (1922). She specifically addressed the importance of sexual pleasure and fulfilment in marriage, advocating birth control to free women from the fears that the emphasis on procreation had caused.[35] Dutch gynecologist Theodore Van de Velde published the first edition of *Ideal Marriage: Its Physiology and Technique* in 1927. He elaborated a whole range of techniques that included oral-genital activity. Consistent with the ethos of romantic love, Van de Velde referred to the "genital kiss" as an essential part of foreplay.[36] This gave both fellatio and cunnilingus a position at the highest plane of emotional and spiritual intensity. In truth, by avoiding explicitness he cleverly blended these practices with the ethos of the time.

Similarly, the word "petting" in the 1920s was used as a broad term to incorporate a wide range of sexual behaviors (that were never specifically described) that were now permissible, or at least practiced in courtship. Alfred Kinsey defined the term as applying to "any sort of physical contact which does not involve a union of genitalia but in which there is a deliber-

ate attempt to effect erotic arousal."[37] While the extent to which petting
was common and how far it included oral sex can be contested, what is in-
disputably clear is that petting led to a "moral panic" in the 1920s, perhaps
because it might very well have included oral-genital practices, but also
because previous sexual boundaries now seemed far more uncertain than
the cultural memory of Victorian mores. Kathleen Bement Davis, in her
survey *2200 Women*, using sparse evidence, noted that "spooning" did not
help happiness later in life.[38] Bohemian Floyd Dell, in an article in *Parents
Magazine*, "Why They Pet," considered how petting was good preparation
for full sex. However, sociologist Ernest Groves argued that girls who petted might not be able to make the move to full sex so easily.[39] Young men
noted the "many codes" they might follow in the 1920s. A YMCA pamphlet, *The Sex Life of Youth*, declared that "the question for all thoughtful
youth . . . is what type and degree of physical—emotional intimacy, if any,
is advisable before the more definite mutual commitment of one man and
one woman to each other in engagement."[40] Numerous articles railed at
college youth, and petting as a practice was always cited as dubious. Yet the
moral uncertainties continued. In visiting *Middletown* for the first time in
1925, the Lynds noted, "a heavy taboo . . . rests on sexual relations between
persons who are not married."[41] However, by their return visit in 1937 they
could note that "the range of sanctioned choices is wider, the definition of
the one 'right way' less clear, causing confusion."[42] Theodore Newcomb
wrote, "If there is a 'typical' attitude of college youth today, it is presumably one of conflict between codes which diverge in greater or lesser degree in respect to the point to which one may not go."[43] The 1920s moral
panic over petting prefigures that over oral sex fifty years later.

Yet efforts to determine behavior itself are problematic. Kinsey, apparently usefully, provided samples that drew on those educated to the age of
8, to between 8 and 13, and 13+. His sample was heavily biased toward homosexuals, toward the prison population, toward Indiana, and, most
significantly, toward the college population, so that the apparently high
and growing incidence of cunnilingus and fellatio in the college-educated
group reflects probably the most Bohemian group in the country, and
those most attuned to the growing social liberalism.

There is a clear trend. In the female study, of those women born before
1900, 26 percent had petted to orgasm. Among the 1900–1909 group, the
figure was 44 percent, and it was 53 percent of those born in the following
decade. Sex surveys conducted in the 1920s do not reveal the more esoteric
practices of premarital cunnilingus or fellatio to be particularly wide-

spread, but the 1954 female study does support the contention that there was some variance of sexual practices among men with women of their own class; in those women educated up to the age of seventeen and over born between 1900 and 1909 who had coital experience less than twenty-five times before marriage, 14 percent of women had experienced cunnilingus, while 26 percent of those born after 1910 had. Among those who had engaged in coitus over twenty-five times, the figures for cunnilingus remained fairly stable. As regards fellatio, instances tripled among the group that had coitus less than twenty-five times, from 7 percent to 23 percent, while among those who had had sexual intercourse over twenty-five times before marriage, the instance was stable.[44] The figures in the male volume are strikingly high. Statistics for marital cunnilingus for those aged 46+ at the time of the interview were 41.4 percent, while for those aged 26–45 the figure was 49.6 percent, suggesting a steady rise.[45] Marital fellatio also showed an increase with 36.3 percent of the 46+ sample having practiced it, as had 45.5 percent of those aged 26–45, again suggesting a steady rise. Of contemporary sex surveys, the only one to refer to the notion of increasing mouth-genital contacts was that of Gilbert V. Hamilton, in which 20 percent of men experienced fellatio, while 22 percent indulged in cunnilingus.[46]

Kinsey argued that "the suggestion that such techniques in our present-day society are a recent development among sophisticated and sexually exhausted individuals is curiously contrary to the specific record."[47] But the figures in Kinsey's sample do indeed show the behavior of "sophisticated" middle-class college elites. So did Gilbert Hamilton's sample, which consisted of visitors to his psychiatric practice. Yet a more varied group, the one thousand married couples reported on by Robert Latou Dickinson, contained only ten (1 percent) who had practiced "fellatio, cunnilingus and soixante neuf."[48] This evidence seems only to confirm that Bohemians and liberals were most likely to engage in these activities.

Others, aside from Kinsey, argued that these practices were appearing more widely in the population. Psychologist Lorine Pruette noted how "many have developed techniques of mutual stimulation which do not carry the danger of impregnation,"[49] while commentator Theodore Newcomb observed the "ample confirmation of the general trend toward increased tolerance of formerly disapproved behaviours in the area of sex."[50] Psychologists Blanchard and Manasses wrote that "even oral manipulations, may all come into sexual play activities."[51] Yet these observers—a psychiatrist, a doctor, and two social psychologists—were themselves steeped in the behavior of urban elites. It seems that oral-genital contacts appear to have spread to these groups, which, increasingly, were adopting a more liberal approach to their sexual lives. In this context, psychologist Lewis Terman provides us with a tantalizing piece of evidence. He suggested in 1938 that "the fault of excessive modesty is rapidly disappearing among women of the populations sampled by our group. The proportion of husbands reporting the wife to be overmodest or prudish decreased from 21.9% from husbands born before 1890 to 12.3% for those born after 1909."[52] Americans were starting to experiment.

Clearly, essentially contemporary-style oral sexuality was spreading by the second quarter of the 20th century, against a long-standing oppositional cultural and regulatory backdrop. The causes of change rested in the steady buildup of emphasis on sexual pleasure, which also generated increasing tolerance for diverse experiences within and without marriage and which tended as well to encourage defiant novelty for its own sake. Other developments, such as improved opportunities for personal hygiene—another big emphasis in these decades—also entered in, helping to mitigate the potential tension between growing concerns about cleanliness and the new interest in oral-genital contact. At the same time, however, the patterns were not yet fully adjusted, both in terms of continued public reticence and in terms of considerable variety according to social class.

Kinsey's surveys are admittedly of very limited value to us in their inclusion of a group educated up to the age of eight and identified as working class. For this is a heavily rural group because of the bias toward Indiana and does not have to reflect the mores of the urban working class. Kinsey reports very little oral-genital contact among this group.[53] Were hygiene standards not so high in this area? Fellatio and cunnilingus were growing in practice among middle-class elites. An intense romantic love, not unlike that valued by the Victorians, remained the dominant ethos because the lines between what was respectable and unrespectable were still drawn. By the 1930s, to be sure, "the genital kiss" trope became well known in the middle class but in the context of romantic love. It countered the nonrespectable dance-hall subculture, the successor to the Victorian underworld that exacted the same disapproval among decent Americans as it had done in the 19th century. Quite simply, nongenital sexuality remained a bad habit to many groups.

However, there is a wealth of qualitative data with which to decide the meaning of oral-genital activity for the urban working class, especially in

New York and Chicago. In this world, there appears an entirely different discourse on oral-genital sexuality to the emerging one higher up the social scale. Such behavior was linked to prostitution, seen guiltily as inappropriate for women. As well, it was the most common practice in the illicit gay world.

As George Chauncey Jr. has shown in his study of *Gay New York* between 1890 and 1940, fellatio was a practice performed on straight men by female prostitutes or gay men, who were known as cocksuckers. The practice didn't challenge straight men because it was argued that their sexual satisfaction was more important than "the gender or character of the person who provided that satisfaction."[54] Furthermore, the behavior was simply often not available from women—obviously not from their girlfriends or wives because it was regarded as causing loss of status, but the taboo was also strong among many prostitutes. Indeed, vice commissioners apparently referred to those prostitutes who performed the acts as "perverts," the same term that they used for gay men, reflecting medical opinion. Chauncey points out that straight men could easily lose status, too, if they engaged in such acts. But as he also noted, part of the thrill of such acts was because they were "transgressive."[55] Yet it was easier for straight men to engage in such disputed practices. They could get away with it; gay men and women could not do so easily.

Chauncey's classic study exposed the simple dichotomy by which the passive role in fellatio or in anal intercourse denoted the effeminate "fairy," while the active role in fellatio ("to be fellated," the passive infinitive) denoted a masculine man, a straight, as it did in the rarer anal intercourse. Chauncey of course has also clearly shown how increasingly an act itself did not inform identity, but that gender choice did as people began to see themselves as homosexuals and heterosexuals. However, there is much evidence from interviews carried out with men in the Chicago dance-hall subculture of the 1930s and 1940s that great tensions surrounded sexual behavior and practice, and that, in particular, the meaning of fellatio was being contested because the behavior was the site of newly emerging, more equalitarian identities. Gay men were at the cutting edge of such change:

> He was a "French queen." When I had known him for two months I had my first sex experience. I was never so thrilled in my life, but wondered what thrill he got in return. In this doubt as to what pleasure he received I grew curious, and then he told me to 'go down' on him. To cure my curiosity I

tried his way of satisfaction thus finding it more thrilling to French than being Frenched.[56]

Given this mutual sharing of sexual behavior and pleasure, the new Chicago gays indulged in the ultimate egalitarian sexual practices: "After we both had the same sort of sex love or satisfaction, we began carrying on the sixty nine fashion."[57] Another young man reports a similar experience:

> I had my first sex party (69) with a boy I fell in love with about 8 mos ago in Oct 1932. He Frenched me and wanted me to French him and I thought it would be disgusting at first but then I Frenched him just because I loved him so much and then it seemed to me it wasn't half as bad as I thought it would be.

But he still felt the need to qualify his enjoyment of Frenching: "I only get a kick out of Frenching a person I love real well the old aunties (sic) make me almost throw up to look at them." He, too, indulged the now-fashionable "69." "I like to have sex parties of the 69 type with a young clean cut fellow of my own type. I like 69 best."[58] Those who did not indulge the "69" vogue were described as "green, for instead of suggesting '69' he first Frenched me and then I Frenched him."[59] Others were not so confident, still trying to differentiate their behavior from that of "queens"; "I use only the tip of my tongue, sharp swift movements. Queens usually use their whole tongue, tap like dogs. I use my chin as a support."[60] And there was plenty of hostility in this period of change:

> One time while a fellow was sucking me off he turned around in 69 fashion and started pushing my head towards his penis. He said, "Go ahead and put your mouth over it. Everybody is doing it now!" I almost did it. I said to myself should I or shouldn't I. Then I got a choking feeling in my throat. My throat closed up on me just as I would want to throw up—I thought I might acquire the habit of Frenching if I got bitchy enough. I have learned to like queer people.[61]

One Leonard participated in both active and passive behavior: "For a number of times it was disgusting to French. But then I got 'hard' to it. I have Frenched in the past few months."[62]

With sexual activities now no longer defining masculinity or femininity, straight or gay, clearly a greater egalitarianism of pleasure had developed in Chicago. While this parallels development among the heterosexual liberal elites at the time, the ethos also broadly pioneers later sexual mores. One young man in 1930s Chicago seemed especially savvy and prescient in deciding that, "as is the case with a lot of homosexuals—people I know—I like to believe that I am bisexual. I have had normal sexual relations with women and enjoyed them. However, in actual number, I do not believe that they exceed 10—by that I mean actually intercourse 10 times. I have always been attracted to men and there is no question but that they are my preference where sex is concerned."[63]

Thus, ultimately, the early 20th century began the opening up of the tabooed sexual practices of fellatio/cunnilingus. There is evidence from doctors and the popularizers of their ideas, the marriage manual writers, that these behaviors were being suggested, while some sex surveys suggest that behavior may have been changing across generations to a very limited degree. In the dance-hall subculture, beneath the bounds of respectability, such practices remained taboo but were nevertheless engaged in. Strict rules, because of the links to identity, applied to what active or passive practice meant. However, increasingly, active and passive practice was subsumed into new identities, homosexual and heterosexual, that subverted former clarities because they heralded looser definitions of masculinity and femininity. This was, however, purely evolutionary. The fermentation of the underworld got little more publicity than its equivalent had done in Victorian times. Not only this, but in many ways the whole social system, while breached in certain ways, remained intact. Unless in veiled or euphemistic terms, discussion of nonprocreative sexual behaviors remained out of order. It might have been okay for doctors writing marriage manuals to encourage the "genital kiss." Dr. Kinsey's eccentricities were tolerated in many circles. Yet Victorianism as ideology remained powerful. These practices were bad habits not to be indulged. But this was soon to change dramatically.

In the late 1960s the veils of sex censorship came crashing down. A series of censorship cases lifted bans on literature (*Lady Chatterley's Lover*), on pornography (*Fanny Hill*), in the theater and in the movies. Perhaps even more important an event in the history of sexuality was the introduction of the pill in 1961. Far more than other kinds of prophylactics and contraceptives, the pill showed human imaginative inventive intervention in the process of the creation of human life itself. Suddenly to argue that procreation was the sole or even the main purpose of sexual intercourse seemed passé. Sex was for pleasure, not procreation. Sex therefore need not be heterosexual nor need it be penetrative (anal intercourse has continued, interestingly, to be taboo as a topic of discussion). Without babies being so likely, this was "plastic sexuality."

In this context, oral-genital sexuality for the first time ever in history from 1968 onwards became a subject of a number of open and public discourses. The still transgressive nature of the practice made it perfect fodder for discussion by the cultural elites. It vaguely meant rebellion against the commitment to procreative heterosexuality and family. Oral sex could be "just love or sex or just food," it represented the perfect behavior for the latest discourse of romantic love, which Anthony Giddens has dubbed "confluent love." This was the right adaptation for the era of sex as primarily for pleasure rather than for procreation. Confluent love is "active, contingent love, and therefore jars with the 'for-ever', 'one-and-only' qualities of the romantic love complex," he has written.[64] Confluent love emphasizes the importance of emotional closeness and intimacy. It can only persevere for the while that the partners feel fulfilled and sexually satisfied. In the *Transformation of Intimacy,* Giddens usefully compares the ethos of confluent love with that of "romantic love." Under the "confluent love system love only develops to the degree to which intimacy does, to the extent to which each partner is prepared to reveal concerns and needs to the other and to be vulnerable to that other." In other words, both partners needed to be prepared to discuss sex together. Giddens continues, "Confluent love presumes equality in emotional give and take." Procreative heterosexuality is in many ways inappropriate here, because oral sex—fellatio and cunnilingus—is much closer to a liaison of "give and take," but also because oral sex is what same-sex couples do, too. Giddens explains, "confluent love has no specific relation to heterosexuality." Giddens, compellingly, comments that, if "romantic love is sexual love i.e (that) brackets off the ars erotica. . . . Confluent love for the first time introduces the ars erotica into the core of the conjugal relationship and makes the achievement of reciprocal sexual pleasure a key element in whether the relationship is sustained or dissolved." In this context, "the cultivation of sexual skills, the capability of giving and experiencing sexual satisfaction, on the part of both sexes, become organised reflexively via a multitude of sources of sexual information, advice, and training."[65]

Why did this happen? French theorist Pierre Bourdieu has provided a useful backdrop in *Distinction* (1984).[66] This work is a study of France after the Second World War, but it can usefully be applied to the United States. Following American scholars of class formation such as Robert Wiebe and Stuart Blumin, Bourdieu sees his "new petite bourgeoisie" as emerging from a context in which commercial profits and power depend on both production and consumption.[67] Bourdieu adapts Max Weber's concept of the lifestyle as central to the "new petite bourgeoisie" that he denotes: how people choose to live and what their cultural preferences were determined "status." People were to be judged "by their capacity for consumption, their 'standard of living' (and) their lifestyle, as much as by their capacity for production." Because they did not have the cultural capital of the older bourgeoisie, the new class quickly built up its own status by dominating occupations such as advertising, the media, journalism, and fashion. With leadership in these areas the "cultural intermediaries" spread the values and tastes, that is "the new model lifestyles" of their class. They embraced leisure, sport, and especially valued cleanliness and hygiene as a means of differentiating themselves from other groups, a trait that had been growing since the 19th century, according to Alain Corbin,[68] but one which made oral sex much more appealing.

Jackson Lears confirms this for the American middle class. After the war, there were more opportunities for "institutionalized employment of intellectual expertise than ever before: . . . in advertising, publishing and the mass media," as well as in service industries dedicated to cultural production.[69] Drifting apart from older moralities, these cultural intermediaries advocated a "fun ethic" as the hub of their new lifestyle, confirmed by contemporary commentators like Martha Wolfenstein.[70] Michele Lamont has recently usefully corrected that in the American context the ethic of pleasure must be qualified as including a serious work ethic, again confirmed by contemporary commentators such as Brissuet and Lewis.[71] What is clear, however, is that for the "cultural intermediaries" in the media, oral sex emerged as the preferred behavior for the new "lifestyles" the cultural intermediaries recommended.

From the end of the 1960s, therefore, American popular culture was steeped in alternative sexualities, including oral sex, as socially subversive and hip. The change in the presentation of this behavior was sudden and dramatic. The celebrated comedian Lenny Bruce included jokes about oral sex in his notorious stage act from the 1960s. *Hair,* the generation-defining

1969 musical, was direct in its agenda: "Sodomy, fellatio, cunnilingus, pederasty. Father, why do these words sound so nasty?" In *Che,* which had the tagline "Don't Bite the Cock That Feeds You," actors simulated sex, including oral sex. The actors were charged under the sodomy laws. They were acquitted after masses of publicity.

Modern masculinist writers such as John Updike and Philip Roth, as they offered trenchant critiques of new erotic sensibilities, also expanded boundaries in their discussion of a range of activities: from masturbation, adultery, swinging, and, of course, oral sex. Consistent with the new ethic of confluent love, the male characters in the novels tried to find in women not only sex, but also meaning and self-awareness. Hence Philip Roth's *Portnoy's Complaint,* a major best seller in 1969 whose notoriety helped move sex talk even further into the public sphere. Portnoy's complaint, of course, is what we, today, would call sexual addiction, most commonly shown as a propensity to masturbation. The novel is a brilliant spoof of both Jewish sexual guilt and of sexual liberation, but it does contain a few plays on oral sex, which is seen as a sign of male confusion and helplessness. Portnoy tries desperately for one girlfriend to perform fellatio on him. After three months, she finally says, "'Alex . . . I will.' . . . I will what? But she was gone, down beneath the covers and out of sight: blowing me!" The performance of cunnilingus was seen as guilt inducing. Of another girlfriend, Portnoy commented, "A Jewish man, who cared about the welfare of the poor of the City of New York, was eating her pussy!"[72] However, for John Updike, especially in *Couples* (1968), its appeal is in its transgressing as well as its pleasurability. Updike saw the role of oral sex in the novel as a symbol of changing times. *Couples* is a take on couples forming relationships with each other and other couples. One husband declares to another husband:

> I like it to be long, to take forever, have a little wine, have some more wine, fool around, try it on backwards, you know, let it be a human thing. She comes too quick. She comes so she can get on with the housework. I gave her the Kama Sutra for Christmas and she wouldn't even look at the pictures. The bitch won't blow unless she's really looped. What did the Bard say? To f**k is human, to be blown, divine."[73]

At the end of the 1960s, rock musicians began to write lyrics of sexual rebellion that included oral sexual behavior on the cusp of such revolt.

Since their inception, the Rolling Stones had written vivid and realistic lyrics to their blues-based tunes. After 1969, however, as Mick Jagger culti-vated an image of shifting sexual identity to his hip and leering persona, he and Keith Richards played with alternative sexual behaviors in their lyrics. According to Stephen Donaldson, their huge 1969 hit "Honky Tonk Women" contains references to oral sex given by transvestites in the lines "she blew my nose and then she blew my mind."[74] "Brown Sugar" from 1971, again a Stones classic, refers obviously to cunnilingus. "Start Me Up" from ten years later may also be about fellatio. However, it is the urban legend surrounding a song from 1970 that links the Stones to discussion of this area of sexual behavior. Decca had demanded one more record out of the Stones and, just to spite them, the Stones are supposed to have recorded an unreleasable song, "Cocksucker Blues," that included the rhyming lyric:

> I want to get my
> C**k S**ked
> I want to get my
> A**e f**ked

This track has, according to Wayne Studer, occasionally appeared in boot-leg versions with "a cover showing a sweating Jagger with his head tossed back and mouth wide open (and I do mean wide open as if to—well, you know)."[75]

The sexual/marriage manuals of the 1970s placed oral sex at center stage. For David Reuben's *Everything You Always Wanted to Know about Sex but Were Afraid to Ask,* the goal of sex was orgasm, to which he added his own concept of "total sexual stimulation." "This is a means of intensi-fying sexual pleasure by utilizing all the available erotic pathways to rein-force and add to the cumulative gratification of the sexual experience," he continued. Cunnilingus was vital to scaling the heights. How could one re-sist Reuben's description: "Taking the example of cunnilingus first, as the tongue is applied to the clitoris the man feels the delicate trembling of that organ in response to the touch of his tongue. The slightly salty but not un-pleasant taste also reinforces his excitement, especially if it brings back as-sociations of the couple's last sexual experience together."[76] Reuben's sense of the freshness of the openness of this discourse is infectious. "What about the woman?" asked Reuben. "She can perform the same kind of stimulation on him." How democratic. Reuben goes on to recommend that the man and the woman stimulate each other "at the same time," in the reciprocal spirit of confluent love.

In 1969, A New York–based Bohemian called Terry Garrity published a manual under the pseudonym "J." Titled *The Sensuous Woman,* it became a bestseller. British writer Linda Grant called it "the book that taught American women how to do blow jobs." This work is a real curiosity now, strangely innocent and entirely lacking the feminist edge that was around the corner. "J," in her cutely knowing way, proposed various means of oral sex: the Whipped Cream Wriggle, the Butterfly Flick, the Silken Swirl, and the Hoover of "gnawing." "J" wrote, "Rough handling here may give him a slightly negative attitude towards you as a bed partner. Of course, if you're tired of him, this is an excellent way to discourage further advances."[77] The work of "J" is important because it actually put oral sex at the heart of her advice. She wished for women's pleasure, which she trusted could be delivered by men. In the Puritan tradition, it all seemed like so much hard work.

After 1969, there was a growing readiness to discuss sexual topics in Hollywood films, including oral sex. Much of these discussions (not depictions) reflected the hip and happening dissonant world-weariness of contemporary actors and directors. Thus, oral sex was pictured negatively. In *Serpico,* oral sex is depicted as "rape" at gunpoint. *Taxicab* features fellatio bought from a streetwalking prostitute. In *Midnight Cowboy,* oral sex is purchased from a male prostitute in one of the film's most torrid scenes. In *Saturday Night Fever,* fellatio is presented as the expectation of a young man if his girlfriend is not on the pill.

Many films incorporated oral sex much more positively. Just as in *Couples,* Warren Beatty's *Shampoo* (1975) features oral sex as the preferred activity for the Bohemian middle class. Julie Christie disappears under a table in an effort to perform fellatio on Warren Beatty. There are suggestions of cunnilingus in *Coming Home* (1975) between Jon Voight, who plays a paralyzed Vietnam veteran, and his girlfriend, played by Jane Fonda. Cunnilingus here was sensitive alternative sex for the crippled.[78]

These scenes were significant, yet they were little more than intimations compared to the film *Deep Throat* (1972). This film lasted for seventy minutes and, out of fifteen sex acts, contains four of coitus, seven of fellatio, and four of cunnilingus. It was meant to play in a few porn houses but soon became a cause célèbre that showed how Americans from all walks of life were keen to participate ("however vicariously") in the sexual revolution. While the film made $25 million and became the inspiration for the burgeoning porn movie/video industry, it, of course, became hugely controversial, not least when Linda Lovelace revealed the contortions and abuse that she had had to undergo in the making of the film. There were efforts to ban it. Psychologists even raved at the risk it posed of encouraging the development of fascism. One judge declared: "This is one throat that deserves to be cut." The film also raised the ire of the growing women's movement. A veritable moral panic arose around its key theme of oral sex. All this, however, was simply fuel to the engine of publicity as the movie became an international hit.[79]

Swedish publishers introduced modern mass-market hardcore pornography in 1967. In 1969, with the development of the loop, it became possible to purchase movies to watch at home. The first films that showed explicit gay sex, produced by Joe and Sam Gage of San Francisco, appeared in 1969: *Kansas City Trucking Co., El Paso Wrecking Co.,* and *L.A. Tool and Die.* Randy Metzger's *Score* (1969) included both hetero and homo sex. By 1973, according to a U.S. survey, about one quarter of the respondents claimed to have seen an X-rated film in the previous year. However, it was to be 1976 before Sony brought in the videocassette recorder, so that, by 1980, 40 percent of VCR owners admitted to having bought or rented an X-rated film: the video version of *Deep Throat* is supposed to have sold 500,000 copies. By the mid-1980s, the dens of Middle America were full to the brim with pornographic video films with their ersatz depictions of oral sex, which behavior had now become a key symbol of sexual revolution and sexual liberation.[80] Yet oral sex as behavior drew out other discourses. Particularly striking was the conversion of sexual advice literature and considerable feminist commentary to an active, usually approving commentary on oral sex—conveying some actual behavioral response as well.

In 1966, Washington University in St. Louis researchers William Masters and Virginia Johnson published *Human Sexual Response* (1966), a carefully calculated work that had an explosive impact on sexual ideologies linked to women's liberation. Masters and his formally unqualified assistant Johnson, who later became the wife he divorced, attempted to reify women's sexuality at the cost of rendering men's redundant. They first pointed out the growing literature that stressed the role of the clitoris in female sexual response. Speciously, they claimed, "Unfortunately, the specific roles previously assigned clitoral function in female sexual response were designed by objective male consideration uninfluenced by and even uninformed by female subjective expression." They then proceeded to summarize the work that emphasized the importance of the clitoris: "It terminates in a plexus of nerve endings within the substance of the glans and the corpora cavernosa." In nerve endings of course, lay sensation. Further, "The most significant physiologic reaction of the clitoris to effective sexual stimulation occurs in the plateau phase of the sexual cycle (that is the orgasm) and develops with universal consistency." But, most explosively, "the penis could not be responsible for this: regardless of clitoral body positioning the penis rarely comes in direct contact with the clitoral glans during active coition. In fact, clitoral retraction, which always develops during the plateau phase and elevates the clitoral body away from its normal pudendal-overhang positioning, further removes the glans from even the theoretical possibility of direct penile contact." The message was clear: penetrative male heterosexuality was not the best way for women to obtain sexual fulfillment and orgasmic satisfaction: "Unless the male partner makes a specific effort to bring the shaft of the penis in direct opposition to the total mons area, the clitoris is not stimulated directly by penile thrust with the female in the usual supine position."[81]

To underline the point, Masters and Johnson famously introduced the idea of the multiorgasmic female who might best obtain satisfaction through masturbation. Men simply were no longer necessarily part of the equation. They went on to positively mock the inept younger male: "The clitoral-body retraction reaction frequently causes even an experienced male to lose manual contact with the organ. Having lost contact, the male partner usually leaves active stimulation of the general mons area and attempts manually to relocate the clitoral body. During this 'textbook' approach, marked sexual frustration may develop in a highly excited female partner. By the time the clitoral shaft has been relocated, plateau-phase tension levels may have been lost."

Masters and Johnson's work touched an immediate nerve. Short of masturbation or lesbianism, oral sex—cunnilingus—was the only way to keep men in the frame at all. In 1967 the first edition of McCary's *Human Sexuality* referred to "sexual oralism" as a "sexual aberration." When McCary revised his book in 1973, oral sex was discussed under the heading of "sexual variance."[82] The immediate impact of Masters and Johnson was to establish oral sex in sex and marriage manuals as the ideal sexual activity for confluent love. Men's redundancy was initially interpreted as a chance of greater sexual egalitarianism and as a chance to expand opportunity for women.

The most important and commercial manual of the period is Alex Comfort's 1972 *The Joy of Sex,* which is the template for future such works. It was the first to show engagement with Masters and Johnson. Comfort, in the spirit of confluent love and plastic sexuality, trusted men and women to work out sex together. Sex was egalitarian, but it was also like eating food. Comfort's book is divided into several sections as if it is a menu: ingredients, appetizers, main courses, sauces, and menus. Oral sex was just one of these, famously described as "mouth music." Sex is now a complex negotiation:

> Who goes first is clearly a matter of preference, but one can give the woman dozens of purely preliminary orgasms in this way, as many as she can take, and she will still want to go on from there, so the man had better save himself for later. A few men can't take even the shortest genital kiss before ejaculating—these should save it until they need a new erection, when it is a uniquely effective way of raising the dead.[83]

The risks of failing in the negotiation were high:

> Some women do and some don't like the man to go all the way and ejaculate (if they love him very much, that may make all the difference, but not always). . . . Others once they are used to it don't find the experience complete unless their lover does ejaculate. . . . With experienced women we guess it is about fifty-fifty, come or not come; in any case you can always ask, and partners soon learn each other's tastes. . . . The various types of nibbling, etc., described in sex books come naturally to most people. One finds them out on the basis of learn and teach.[84]

Comfort's manual was and still is the perfect one for the era of confluent love. Its only morality is pleasure, which Comfort argues can be gained from experience and technique. Comfort's sex is democratic and free and secular. It is no longer sex as rebellion, but sex, any sex, as public virtue, and, as ever, hard work.

Masters and Johnson also stimulated the feminist takeover of the sexual revolution. For the egalitarian ethos of confluent love could readily be adopted to feminist demands for recognition of female sexuality.

Masters and Johnson's famous charge that "phallic phallacies" had dominated writing about sexuality before their (or at least Kinsey's) work was seized by feminist writers around 1970 to blur the divisions between the public and the private arena. If the personal was political, as the feminists claimed, then sex itself was the main battleground. In the new paradigm, orgasm was the main goal of sexuality, so building up sexual technique was the way to develop this goal. Women wished to reclaim their bodies from male domination and oral sex became the symbol of women's liberation and the preferred route to orgasm. The famous Boston Women's Health Collective's *Our Bodies Ourselves* (1971) was the first classic feminist statement from the United States on women's sexuality in the 1970s. This book was very much in the mold of confluent love. It stressed mutuality between men and women. It is cautious and tentative about oral sex. The writers admitted that the penis inside the vagina might "stimulate the clitoris enough to reach orgasm."[85] The authors then refer to a work which they regarded as so important that they indicated an address where it could be obtained via mail order. Ann Koedt's classic *The Myth of the Vaginal Orgasm* followed the logic of Masters and Johnson: that if the clitoris was the central site of female orgasm, oral sex was not only the best way to obtain that goal, but oral stimulation did not need to be performed by a man. Koedt was blunt about this: "Lesbian sexuality, in rubbing one's clitoris against the other, could make an excellent case, based on anatomical data, for the extinction of the male organ. . . . It forces us to discard many physical arguments explaining why women select men (to) the exclusion of other women."[86]

Other feminists criticized this approach, in Europe and in the United States.[87] Early on in the debate, Germaine Greer argued that "real gratification is not enshrined in a tiny cluster of nerves but in the sexual involvement of the whole person."[88] Oral sex, far from offering a real liberation, was by this account mimicking the male-defined orgasm-focused language of the sexual revolution. The cultural intermediaries were gender blind, according to Greer. In their respect for sex as work, these feminist cultural intermediaries resembled the Puritans. But their system took away the magic of things.

In 1976 "cultural historian" Shere Hite published *The Hite Report* on women's sexuality, a tome that entirely justifies the ridicule that has been heaped on it for shoddy methodology and extreme claims. Yet the book now has value for historians, for despite a sampling technique that would have made Kinsey blush, it is a fascinating insight into the thinking of elements of the feminist elite in the 1970s (complete with commentary from Ms. Hite).

Significantly, Hite launched her attack on reproductive sexuality in her chapter on cunnilingus. "It is very clear by now that the pattern of sexual relations predominant in our culture exploits and oppresses women. The sequence of 'foreplay,' 'penetration,' and 'intercourse' (defined as thrusting), followed by male orgasm as the climax and end of the sequence, gives very little chance for female orgasm." Clitoral stimulation was obviously an ideal situation for her either as foreplay or as an end in itself. Yet she opined, "Our culture has discouraged clitoral stimulation. . . . Our language for, as well as our respect for clitoral stimulation, is almost non-existent."[89]

However, while Hite's sample confirms the complexity of negotiation, it suggests that such practices were catching on in the new culture of erotic give and take, but that their implementation was not without difficulty. Men's motives were suspect: "I resent men engaging in some activity because they think it will stimulate me. I doubt that clitoral stimulation is even remotely interesting to men except that it makes them feel powerful in getting a reaction from the woman. I do not cooperate with patronizing nonsense."[90] Once the difficulties of negotiation were over, women in fact saw cunnilingus in a very positive light:

"Cunnilingus is very sweet, tender and tense."

"It's sexy! What can I say?"

"It's erotic because it's forbidden—another kind of 'soul kissing.'"

There were some vestiges of guilt; "I think perhaps it seems a little gross, or I think it isn't 'ladylike,'" or "I guess my generation was not taught that the genital area was beautiful, so I have a few hang-ups." But those who overcame their problems responded that "the fact that someone can love 'that' part of me means a lot." Another noted that "I enjoy cunnilingus immensely for the obvious physical reason, and for a mental reason as well. The male is exhibiting positive feelings to my femaleness."[91] In this group there was very little resistance to behavior change.

Shere Hite's women, despite their doubts, go-gettingly joined in. But Hite's 1979 *Report on Male Sexuality* is the culmination, the acme of the clitoral wars. In this work, men responded to yet another questionnaire on their sexual relations. Men responded with incredulity when asked the question, "Do men want intercourse when they have sex?" So established was the idea of penetrative sex in the culture. A typical response was, "After sex is begun, there must be some mutual understanding of what will result, and if I have an erection I am in arousal and therefore I expect full intercourse to its conclusion."[92] To men, penetrative sex seemed natural. Others were clearly, obligingly starting to see sex in other ways: "I try to look at sex as a broader range of activities including masturbation, oral and manual stimulation." This clearly showed the influence of the zeitgeist, "I used to feel intercourse was expected, but anymore I don't.[93] There was plenty of support for fellatio: "My favorite thing? Blow jobs!" "Fellatio is the best." "Fellatio! Oh yea!"[94] Yet again this area was a place of conflict. Many men did not appreciate women not being into it. However, it was regarding cunnilingus that Hite reserved her greatest ire. Hite's interpretation of Masters and Johnson was to take their perspective even further:

> Basically, Masters and Johnson have said that women should get sufficient indirect clitoral stimulation from the penis's traction on the skin surrounding the vagina, which is indirectly connected to the skin covering the clitoris, to reach orgasm; however, the *Hite Report on Female Sexuality* based on a much larger sample, found that, in practice, this was not effective for the large majority of women, who need more direct clitoral stimulation for orgasm.[95]

But men didn't know where the clitoris was; the "overwhelming majority of men preferred the woman to orgasm from intercourse/coitus"; as Hite went on, contemptuously, "But most men in this study had not had the actual experience of giving a woman an orgasm from specific clitoral stimulation, and thus were answering theoretically."[96] Further, men revealed how they felt when they first discovered that women needed "clitoral stimulation apart from coitus." Guilt and shock seem to have been the main reactions from these poor guys:

> I used to think I understood feminine sexuality—you know, I was gentle, patient, understanding, etc.—if they couldn't orgasm it was 'OK'! I let them get on top during intercourse and *everything* (a real sport wasn't I?). Anyway, now I see that the sensitivity I had that I thought was about 90 percent was more like 10 percent. [Age twenty-two]

"The other day a friend of mine told me that I was making a mistake expecting women to orgasm during intercourse with me, and that I should try to stimulate them some other way. This was radical news to me." A married man noted his wife could not orgasm with him: "When I come and she does not, which does make me feel alone in ecstasy, sometimes lonely. I desire my body, myself and my lovemaking to be in part hers, the gift of myself to her." Fortunately, the Hite Report had come to the rescue:

> Since we are both aware of the *Hite Report on Female Sexuality*, my wife no longer feels the pressure or feels inferior about not being able to come with me. Now, I feel good about this fact and more realistic about the reality of female orgasm.[97]

How remarkably easy it was to bring about behavioral change for some people.

Hite's works are far and away the most strident documents of the clitoral wars. She could not have made her disregard for the penis or for reproductive heterosexuality clearer. Intercourse "has been symbolic of men's ownership of women for approximately the last three thousand years. It is the central symbol of patriarchal society; without it there could be no patriarchy." Hite, the most populist of the sexual cultural intermediaries, outrageously wished to redefine sex itself. And oral sex was at the heart of this redefinition: "Our definition of sex is, to a large extent, culturally, and not biologically, created. Women's need for orgasm and for specific clitoral stimulation to reach that orgasm is not honored or respected in the traditional definition of sex." She pleaded in her cloying way:

> Why does our society consider it perfectly acceptable to assume that "sex" can be defined as intercourse, to male orgasm "every time," with clitoral stimulation to female orgasm included only "sometimes" or not at all—while considering it outrageous to define "sex" as clitoral stimulation to female orgasm "every time" if it almost never or only rarely included also penis stimulation/intercourse to male orgasm.[98]

In Hite's world, oral sex was the ultimate symbol of women's liberation, and here the once preferred and unmentionable behavior became mainstream.

Other feminist writers followed Hite's lead in seizing the momentum of women's liberation. Nancy Friday specialized in recording women's sexual fantasies in a series of works, notably *My Secret Garden* (1973) and *Forbidden Flowers* (1975). Oral sex figures prominently in these fantasies, which are shown very vividly and explicitly; though the works were presented as legitimate, they truly were pornographic. Overall, her works seem to confirm many of Hite's observations. Women wrote of their experiences of cunnilingus and fellatio, though Friday noted that

> this kind of lovemaking comes as a later, liberated step for many women. They have resisted oral sex earlier in their sexual lives, before they grew confident enough to become experimental. Perhaps they felt that it was "wrong" or that there is something . . . unattractive about themselves "down there."[99]

Fantasizing about oral sex could bring women through to the full sexual liberation that engaging in such activity symbolized.

Erotic novels for women also developed this trend. Carol Thurston, in her study of these works, has noted the extent to which oral activities impacted on the field. Linda Lael Miller's *Corbia's Fancy* (Pocket Tapestry, 1985) "contains eleven separate episodes of sexual intercourse, five of cunnilingus and four of fellatio, all within two hundred and seventy pages." Oral sex appears in 43 percent of the books that Thurston examined. Thurston notes that the heroines in these novels tend to be multiorgasmic. Therefore, the multiorgasmic heroine leads naturally to variety, since it is a foregone conclusion that even the most virile of heroes cannot hope to keep up with her, with the result that cunnilingus is portrayed as both foreplay and stimulation to orgasm. It is not something delayed into a relationship, but can occur the first time. In Pat Wallace's *Sweetheart Contract* (1983, 121), a first encounter is described:

> With teasing, excruciating leisure that unseen mouth moved open—lipped and moist over her vibrant flesh, licking her knees and her upper legs, travelling upward in a narrowing path, nuzzling the golden luxuriance of her secret body for so long that she felt a scream would be torn from her lips.[100]

Oral sex is used in the works to extend and to vary the sex scenes. Barbara Cartland this wasn't.

Feminist contributions to discussions and (to a lesser degree) practice of oral sex were matched by gay commentary. Even more than with feminism, however, there were countercurrents. The later pressure of the AIDS epidemic added yet another element. The gay "community" had pioneered at midcentury the development of more egalitarian roles reflected in actual sexual behavior. Gay liberation made this compulsory. David Bowie, who created the early seventies fad for glam rock that, after Jagger, dabbled with alternative gender identities and sexual behaviors, was a major figure in spreading gay values. In a famous interview in 1972 he claimed to be "gay." He adopted this pose because he understood that gay liberation was helping drive the changes in acceptable sexual behavior. Contained in many of his songs is a trenchant critique of the sexual revolution.[101] Throughout the seventies, Bowie dabbled in differing gender and sexual identities, but as Ziggy Stardust and his alter ego, Aladdin Sane, he toyed with alternative sexual behaviors, including, notoriously, oral sex. On stage as Stardust, he used to "fellate" the guitar of musician Mick Ronson. In "Cracked Actor" from Aladdin Sane, Bowie becomes an aging gay actor who begs a hustler to "suck, baby, suck, give me your head." As Wayne Studer noted, "I couldn't believe my ears the first time I heard *that* on my college radio station back in 1973."[102] Bowie also produced Lou Reed's 1973 album *Transformer* from which the song he produced, "Walk on the Wild Side," comes, a song that brings alive to a wider audience the gang around Andy Warhol and alternative behaviors.

The gay community was indeed in the vanguard. Carl Wittman's *A Gay Manifesto,* the most important essay from the time, suggests that confluent love was so advanced in the gay community that older practices could be condemned:

"I like to make it with straight guys."

"I'm not gay, but I like to be done."

"I don't like to be touched above the neck."

"This is role playing at its worst, we must transcend these roles. We strive for democratic, mutual, reciprocal sex."[103]

But by the mid-70s, oral sex was old hat. According to Gabriel Rotello, the right-on world of gay lib meant that

more and more men began having sex with each other rather than with trade, and as more and more adopted anal sex as part of their sexual repertoire, activists called upon men to strive for sexual equality and strict role separation.[104]

Versatility as well as lubrication was the word. Author Edmund White's 1977 period piece *The Joy of Gay Sex,* modeled as an imitation of Alex Comfort's book, relegated oral sex to the aperitifs. Of "blow jobs," White wrote,

> At some point in almost every gay encounter someone will play a little mouth music. It is the preferred method for quickies or when there is a sense of danger or discovery. But its attractions are by no means merely functional. As a prelude to the full symphony of intercourse, as the theme played in the duet of soixante-neuf, or as the way to resuscitate a dead body, a good blow job (which does not require blowing and should seem more a vocation than a job) is the ideal technique.[105]

White commented that in France oral sex had been known until the 1960s as *le vice américain,* but that "today this generalization seems less common, and a purely suggestive and piecemeal survey would suggest that Americans are now much more into f**king." Apparently, there used to be a "quip—that sixty-nineing is what Princeton boys like to do since it's so fair." Sixty-nineing had "its own distinct charms—there is total reciprocity," mocked the bon viveur White.[106] Oral sex was so last year to postgay liberation intellectuals like White.

To the gay on the street or in the bar, this was not the case. In the late 1970s in the wake of the medical crisis wrought by Hepatitis B, several studies were carried out in major American cities on the sexual behaviors of gay and bisexual men. These revealed that oral sex was still the most popular practice among gay men, especially among white men. Seventy-two percent of white men practiced insertive oral with a nonsteady (an active role). This compared with only 41.2 percent who practiced insertive anal with a nonsteady (also an active role). Among black men, the practice was notably less popular: a mere 50 percent practiced insertive oral, while only 46.7 percent practiced insertive anal.[107]

Yet as the AIDS crisis of the 1980s got underway, the gay liberation ideologists continued to stress militantly that anal sex was the major expression of gay intimacy. In an article in the hysterical *New York Native,* Joseph Sonnabend declared that the rectum is a sexual organ, and it deserves the respect a penis gets and a vagina gets. Anal intercourse has been the central activity for gay men and for some women for all of history. . . . We have to recognize what is hazardous but at the same time, we shouldn't undermine an act that's important to celebrate.[108]

When the associate director of education of a large AIDS organization was queried about whether he would recommend the abandonment of anal sex, he responded that he "would never recommend avoiding anal intercourse." To do this would mean the absorption of "the larger society's hatred of gay sexuality."[109] Nero fiddled. And Rome burned. Instead of adopting a regime such as that of Holland, which encouraged the stopping of anal intercourse in favor of oral sex or masturbation, the United States developed what David L. Chambers has called "the code of the condom."[110] The safer-sex industry was born.

As Karolynn Siegel has noted, safer-sex literature was remarkably consistent in its recommendations. There were risky practices: anal sex, rimming, and ejaculation in the mouth; there were "probably safe" practices, which largely included using a condom, while there were "completely safe" practices such as hugging or kissing.[111] With the "use a condom" soundbite, the safer-sex industry took off. But it would have been far better to have given greater precedence to oral sex as most men's favored sexual practice. The industry simply could not move away from gay-lib ideology. Typical was a collection of stories called *Hot Living,* subtitled *Erotic Stories about Safer Sex,* edited by John Preston (1985). One tale by Marty Rubin, called "A Nice Jewish Boy from Toronto," featured many scenes of anal intercourse (with a condom, of course). The older man requested of his younger conquest whether he would like oral or anal sex. "First the appetizer," he replied, "then the main course."[112] This paralleled Edmund White's 1977 advice in the *Joy of Gay Sex.* Yet it did not reflect the reality of most gay men's lives.

Oral sex without a condom or ejaculation in the mouth was considered only "probably safe." But the word around the gay community was that it was pretty safe. Still, doctors and safer-sex advocates demanded behavior change even regarding oral sex. Tantalizing evidence suggests that gay men in San Francisco resisted such advice, especially if they were in monogamous relationships. In 1985, 36.3 percent of men in monogamous relationships performed oral-genital intercourse, while the figure in 1986 was 47.4

percent, a difference of +11.1 percent. Differentials of +14.9 percent occurred in the core relationship of men in nonmonogamous relationships,
of +19.2 percent in their outside relationships, and of +16.7 percent of men
not in relationships.[113] This could be interpreted as men reverting to form
and probably engaging in a safer sex practice, anyway.

Sociologist Pepper Schwartz confirms that gay men's relationships in
the 1980s continued in the mold of confluent love they had helped pioneer. They inevitably conflicted, "Why am I always the one who does it?" "I
thought that's what you wanted to do." "69" was the perfect solution. "Im-
balance in performing oral sex is avoided and the couple is happier with
their sex life."[114]

There's no question that all forms of what had been deviant sexuality
were named via the 1980s/1990s Safer Sex movement. The prevalence of
oral sex would not have been made possible without the vital backdrop
wrought by the 1970s discourse on oral-genital sexuality and the clitoral
wars.

Yet a final core question remains: How far did sexual practice and behavior change in the American heterosexual mainstream? What was the
meaning of oral sex to mainstream America in the 1970s/1980s? How great
was the influence of the cultural intermediaries? On a deeper level, what
was the emotional meaning of any behavior shifts?

There is a vast amount of contemporary literature on these themes,
which broadly points in the same direction. The best survey of American
sexual behavior, *Sex in America* (1994), by Robert Michael and John
Gagnon, draws out the key themes that emerged after 1970.[115] Their study,
with high reliability and validity, confirms that oral sex had definitely been
part of the sexual script since 1970. Yet the work confirmed the overwhelming popularity of vaginal sex, indeed as a cultural universal. Experience of oral sex differed according to education, race, and age. It was by no
means universal.

With regard to education, the same trope used by Kinsey to indicate
class, 59 percent of men who had failed to graduate high school had never
experienced oral sex, compared to 81 percent who had had any college.
Only 16 percent of women who had not graduated high school had performed oral sex in their last experience, compared to 27 percent of men
with some college. For women who had failed to graduate high school, 41
percent had experienced active oral sex, while 78 percent of those who had
been to college had. In their most recent sex event, the figure was 10 percent to 22 percent.[116]

In her 1976 study of San Francisco working-class married couples, Lilian Rubin reported strong resistance to oral sex among the women she interviewed. Rubin's study compared twenty-five working-class couples with twenty-five middle-class couples and found similar levels of oral sex. But the study is most important for qualitative data. Blue-collar women noted a great deal of ambiguity: "I sure wish I could stop him pushing me into that," remarked one.[117] Equally, the men revealed they did not think their wives really liked oral sex, so did not engage in the practice very often. This reflected Kinsey's view that the working class was much more ambivalent about oral sex.

The resistance to oral sex practices among African Americans is even more striking. While 81 percent of white men had engaged in active oral sex over their lifetime, the same applied to only 51 percent of black men, and only 22 percent of black men had performed oral sex as part of their last sex experience. For white women, the figure for active sex was 75 percent and for black women 34 percent, with only 10 percent experiencing active oral sex. Indeed, within the African American population, oral sex seems to have been associated with the undesirable practices of white people.[118] Geoffrey Coles, conducting a number of interviews with teenagers in 1985, managed to obtain some very frank comments: "Black boys do not like cunnilingus," he reported a black boy telling him. "A lot of white people do that. Black people, I don't know. I wouldn't, I'll tell you that." Asked why he thought the practice was more popular with white than black people, the response came, "I don't know—'cause white people are more freaky than black people, I guess."[119]

Religion was also an important variable in determining the extent of oral sex practice among men and women. Unsurprisingly, Catholics and mainline Protestants were enthusiastic. But only 67 percent of all Protestants had experienced active oral sex at any time, and only 56 percent of women. But for men, only 22 percent had performed active oral sex in their last sex event, and only 13 percent of women. Presumably, evangelical Christians practiced what they preached?[120]

Sex in America revealed the extent to which there was a generational component to frequency in practice of oral sex. Eighty-five percent of men aged 25 to 29 had experienced active oral sex, with 32 percent engaging in it for the last sex event, compared to a 59 percent of men aged 50 to 59 who had experienced it at any time, with only 13 percent engaging in it at their last sex event. For passive oral sex, the figure was 85 percent against 62 percent, with only 34 percent against 14 percent in the last sex event.

For women aged 25 to 29, the figure for active oral sex was 76 percent; for those aged 50 to 59, 44 percent. But for the last sex event, the figure was 24 percent versus 9 percent. With regard to passive oral sex, the figure was 80 percent against 52 percent, with 24 percent against 10 percent for the last event. This confirms not only the prevalence of these practices among mainstream America, but that a significant change over time had occurred.[121]

Other commentators confirm the same point. As Lilian Rubin noted in a 1990 study, "The boundary of the unacceptable continues to recede, and behaviors that were almost unheard of yesterday have become commonplace today." She confirms this with some useful historical data: "Oral sex? In those days? Are you kidding? I can't even imagine any of the girls I knew getting into that then." For girls especially, there might be a high price to pay: "I remember doing it because this guy I liked so much wanted me to. . . . I felt so dirty, it was awful." With each generation, inhibitions have been reduced, but still some wariness remained. "I couldn't even think about it then—it seemed dirty, revolting," said a thirty-five-year-old man. However, newer generations were better adjusted, "I thought it was yichhh, you know, yucky . . . but I was curious about it . . . it was kind of fun, like sucking on a lollipop."[122]

Anthony Pietropinto, in a pioneering study of male sexuality, noted that "oral sex is on its way to becoming the new standard of intimacy." He would have better said "a" new intimacy standard; still, he had a point. He confirmed the age differential: "One of the most striking findings of the study was the percentage of men under forty who consider oral sex the most pleasurable part of foreplay is triple that of men over the age of sixty-five." He went on: "A generation ago, a man might have found this . . . threateningly passive and feminine, but most men today feel they are entitled to a pleasant respite from constantly proving their prowess."[123]

In two areas, oral sex practices seem to have particularly infiltrated; that is, among college youth and younger married or cohabiting couples. The growth of the practice was first identified in a study of college youth conducted in 1967 by John Gagnon, not published or interpreted until 1987. Gagnon sees oral sex as entering into the "sexual script" of Americans about 1970. "What we may be observing here is the emergence of a historically new set of decisions about various forms of sexual conduct that needed to be made by cohorts of young people in the middle to late 1960s." Because young people in college were to have more emotional-erotic involvements, this required "more complex distinctions between sexual partners and what the appropriate sexual techniques might be in differing relationships."[124]

Gagnon noted, too, a difference in the oral-genital script between men and women. For men, engagement was really straightforward: "The more partners these men had, the less religious they were, and the more often they had been in love, the more likely they were to have had oral-genital sex."[125] Men seemed to respond to less-inhibiting moralities and great opportunity. Many men generally appeared to have relished the practice, but for women their involvement depended on the nature of the relationship they were in. Edward S. Herold and Leslie Way indeed noted that "the strongest predictor of having experience (for women) was personal ideology regarding the acceptability of oral sex."[126]

S. Newcomer and J. Udry in the 1980s confirmed the consistency of studies of adolescent engagement in oral sex.[127] Most studies had suggested that cunnilingus for males had more than quadrupled, while for women it had more than doubled. The practice of fellatio had more than doubled for women and had gone up 50 percent for men since the 1960s. The richest qualitative resource is Geoffrey Coles's 1985 study, *Sex and the American Teenager.* Many teens saw oral sex as a means of birth control. A seventeen-year-old New York girl said that she preferred oral sex, "definitely both ways. . . . That's what we used to do before we could start having sex, because we didn't have protection and stuff." Another girl, on rejecting intercourse for lack of protection on a camping trip, piped up, "There's always oral sex."[128] Rutgers students interviewed by Michael Moffatt in the 1980s confirmed that "oral sex" was a kind of new sex. One female co-ed said, "I truly believe that I have had good sexual experiences with my past boyfriends. My experiences go from kissing to 'everything but' intercourse. I don't think that my relationships have left my partners sexually frustrated because I take much pleasure in giving and receiving oral sex."[129]

Yet oral sex was a source of conflict for teens. Vaginal intercourse was still the standard. One sixteen-year-old noted that "it's hard for me to deal with it, because, you know, when you know that a guy doesn't want to give you head but you're giving him head, you wonder if it's because he doesn't like *your* vagina or what. I mean, you wonder if it's personal or if that's the way they feel about every girl. So it's real hard."[130] It is clear that by this time, oral-genital sexuality became the acceptable last boundary before full intercourse, or a respectable alternative. What was it like for these teenagers once they grew up? As Michael and Gagnon's study made clear,

vaginal intercourse remains "special" to Americans: "No other genital sexual activity even approaches it in prevalence." According to their figures, 95
percent had had vaginal intercourse when they had previously had sex.
Eighty percent said they had had vaginal intercourse each time they had
had sex last year, while a further 15 percent "usually" had vaginal sex.[131]
Reading between the lines, the major studies of the 1980s do reveal,
though rather grudgingly, that this is the case. Even the radical Lilian
Rubin accepted that "among the older generation the range of acceptable
behaviors was narrow."[132] Sociologist Pepper Schwartz assumed that sex
meant vaginal sex, but insisted on examining "various kinds of sexual acts
to understand why performing them is important to the well-being of the
relationship," and the majority of the problems that she discusses are
about traditional heterosexual intercourse (discussions of its reproductive
capacity are hardly present at all). One of her respondents indicated that
"ninety percent of the time when we make love it includes intercourse."
Another notes that "intercourse is great. . . . I love intercourse because it's
the time we communicate the best."[133]

This was important, but it was confluent love that dominated the
agenda. And oral sex practice was on the rise. In this ideology of intimacy
and ethic of pleasure, partners have the right to freedom of choice. They
negotiate with each other what they should do to maximize orgasmic potential. It is no wonder that in the world of confluent love, sexuality is
contested. And Rubin and Schwartz's samples, drawn from more mainstream Americans, show 1980s behaviors.

Indeed, sexuality is about the "balance of power" (between the genders)
in the bedroom. Men seemed to have been the better-adjusted gender.
Positive comments abound from this better-selected sample: "When she
gives me oral sex I view it as an expression of her feelings for me." But
cunnilingus, too, was popular: "I enjoy giving it . . . I don't feel degraded
going down on her and she shouldn't either."[134] This probably reflects that,
by the 1980s, fewer men associated the practice with prostitution.

Women were still far less happy: "I've never initiated it. I want it, but I
always wait. But my partner does it frequently and predictably." For
women, the ancient taboos still held strong: "His genitals don't attract me
in and of themselves. I don't equate it with a sale at Bloomingdale's. That I
could do all the time. But it's not like going to the dentist either. It's between two extremes. Closer to Bloomingdale's than to the dentist." Some
women might regard cunnilingus as "submissive on his part." Significantly,
Schwartz noted that "overall, our women do not perform oral sex on men

as often as men perform it on them." Therefore, many women were uncomfortable with the reciprocity demanded by the ideology of confluent
love. Yet, oral sex was virtually the sexual practice of choice for sexually
liberated women. For them, the behavior reflected the highest standards:
"I like oral sex very much because it is extremely intimate and I'm moved
by it as an act of intimacy." For another woman it was much the same: "It
almost starts with him going down on me, and then he may do it more to
me . . . prior to intercourse. Two to one in favor of me. Being the 'eater' I
think I require more revving up. I'm a little slower to get started."[135]
Schwartz summed up her findings about women:

> Because there are so many meanings that heterosexual women can attach to
> cunnilingus and to fellatio, their willingness to engage in oral sex varies
> greatly. For some there are no obstacles—for others it is inconceivable; and
> for most it is a source of ambivalence. Because of this diversity we find that
> *on average* oral sex neither contributes to nor detracts from the quality of
> these women's lives.[136]

In the end, for Americans, as the wave of egalitarianism in relationships
bore on, bolstered by the democratic potential of oral sex, it is clear that
reciprocity, the stress on orgasm and intimacy, made the bedroom a very
contested area. And Americans of both genders were not necessarily any
happier than before. These important and pioneering studies show that,
while traditional penetrative heterosexuality was most popular, oral sex
had caught on as a behavior since 1970, though not as fast as popular discourse about it had.

Oral sex has achieved unprecedented importance in contemporary American culture, building on a first set of changes from the later 19th century,
then on a fresh wave of innovations from the 1970s onward. Disparities remain, reflecting differential impacts of earlier cultural values. Public discussion has outstripped actual behaviors, but these too have shifted; and
for some groups, oral sex has become a key measurement of sexual liberation and expressiveness or a related standard that must be acknowledged
even if with private reluctance. General changes in sexual goals and discourse and in bodily presentation have combined with special inputs from
youth culture, feminism, and gays.

The history of oral-genital behavior offers us a fresh perspective on
American sexuality while confirming certain patterns that scholars have

been establishing over the past twenty-five years. The most straightforward reading, notably followed by John D'Emilio and Estelle Freedman in their classic account *A History of Sexuality in America* (1988), is what Barbara Ehrenreich once described as "Whiggish"; we are moving toward the best of all possible erotic worlds. This is no doubt what the "lifestyle gurus" of the cultural intermediaries thought.[137]

The most common alternative scenario used in the early 21st century derives from rascally French sex philosopher/svengali Michel Foucault, who sees one form of regulation giving way to a further form of regulation by means of discourse, which generates multiplicities of sex talk, leading to further regulation. Liberation is impossible. According to this scenario, the cultural intermediaries, while posing as sexual liberators, in fact served to repress sexuality.

There is a great deal in this. Foucault, however, as a gay man and a gay revolutionary in the tradition of Jean Genet, was essentially a sexual pessimist who, as such, could offer numerous insightful vignettes into the behavior of the "normal" he so despised. What Foucault forgot was the role of the social construction of love in the history of sexuality. This article provides an excellent example of the "disciplining" of this emotion. Victorian "romantic love" appears to have involved unprecedented emotional intensity. That we don't know much about actual Victorian sexual behavior merely underlines the point. What was kept secret only served to heighten intensity.

But it did so too much. By late Victorian times, pornography suggests an obsession with oral sex within the middle class. In the first half of the 20th century, "romantic love" seemed under strain as marriage manual writers proclaimed the "genital kiss" as the height of ecstasy. There were many factors aside from representations of oral-genital sexuality that drove the construction of love. But, from the 1960s, oral-genital sexuality was vitally important as the most appropriate sexual behavior for the new era of confluent love that measured its success by the intensity of orgasm. Ancient taboos, breached in the early 20th century, now collapsed. Such an approach was widely criticized as ignoring the fervor of the whole relationship at the expense of a quick-fix, thrills, fleeting pleasure. Americans thought they were being liberated, but, in reality, they were being regulated into accepting less.

Such love was passing, briefly intense, and involved negotiation of roles and behaviors. It was the perfect sexual practice for the divorce of sexuality from procreation that the era heralded. Immensely pleasurable, it was reciprocal and democratic, and its different permutations meant that there was plenty of choice, which was essential for these rather spoiled people.

The period around and after 1970 is key. Here the crucial move of oral sex from the private world out into the public world and back again took place as the cultural intermediaries spread the ideology of the new "lifestyle" of confluent love and as it was debated and contested by ordinary Americans in the "clitoral wars" of that decade. Angus McClaren has spoken of the importance of "moral panics" to bringing about sex change, and the "clitoral wars" and other concerns over oral-genital sex, notably in the film *Deep Throat,* in the 1970s confirm this view.[138] These debates were present at the birth of confluent love.

Ultimately, confluent love was about power shifts, especially in gender power. And this chapter has shown how the power relations between men and women were contested in the bedroom itself from the 1970s. For men, confluent love, more readily available oral sex, and the pill could mean irresponsibility or lack of commitment. Some men genuinely worried that their partners should get the best out of oral sex.

But for feminists, "oral sex" became a key symbol of women's liberation. It meant that they did not have to commit to a man. Also, men could be the passive partners in sex. Above all, "oral sex" meant that male domination need not be perpetuated in the act of penetrative heterosexuality. This was most notoriously articulated in Andrea Dworkin's 1983 novel *Intercourse,* in which she compared penetrative intercourse, be it consensual or not, to rape.[139] While the feminist emphasis conjoined with a wider zeal for sexual experimentation among many middle-class women after the introduction of the pill, many women were also wary of the new emphasis on oral sex despite the rhetoric of liberation.

The spread of oral sex also puts into sharp relief the influence of gay sexual behaviors on heterosexuality. Fellatio had been seen, on the rare occasions that it had been referred to, as a disgusting homosexual practice. But gays, by midcentury, pioneered confluent love by adopting more egalitarian roles in sex. It is ironic that in the 1970s, in the vanguard of sexual behavior as in disco music, gays moved on (sort of) as their leaders encouraged them to practice more anal intercourse (probably with lethal consequences, at least before safer sex came in). Yet average gays continued to practice oral sex as part of confluent love during the crisis. And average American couples did not experience the sorts of vehement politicized conflicts that elite readers of Shere Hite had.

AIDS forced a massive outpouring of work on sexual behavior from sociologists and medics, so that Shostak's fruitless 1981 computer search on Medline File for any material on oral-genital sex has now been rectified.[140] But not among historians, for whom the history of sexuality has largely been about identity, ideology, and sexual meanings. Hence the focus has been on the construction of homosexuality, then on heterosexuality, and now the hot sexual history (nay, the hot history) is on transsexuality.

But a focus on behavior can entirely change our reading of history. There seems to be an initial cultural lag between the burst of oral sex talk around 1970 and increasing practice which was decisive but slower. Anyway, as most Americans seem overwhelmingly to engage still in penetrative heterosexuality rather than in alternative practices such as oral-genital sex (which can be part of foreplay), we can see clearly that the early 1970s moral panic did not create vast swathes of behavior change. As the AIDS industry has discovered, alterations in behavior are hard to instigate, though sex talk is easy.

Yet we still have to read the cultural messages. Oral-genital behavior has been an option at all times in history. But it was unmentionable, at least in Western civilization. The current openness of discourse (if only relative, and still limited even in the media and largely confined to the United States) is historically unprecedented. As such, Americans are in entirely uncharted territory. Starting over again, breaking ancient molds of conduct may be egalitarian and hip (and characteristically American), but how can we know its consequences? Behavioral history helps identify the timing and magnitude of change, along with distinctive causes and differential reactions. In a current sexual system that is far too recent to reify, it cannot as easily evaluate the quality of the results.

NOTES

1. Alex Comfort, *The Joy of Sex* (London, 1972).

2. "Lukas Story I" (Santa Fe, CA, DVD, 2003). The influence of pornography on pop videos might very well be studied. Most interestingly, the Spring 2004 "gay" storyline on *Coronation Street,* the top TV show in Britain, and broadcast all over the English-speaking world (excluding the USA) reflects the influence of gay porn in both the moves and the casting of the actors, Chris Finch and Bruno Langley, who resemble Ridgeton and Paulik, respectively. There were jokes about oral sex, possibly understood by Lancashire grannies. The storyline caused a sensation (see www.digitalspy.com/soap forums "Corries Unhappy Gay Father Todd Gets

Snared," Parts I and II and now III, which was argued to be the biggest Internet forum of all time).

3. Ian Kerner, *She Comes First: The Thinking Man's Guide to Pleasuring a Woman* (New York, 2004).

4. Michelle Weiner Davis, *The Sex-Starved Marriage* (New York, 2004), 118.

5. Anthony Giddens, *The Transformation of Intimacy* (London, 1992).

6. Bill Clinton, *My Life* (London, 2004), 80.

7. John Gagnon, "The Sexual Scripting of Oral-Genital Contacts," *Archives of Sexual Behavior* 16:1 (1987): 1–25.

8. Michel Foucault, *The History of Sexuality*, vol. 1 (London, 1986), 47–48.

9. Gilbert Herdt, *Guardians of the Flute* (New York, 1987).

10. Plato, *The Symposium* (London, 1998), 182.

11. Michel Foucault, *The Care of the Self* (London, 1988).

12. Wayne Dynes, "Fellatio," *Encyclopedia of Homosexuality* (London, 1990).

13. St. Paul's letter to the Corinthians 7:2.

14. St. Augustine of Hippo, *Confessions* (London, 1992), 71.

15. St. Thomas Aquinas, *Summa Theologica*, ed. A. M. Fairweather (London, 1954), 429.

16. Alan Bray, *Homosexuality in Renaissance England* (London, 1982); Thomas Carew, "A Rapture," in Hugh Kenner, ed., *Seventeenth Century Poetry: The Schools of Donne and Jonson* (New York, 1964), 343.

17. Max Weber, *The Protestant Work Ethic and the Spirit of Capitalism* (New York, 1956).

18. Edmund Leites, *The Puritan Conscience and Modern American Sexuality* (New Haven, 1986), 79.

19. Ibid., 16.

20. Ibid., 16.

21. Karen Lystra, *Searching the Heart: Women, Men and Romantic Love in Nineteenth-Century America* (New York, 1989), 66.

22. Ibid., 86.

23. Ibid.

24. Ibid.

25. Auguste Debay, *Hygiène et physiologie du mariage* (1848).

26. Lystra, *Searching the Heart*, 63.

27. Foucault, *The History of Sexuality*, 29.

28. Giddens, *The Transformation of Intimacy*, 44.

29. Cited in Jonathan Ned Katz, *Gay/Lesbian Almanac* (New York, 1983), 214.

30. Ibid., 233.

31. Ibid., 204.

32. Richard Posner, *A Guide to America's Sex Laws* (New York, 1996).

33. Sigmund Freud, "Three Essays in the Theory of Sexuality," in Peter Gay, ed., *The Freud Reader* (London, 1995), 239–93.

34. Havelock Ellis, *Studies in the Psychology of Sex*, vol. 6 (New York, 1936).

35. Marie Stopes, *Enduring Passion* (London, 1928); Marie Stopes, *Married Love* (London, 1922).

36. Theodore Van de Velde, *Ideal Marriage: Its Physiology and Technique* (London, 1928).

37. Alfred C. Kinsey, *Sexual Behavior in the Human Male* (Philadelphia, 1948), 531.

38. Katharine Bement Davis, *Twenty-Two Hundred Women* (New York, 1972).

39. Lewis Terman, *Psychological Factors in Marital Happiness* (New York and London, 1938).

40. Ernest W. Burgess, "Sociological Aspects of the Sex Life of the Unmarried Adult," in Ira Wile, ed., *Sex Life of the Unmarried Adult* (New York, 1934), 125.

41. Robert and Helen Lynd, *Middletown: A Study in American Culture* (New York, 1929).

42. Robert and Helen Lynd, *Middletown in Transition* (New York, 1937).

43. Theodore Newcomb, "Recent Changes in Attitudes towards Sex and Marriage," *American Sociological Review* 2 (1937): 659.

44. Alfred C. Kinsey, *Sexuality in the Human Female* (Philadelphia, 1953), 281.

45. Ibid.

46. Gilbert Hamilton, *A Research in Marriage* (New York, 1929), 178.

47. Kinsey, *Human Male*, 76.

48. Robert Latou Dickinson, *A Thousand Marriages* (Baltimore, 1931), 366.

49. Lorine Pruette, "Conditions Today," in Wile, ed., *Sex Life in the Unmarried Adult*, 289.

50. Newcomb, "Recent Changes in Attitudes towards Sex and Marriage."

51. Phyllis Blanchard and Carolyn Manasses, *New Girls for Old* (New York, 1930), 59.

52. Lewis Terman, *Psychological Factors in Marital Happiness* (New York, 1939), 321.

53. Kinsey, *Human Male*, 371.

54. George Chauncey Jr., *Gay New York: The Making of the Gay Male World, 1890–1950* (New York, 1994), 85.

55. Ibid., 85.

56. "At the Age of 6," Homosexuality Interviews, Box 98, Folder 2, Ernest Burgess Papers, Regenstein Library, University of Chicago.

57. Ibid.

58. Ibid.

59. Ibid.

60. Added material, Homosexuality Interviews, p. 8 in ibid.

61. March 1933, 13, Homosexuality Interviews, Box 98, Folder 3, Ernest Burgess Papers.

62. Ibid.

63. "As is the Case," 2, Homosexuality Interviews, Box 98, Folder 4, Ernest Burgess Papers.

64. Giddens, *Transformation of Intimacy,* 62.

65. Ibid.

66. Pierre Bourdieu, *Distinction* (London, 1984).

67. Robert Wiebe, *The Search for Order* (New York, 1967); Stuart Blumin, *The Transformation of the Middle Class* (New York, 1989).

68. Alain Corbin, *Time, Desire and Horror: Towards a History of the Senses,* trans. Jean Birrell (London, 1995).

69. Jackson Lears, "A Matter of Taste: Corporate Cultural Hegemony in a Mass-Consumption Society," in Lary May, ed., *Recasting America* (Chicago and London, 1989), 50.

70. Martha Wolfenstein, "Fun Morality: An Analysis of Recent American Child-Training Literature," reprinted in Margaret Mead and Martha Wolfenstein, eds., *Childhood in Contemporary Cultures* (Chicago, 1954).

71. Michelle Lamont, *Money, Morals and Manners: The Culture of the French and American Middle Class* (Chicago and London, 1992); Dennis Brisset and Lionel S. Lewis, "Sex as Work," *Social Problems* 15 (Summer 1967): 8–18.

72. Philip Roth, *Portnoy's Complaint* (London, 1999), 238–39.

73. John Updike, *Couples* (New York, 1968).

74. Stephen Donaldson, "Fellatio," in Wayne Dynes, ed., *Encyclopedia of Homosexuality.*

75. Wayne Studor, *Rock on the Wild Side* (San Francisco, 1994).

76. David Reuben, *Everything You Ever Wanted to Know About Sex but Were Afraid to Ask* (New York, 1969), 50–52.

77. "J", *The Sensuous Woman* (New York, 1969); Linda Grant, *Sexing the Millennium* (London, 2003), 120.

78. Arthur B. Shostak, "Oral Sex: New Standard of Intimacy and Old Index of Troubled Sexuality," *Deviant Behavior* 2 (1981): 127–44.

79. David Allyn, *Make Love Not War: The Sexual Revolution, an Unfettered History* (New York, 2000), 126.

80. Ibid.

81. William Masters and Virginia Johnson, *Human Sexual Response* (New York, 1966), 45.

82. Shostak, "Oral Sex".

83. Comfort, *The Joy of Sex,* 82.

84. Ibid.

85. Boston Women's Health Collective, *Our Bodies/Ourselves* (Boston, 1971), 114.

86. Ann Koedt, "The Myth of the Vaginal Orgasm."

87. Lynne Segal, "Sexual Uncertainty, or Why the Clitoris Is not Enough," in Sue Cartledge and Joanna Ryan, eds., *Sex and Love* (London, 1983), 27.

88. Germaine Greer, *The Female Eunuch* (London, 1999).

89. Shere Hite, *The Hite Report: A National Study of Female Sexuality* (London, 1977), 384.

90. Ibid., 333.

91. Ibid., 361.

92. Shere Hite, *The Hite Report on Male Sexuality* (London, 1979), 419.

93. Ibid., 421.

94. Ibid., 424.

95. Shere Hite, *Female Sexuality,* 640.

96. Ibid., 642.

97. Hite, *Male Sexuality,* 477–78.

98. Ibid.

99. Nancy Friday, *My Secret Garden* (New York, 1975), 254; Nancy Friday, *Forbidden Flowers* (New York, 1994).

100. Carol Thurston, *The Romance Revolution: Erotic Novels for Women and the Quest for a New Sexual Identity* (Urbana, IL, 1987), 142.

101. David Bowie's classic song, "Drive-In Saturday" (1973), is about how, following a holocaust, 21st-century people learn how to have sex from watching early 1970s pornography.

102. Wayne Studor, *Rock on the Wild Side* (San Francisco, 1994), 41.

103. Carl Wittman, "A Gay Manifesto," in Mark Alasius and Shane Phelan, eds., *We Are Everywhere: An Historical Sourcebook in Gay and Lesbian Politics* (London, 1995).

104. Gabriel Rotello, *Sexual Ecology: Aids and the Destiny of Gay Men* (New York, 1998), 53.

105. Dr. Charles Silverstein and Edmund White, *The Joy of Gay Sex: An Intimate Guide for Gay Men to the Pleasures of a Gay Lifestyle* (New York, 1977), 26.

106. Ibid., 169.

107. Linda S. Doll, "Sexual Behavior before Aids, the Hepatitis B Studies of Homosexuals and Bisexuals," *AIDS* 4:11 (1990): 1069.

108. Joseph Sonnabend, "Looking at AIDS in Totality: A Conversation," *New York Native,* October 7, 1985. Cited in Rotello, *Sexual Ecology,* 101.

109. Cited in Rotello, *Sexual Ecology,* 102.

110. Ibid., 100.

111. Martin P. Levine and Karolynn Siegel, "Unprotected Sex: Understanding Gay Men's Participation," in Joan Huber and Beth E. Schneider, eds., *The Social Context of Aids* (Beverly Hills, CA, 1992), 47–71.

112. Marty Rubin, "A Nice Jewish Boy from Toronto," in John Preston, ed., *Hot Living: Erotic Stories about Safer Sex* (Boston, 1985), 106–32.

113. L. McKusack et al., "Aids and Sexual Behavior Reported by Gay Men in San Francisco," *American Journal of Public Health* 75(5) (May 1985): 495.

114. Philip Blumstein and Pepper Schwartz, *American Couples* (New York, 1983), 235.

115. Robert T. Michael, John Gagnon, et al., *Sex in America: A Definitive Survey* (Boston, 1994).

116. Ibid.

117. Lilian Rubin, *Worlds of Pain* (New York, 1976), 138.

118. *Sex in America,* 141.

119. Geoffrey Coles, *Sex and the American Teenager* (New York, 1985), 62.

120. *Sex in America,* 142

121. Ibid., 174.

122. Lilian Rubin, *Erotic Wars* (New York, 1990), 33.

123. Anthony Pietropinto, *Beyond the Male Myth* (New York, 1977), 38.

124. John Gagnon and William Simm, "A Sexual Scripts Approach," in *Theories of Human Sexuality,* ed. J. H. Geer and O'Donohue (New York, 1987), 27.

125. Ibid.

126. Edward S. Herold and Leslie Way, "Oral-Genital Behavior in a Sample of University Females," *Journal of Sex Research* 19(4) (1983): 336.

127. S. Newcomer and J. Udry, "Oral Sex in an Adolescent Population," *Archives of Sexual Behavior* 14 (1985): 41–46.

128. Coles, *American Teenager,* 60.

129. Michael Moffatt, *Coming-of-Age in New Jersey: College and American Culture* (New Brunswick, NJ, 1989), 199–202.

130. Coles, *American Teenager,* 60.

131. *Sex in America,* 135.

132. Rubin, *Erotic Wars,* 33.

133. Schwartz, *American Couples,* 194.

134. Ibid., 227.

135. Ibid., 269.

136. Ibid., 235.

137. John D'Emilio and Estelle Freedman, *A History of Sexuality in America* (New York, 1988); review of book by Barbara Ehrenreich in *Tikkun,* September 1988.

138. Angus McClaren, *Twentieth-Century Sexuality: A History* (New York, 2000).

139. Andrea Dworkin, *Intercourse* (London, 1987), 82.

140. Shostak, "Oral Sex."

About the Contributors

Gary Cross, Distinguished Professor of Modern History at Pennsylvania State University, is author or editor of eleven books of retrospection on contemporary American and European society, popular culture, work, and leisure. His books include *The Playful Crowd: Pleasure Places Across the Twentieth Century* (with John Walton), *The Cute and the Cool: Wondrous Innocence and Modern American Children's Culture, An All-Consuming Century: Why Commercialism Won in Modern America, Kids' Stuff: Toys and the Changing World of American Childhood,* and *A Social History of Leisure: Since 1600.*

Paula S. Fass is Margaret Byrne Professor of History at the University of California at Berkeley. She is the author of several books, including the *Damned and the Beautiful: American Youth in the 1920s, Kidnapped: Child Abduction in America, Outside In: Minorities and the Transformation of American Education,* and the editor of *The Encyclopedia of Children and Childhood in History and Society* and *Childhood in America.* She is currently working on children and globalization.

Steven M. Gelber is Professor of History at Santa Clara University in California. His most recent book is *Hobbies: Leisure and the Culture of Work in America.* He is currently working on a study of the history of American horse trading and car dealing from which this chapter is drawn.

Susan J. Matt is Associate Professor of History at Weber State University in Ogden, Utah. She is the author of *Keeping Up with the Joneses: Envy in American Consumer Society, 1890–1930.* She currently is writing a book on the history of homesickness in America.

Linda W. Rosenzweig was Professor of History at Chatham College in Pittsburgh, Pennsylvania. She has authored *The Anchor of My Life: Middle-Class American Mothers and Daughters, 1880–1920* and *Another Self: Middle-Class American Women and Their Friends in the Twentieth Century.*

Mark M. Smith is Carolina Distinguished Professor of History at the University of South Carolina. He is author of *Mastered by the Clock: Time, Slavery, and Freedom in the American South,* which won the Avery O. Craven Prize awarded by the Organization of American Historians. His other books include *Debating Slavery: Economy and Society in the Antebellum American South, Listening to Nineteenth-Century America,* and two edited collections, *The Old South* and *Hearing History: A Reader.* He has published articles in the *American Historical Review, Past and Present,* the *William and Mary Quarterly,* the *Journal of Southern History,* and the *Journal of Social History.* His next book, due out in 2006 with the University of North Carolina Press, is titled *How Race Is Made: Slavery, Segregation, and the South.*

Suzanne E. Smith is Associate Professor of History in the Department of History and Art History at George Mason University. She is the author of *Dancing in the Street: Motown and the Cultural Politics of Detroit.* Her current book project is titled *To Serve the Living: A Cultural History of African-American Funeral Directing.*

Peter N. Stearns is Provost and Professor at George Mason University. He has written widely on behavioral history, particularly in areas such as emotion, old age, and dieting/obesity. He is editor of the *Journal of Social History* and past Vice President (teaching division) of the American Historical Association.

Kevin White is the author of *The First Sexual Revolution* and *Sexual Liberation and Sexual License.* He is currently Assistant Coordinator of Access to the Portsmouth University, United Kingdom.

Index